JOHN BLEY

John Bley

of East Leake & London

1674 – 1731

distiller & benefactor

by

Keith Hodgkinson

Rachel Flynn

Ian Flynn

published by East Leake and District Local History Society

www.eastleake-history.org.uk

First edition published 2012 by East Leake and District Local History Society (EL&DLHS)

ISBN 978-0-9531710-3-3

Printed and bound in the UK by Russell Press Ltd., an ISO 14001 environment management system accredited company, on an FSC Paper from a sustainable source.

Front cover: Thames Wharf by Samuel Scott (c. 1757) © Victoria and Albert Museum, London. *This scene has variously been ascribed to the Old East India Wharf near London Bridge and to Custom House Quay. The latter was extremely close to where John Bley lived and worked.*

Back cover: (1) detail from lower part of Bley memorial window in St Mary's church, East Leake (D. Chapman 2012) (2) John Bley's signature and seal.

Contents

Illustrations

Images have been used by kind permission of the following:

Nos. 57, 60 National Archives; 4, 35, 40, 43 Nottinghamshire Archives; 3, 29, 30, 31, 65 University of Nottingham Dept. of Manuscripts & Special Collections; 5 the Diocesan Registrar Diocese of Worcester Collection at Worcestershire Archive & Archaeology Service; 8, 46, 49 London Metropolitan Archives; 22 Aviva Group; 28 the Thoroton Society of Nottingham; 62 Bank of England Archives; 38 Fine & Country, Loughborough and Mrs & Mrs van Laun; 32 the Archivist, Westminster School; 44 the Trustees of St Dunstan's Educational Foundation; 45 the Trustees of the British Museum.

Introduction

East Leake, now and then

East Leake is now a mainly commuter village of nearly 7,000 people close to the border of south Nottinghamshire and north Leicestershire. It lies in a shallow valley running east-west and has a traditional 'b' shape along the main street and stream. Transport links have never been straightforward. The village is not located on any major road route though the Great Central Railway briefly offered links to London and elsewhere. To the north are Gotham (of Wise Men fame) three miles away, Clifton and thence Nottingham at ten miles and across the river Trent. To the south and east are the gently rising Wolds, with to the south-west the river Soar and the market town of Loughborough.

There are many smaller villages within a radius of three miles or so. For our purposes the most significant of these are Bunny, Costock, Rempstone and Hoton which run in this order south down what is now the A60 between Nottingham to the north and Loughborough, Leicester and ultimately London. In John Bley's time this road was little more than a poorly maintained trackway. But it gave travellers a viable if expensive route to London with the twice-weekly Mansfield Carrier, among others, making the connection to Nottingham and taking the post from provincial centre to the national capital at 6d a package. Most heavy goods came to the village via the river Trent (from the Humber and the North Sea) and its tributary the Soar. Either way, London was a good three-day journey by road or even weeks by water depending on weather and season.

The original name 'Leche' means wet land, and the flat valley floor provided good water-meadows. Gentle slopes to north and south gave average to good farmland and here a few hundred villagers survived a barely comfortable yearly round with little to disturb them.

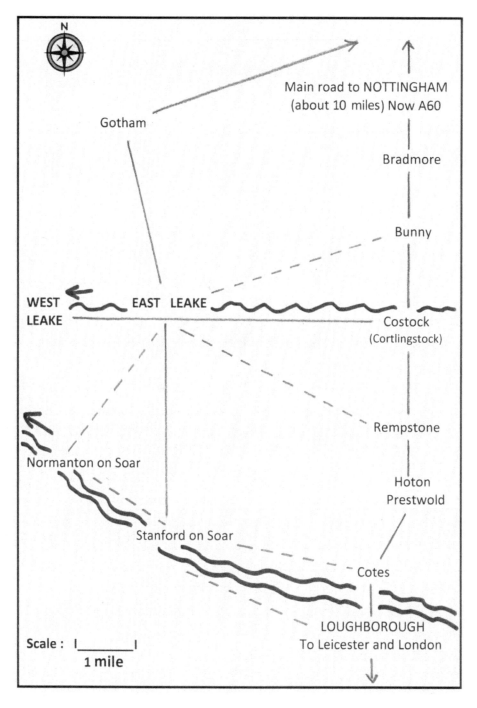

Diagrammatic map showing East Leake and other locations in the book

Throughout history East or Great Leake was always paired with the smaller West or Little Leake a mile away. Ever since the Domesday Book (1086) the village had had the benefit of three manorial Lords. Most of these were absentee landlords whose tenancies had been bought and sold, divided and subdivided many times. East Leake can therefore be considered to have been an open village with a diverse and shifting social structure. The Civil War had made but slight impact while commercialism was no more advanced here than elsewhere in the provinces. Typically for a village of this size, in the late 17th century the grocer Enoch Watson sold sugar, currants and raisins, ginger and pepper and haberdashery. A quiet village then, a backwater even, but not without interest. One rather unusual feature was the fact that the Rectory was then located in West Leake while the main village made do with a resident Curate for its services, record-keeping and social control. This situation gave rise to an occasional tension such as that with which our story begins.

How and why the book was written

Twenty years ago this project would have been well nigh impossible.

'John Bley – who was he?' This was the title of a short article in the Local History Society's journal 'The Leake Historian' published in 2004. A newspaper article in 1934, a members' evening talk in 1993 and the 2004 article all raised the vexed question of John Bley's origins. The authors stated that 'there are few contemporary sources of information ... [his] origins are something of a mystery'. Two years later the evidence of his apprenticeship in London had been located, but little else. Then it was decided to renovate Bley's rather prominent tomb in front of the church's east window. A Heritage/Lottery grant required the local history society to produce something of benefit to local schools, so a short biography was attempted. In the course of this research some new leads were opened up with amazing results. Despite our first impressions, we found an unexpectedly wide range of evidence which involved piecing together little details from many different places. At the same time we widened the scope of our investigations by referring to more general historical sources and to established national history. In this way we were able to link our rather limited local records in East Leake with the national story. Using the internet now enabled us to locate documents in the unlikeliest of places such as Worcester and Lewisham and greatly speeded up some of the searching by allowing us to access many sources digitally. The resulting detail was so interesting, we felt, that it just had to be recorded and the story told in full.

The first four chapters are a chronological account of John's early years. Chapters five and six then break off for an examination of his remarkable relationship with the local squire, Sir Thomas Parkyns, and John's activity as generous benefactor in his home village. Two more sections complete his life-story and these sections end with his death and will, which tell us such a lot about his importance to family and friends in city and village. The penultimate chapter reveals the mysterious bequest to an unknown infant whose own life adds further interest and leads to more unanswered questions. The book ends with a conclusion discussing the more general significance of John Bley's life and work.

The national context

'Local boy makes good.' There are many such stories and they are significant at the local level. What gives John Bley's life additional interest is its scope. The outer boundaries of this tale take us from 1645 in the middle of the English Civil War right through to 1789 at the outbreak of the French Revolution. The inner story, of John's own life, covers the period of Restoration, the Glorious Revolution of 1688/9, the financial revolution and the beginnings of the long Georgian population explosion centred on the metropolis. Few history books cover the same ground; most are based on and restricted to the classic dynastic periods: Stuart, Hanoverian, and Industrial Revolution. The narrative takes us through these period boundaries and shows how one group of people developed their lives in contrasting situations. There is continuity in the village but change and opportunity elsewhere.

The story will take us from village to city, and back to village again. Our hero goes from village schoolboy to millionaire, in fine detail and with several surprises including a little murder and mayhem along the way.

We begin with one mystery and end with another. Neither is entirely resolved.

Spelling, dates and monetary values

In the period covered by this book, writing styles were highly individual. Spelling was varied and inconsistent even between people of high status. There were even variations in the spelling of names, sometimes following regional differences in pronunciation. So for example the name 'Wight' was occasionally spelled 'Weight'. This can lead to problems in research on family histories and in transcribing original sources. Where these occur they have been indicated in the text.

All the dates in the text of this book use the old Julian calendar which differed by 10 or 11 days from the new Gregorian calendar adopted in England in 1752. The New Year is, however, taken to begin on 1 January, although in pre-1752 England the Julian New Year began on 25 March.

To help readers locate events in this story in the national context a timeline has been added at the end of the book.

As far as monetary values are concerned historians are generally agreed that the problem of giving a modern equivalent is too complicated for us to use with any meaning. What could be the equivalent, now, of an 18th century horse, for example, or a house in the centre of the City of London? Nevertheless we think that most readers would still like some idea of the value today of John's estate when he died, so for this we have used the website *www.measuringworth.com/ppoweruk*. This is easy to use and explains the basis of its calculations. The relevant opening page warns, though, that 'there is no single correct measure, and economic historians use one or more different indicators depending on the context of the question.' If we use the changing retail price index as the base, then values in this book would need to be multiplied by 150. But using average earnings as the base gives us a multiple of 1500. Earnings have risen ten times faster than prices since our period, which is one measure of how wealthy we have become.

For the benefit of those brought up after the decimalisation of our currency the following guide to the old monetary system may be necessary:

12d (pennies or pence)	= 1s (shilling)	5p in new decimal
10s (ten shillings)	= half of a £	50p " "
20s (shillings)	= £1 (pound)	
1 guinea = 21 shillings = £1.05		

Accounts were written in a sort of shorthand:

1/6d = 1 shilling & 6d   = 7½ new pence

Acknowledgements

The book is dedicated to our former chairman Tony Grundy, who passed away on New Year's Day 2012. He chaired our society for thirteen years and was a very active member for more than three decades. It was Tony who organised the restoration of John Bley's tomb, a project that more than anything else inspired this book.

We are grateful to all the members of our Local History Society who helped with this project and especially the committee who provided so much support over a long period. Thanks are also due to the late Harry Meadowcroft who did much initial research. Collaboration between many amateur historians has been both necessary and beneficial to the project. We would especially like to thank Peter Foden, a professional archivist who has freely given his time, advice and knowledge (especially his legal Latin!) over several years. We are much indebted to Dr Michael Honeybone for reading and commenting on the text.

Our county archivists are equally unsung heroes. The Archive Offices are (still) free and generous and the following have been especially helpful: Nottingham, Derby (at Matlock), Leicester (at Wigston), Lincoln, York and Worcester. Nottingham University's Dept. of Manuscripts and Special

Collections was both cosy and productive. The National Archives, Parliamentary Archives and British Library were essential sources. The Guildhall Library in London was welcoming and the Bank of England archive was a hidden revelation, where Dr Anne Murphy of the University of Hertfordshire gave us professional guidance. Archivists John Coulter of Lewisham Archives, Pamela Hunter of the RBS Group plc, Raya McGeorge of the Fishmongers' Company, and Elizabeth Wells of Westminster School all went well beyond the call of duty to dig out valuable information for us. Brenda Lewis also did useful work on education in East Leake. The staff of London Metropolitan Archives were unfailingly helpful over the course of several visits. Little Baddow History Centre, the Enfield Society and the Great Yarmouth Local History & Archaeological Society all provided valuable background information. We thank all of them and all the other local history organisations and archivists that we contacted for their help and for their great patience in dealing with our queries.

Finally the authors wish to express their deep appreciation of the unflagging editorial support and constant encouragement provided by Mary Hodgkinson throughout this project.

The publication of this book has been made possible by the generosity of East Leake Parish Council, the East Leake Townlands Trust, Nottinghamshire County Council, Rushcliffe Borough Council, via their Community Fund, British Gypsum and Nottinghamshire Local History Association.

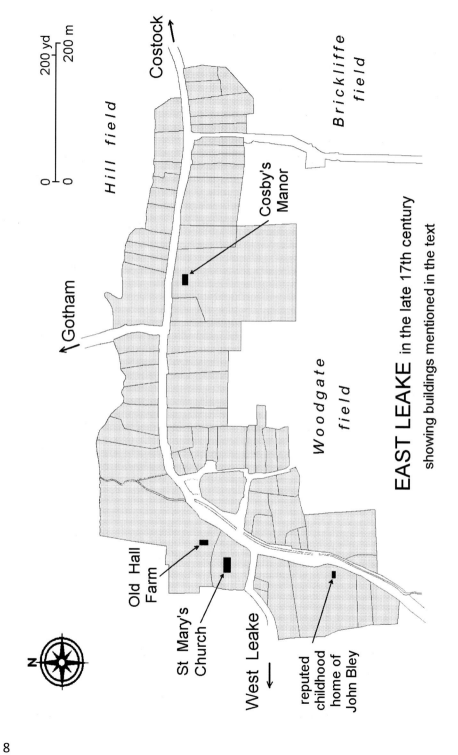

200 yd
200 m

Costock

Hill field

Brickliffe field

Cosby's Manor

Gotham

Woodgate field

Old Hall Farm

St Mary's Church

West Leake

reputed childhood home of John Bley

N

EAST LEAKE in the late 17th century

showing buildings mentioned in the text

Chapter 1

'Born in this Town'

The year 1675 saw two startling events in a small South Nottinghamshire community. A young unmarried woman from a respectable family gave birth to an illegitimate son and would not name the father. A few months later the young curate suddenly left the village, armed with a testimonial from five neighbouring clergymen but with no recommendation from his own rector. He took up another curacy in distant Worcestershire, far away from his roots. The parish register he left behind, and for which he had been responsible, contained no record of a baptism for the child. In East Leake, a village of fewer than 100 households, tongues must have wagged; could the two events possibly be related?

The young woman was Elizabeth Wight, or Weight, both versions almost certainly being pronounced as the modern 'wait', and Elizabeth's disgrace was recorded permanently by the churchwardens in their submission to an archdeaconry visitation:

Leake   April the 20th 1675
          Item we present Elizabeth Weight having a bastard
          she refusing to tell who is the father of it

Had Elizabeth been dependent on the parish, she would have been placed under extreme pressure to name the father, even while in labour, so her silence suggests she had means; indeed she did belong to one of East Leake's main families. Her grandfather had been a yeoman farmer in the village and her uncle George Wight had acted as bailiff to the Armstrongs when they held manorial rights in East Leake. George was also a church-warden, though why he happened to be in prison when he should have been reporting to the archdeacon in 1666 remains a mystery!

But just who was the father of Elizabeth Wight's child? At first sight a curate may seem an unlikely candidate for villain of the piece, but it would not be the first time a clergyman of East Leake had indulged in inappropriate behaviour. A certain Thurstan Chaplain had been Rector of Leake in 1610, when the Archdeaconry of Nottingham presentment bills featured an intriguing reference to the 'supposed daughter of Thurstain Chapleine, clerk'. Indeed, Elizabeth Wight and her child could have fared far worse. Just a few years later, in 1679, the minister of Stanton Lacy near Ludlow was hanged at Tyburn for the gruesome murder of his own infant. Having seduced his young ward and made her pregnant, he spirited her away to London, delivered the child himself, stuffed it down the 'house of office' and returned to Shropshire abandoning the girl to her fate. Had Rev. Robert Foulks of Stanton Lacy been curate of Leake in William Bleay's place there might have been no story of a village benefactor left for us to tell. Certainly, 17th century village clergymen were not above suspicion when there was an unexplained pregnancy.

So what kind of person was William Bleay, the young curate of Leake who left in suspicious circumstances? We know little of his background or parentage, but we do know he was baptised at St Mary's, Leicester in June 1645, at a pivotal point in the English Civil War. The town had declared its support for parliament's struggle against the king and was held by a 1000 strong parliamentary garrison, mostly made up of local recruits. On 30 May royalist cavalry surrounded the town and on the following day Prince Rupert arrived with the rest of the royalist army. A fierce bombardment made a breach in the town wall and an all-out night assault was launched. Twice the attackers were repelled with heavy losses, but at length the defences were overwhelmed and the garrison surrendered.

The king's soldiers then went on the rampage, in the words of contemporary royalist historian the Earl of Clarendon, 'with the usual

Licence of Rapine, and Plunder, and miserably sack'd the whole Town, without any distinction of Persons or Places; Churches, and Hospitals, as well as other Houses, were made a Prey to the enraged, and greedy Soldier'. We do not know exactly where William's mother was or on which day she gave birth, but the experience must have been utterly terrifying. Order of a kind was eventually restored and a royalist garrison installed under Lord Loughborough, while the rest of the king's forces marched south to engage the main parliamentary army. Two weeks later, at Naseby, King Charles suffered a decisive defeat and Leicester was again filled with his troops, this time fleeing from the battlefield. On 19 June the Royalists finally withdrew and shortly afterwards William was baptised.

Following this dramatic introduction to the world, William grew up in Leicestershire along with an elder brother Thomas and sister Elizabeth. We know nothing of his father's occupation, but the family had sufficient means and status to educate both sons at Emmanuel College, Cambridge. The two young men entered university as sizars, performing menial tasks to support their education, so the Bleays were not wealthy though they certainly had an educated background. After successfully completing his studies, William was awarded his degree in 1667 and followed his elder brother into the Church, returning to Leicester to be ordained at St Martin's church on 10 August 1668.

We next catch sight of William three years later when he signed the Bishop's transcripts, copies of the parish registers, as curate of East Leake.

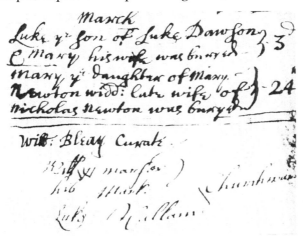

So East Leake was either his first curacy or very close to it. His rector, John Davys, was some 12 years older than William but also new to the area. He had been appointed Rector of Leake in 1668, thanks to family links with Earl Hastings, patron of the living. Davys lived in the rectory at West or Little Leake, a very small village a short distance away from the much larger East or Great Leake. Although the rectory lay in the smaller village, it had the distinct advantage of being very close to the manor house of the Mansfield family, so giving the rector opportunities to socialise with the gentry not available in the larger village where farmers formed the highest rank of society. Hearth tax returns of 1674 confirm this by showing West Leake manor with a dozen hearths whereas no property in East Leake had more than four.

The rector was probably happy to let his curate look after East Leake's parishioners and their fine church, while he devoted his time to more interesting pursuits. A series of letters to the Royal Society between November 1683 and January 1685 reveals Davys as an obsessive inventor, devising machines for weaving lace 'as in a silk stocking frame', making twist, carding wool, pumping water and improving the performance of jacks and balance clocks, as well as inventing musical instruments and lamps. In one letter he enclosed a piece of knitted cloth he had made on his own machine in the rectory at Little Leake. The Royal Society was unimpressed; shown these letters, the famous scientist Robert Hooke commented 'most of the things which he proposed were already practised in London'. Following this rebuff, the industrious rector resorted to writing in Latin in an effort to be taken more seriously, but to no avail.

While written some time after William Bleay's departure, the letters strongly suggest that pastoral responsibilities were not John Davys's first priority. Moreover he was conscious of his social status, marrying into the aristocracy, purchasing one of the three East Leake manors and later engaging in a legal wrangle with Sir Thomas Parkyns over manorial rights. Maintaining his standing with the gentry and aristocracy was probably a much higher priority than tending to the spiritual needs of East Leake's farm workers – something his curate could be left to get on with without close supervision. So Davys was unlikely to spot a burgeoning relationship between a susceptible young curate and a village girl, had it existed, let alone nip it in the bud.

In the normal course of events, being curate of East Leake should have been a useful step on the career ladder for an aspiring clergyman. The next position for William Bleay might be a living of his own, a vicarage at least. So William's sudden departure in 1675 to the curacy of Inkberrow in Worcestershire cannot be construed as a carefully thought-out career move. Preserved in the archives of the diocese of Worcester is the following judiciously worded testimonial:

Written in Latin, the testimonial translates as follows:

> We whose names are subscribed attest that William Bleay, a Priest, Master of Arts, well known to us, has set out on a life and conduct both holy and sober: nor that he has held or believed anything (which we know) whatsoever, except what the Anglican Church now approves and guards. In witness of which we (each in his own hand) have put our names, on the twenty eighth day of August 1675

The signatories were:

John Bridges, Rector of Gotham

John Marler, Rector of Normanton on Soar ('Normanton super Sore')

Charles Wainwright, Minister of Bunny ('Boney')

Thomas Boyer, Rector of Rempstone

Thomas Townsend, Rector of Costock ('Cortlingstock')

These five clergymen were the incumbents of all the parishes neighbouring East Leake, saving only Stanford-on-Soar and West Leake. The testimonial was not signed by William's own rector, John Davys, nor was there any mention of William's curacy at Leake which might trigger a letter of enquiry to Davys. Was William trying to hide something? Had Davys discovered that William was the father of Elizabeth Wight's child and was he unwilling to recommend him? At this distance in time we can only hazard guesses.

The testimonial served its purpose and by the end of 1675 William was safely installed as curate of Inkberrow. But before we can follow William any further we must turn to the career of his elder brother Thomas. For a precise match between the date of William's testimonial and another crisis in the Bleay family raises another possible reason for William's breach with John Davys and departure from East Leake.

Ordained some years before William, Thomas Bleay had served as curate of the Leicestershire village of Lower Broughton before becoming Rector of Hatcliffe near Grimsby. A widow Elizabeth Bleay, thought to be

Thomas' mother, had purchased the presentation of this living from a certain Edward King and, on the death of the previous incumbent, presented Thomas to the living. Accepted by the bishop of Lincoln, Thomas took up his post and earned the approval of his new parishioners. However, the bishop died in April 1675 and shortly afterwards the previous patrons of the living, the Chapter of Southwell, obtained a court decision that overturned Elizabeth Bleay's right of presentation. This made Thomas' position untenable and he resigned on 27 August after just three years at Hatcliffe. The testimonial carried by William Bleay on his flight from East Leake was signed the following day. So there was utter tumult in the Bleay family that month, but was it pure coincidence or was there some link between the two events? At first sight, it is difficult to see what this could be. One possibility is that William had asked John Davys to intervene at Southwell on his brother's behalf and Davys had declined; perhaps this is the true reason the two men parted company.

If we knew Thomas Bleay's next move it might throw some light on the mystery, but an unexplained gap of five years occurs in his career until his installation as Rector of Saxelbye, a Leicestershire village close to where he had been curate. This time he was able to settle and remained there until his death in 1706. He kept his affairs well organised, writing his will over 20 years before he died. His brother William received £100, various religious documents, including bundles of sermon notes, and the choice of half a dozen books from his library. Thomas remembered the poor of the Broughton villages in his will, but there was no mention of Hatcliffe. The rectory at Saxelbye was quite commodious for just Thomas and his wife (they had no children) with two parlours, four chambers, a library and study plus the usual domestic offices. A few livestock were also mentioned in the inventory. His estate totalled £228 18s, a fair enough sum at a time when a young curate was lucky to receive £30 a year. Thomas was no pauper, therefore, but he was not wealthy.

Returning to Inkberrow, it not only gained a new curate around the end of 1675 but also a vicar. The new bishop of Worcester, James Fleetwood, had discovered a number of parish vacancies which he was anxious to fill.

By the end of December, William Bleay was in place as Inkberrow's curate. Then, in February, Fleetwood appointed a vicar in the shape of Henry Mugg(e), a pluralist with livings in other counties for whom the appointment would merely represent a welcome addition to his income; with a large and impressive church, Inkberrow is likely to have been a wealthy living. William was already used to running a church, experience which would appeal to an absentee vicar.

After five years at Inkberrow William was more than ready for a parish of his own. With encouragement and help from his elder brother, he gained the living of Colston Bassett in Nottinghamshire and was inducted there on 22 February 1680 by his friend Rev. Charles Wainwright vicar of Bunny, one of the signatories of the testimonial William had taken to Worcester. Again, one could ask why he should return to Nottinghamshire and a parish within ten miles of Leake, if he really had fathered Elizabeth Wight's son, but perhaps he calculated that such an old scandal was unlikely to reach ears in his new parish.

Colston Bassett was a very different village from East Leake. Throughout the 1670s Lady Mary Golding of Colston Bassett Hall and her extensive household were 'presented' by the churchwardens for being popish recusants and failing to attend the parish church. William was not prepared to carry on with the arrangement his predecessor had made with the Goldings regarding payment of tithes and within a few years had engaged in legal proceedings against Dame Mary and Sir Edward Golding. Being vicar of a parish where the leading family and their household did not support the church could not have been easy. Sir Edward is said to have done much tree planting between 1704 and 1710; one wonders if he was trying to screen the troublesome vicar and his church from view.

William Bleay remained in Colston Bassett for the rest of his days and was buried there on 4 May 1721. As he lay on his deathbed, he gave instructions that all his possessions should pass to his sister Elizabeth, who had married an innholder of Leicester called Joseph Travell. William mentioned no other family – no wife, no son. He lies in an unmarked grave near the ruins of his former church.

The ruins of the old Colston Bassett church

We must now pick up the story of Elizabeth Wight, left behind in East Leake with her illegitimate son John. Elizabeth's father was no longer alive and her brothers were almost certainly in London, so the obvious person to turn to was her elder sister Mary who had recently married John Hopkins, a local farmer, and was thus in a position to give Elizabeth a home. The lack of any Wights in the 1674 Hearth Tax return supports the idea that Mary Hopkins was Elizabeth's only near relative in the village. If Mary did take the pair in, they had good reason to be grateful; half a century later, Elizabeth would leave money to her sister's family in preference to other relatives and her son John himself left very generous bequests to his Aunt Mary's descendants.

The village in which John grew up was small by today's standards, though a little larger than its immediate neighbours. Perhaps 90 timber-framed cottages and farmhouses, mostly thatched, were strung along the main street and huddled around The Nook opposite the church. The days of fully brick construction were only just beginning in this area. Local archdeacon Robert Marsden's commonplace book entry of 1731 tells us there were some 15 farmers of sufficient substance to have their own ploughing team and they would be the main employers in the village. The rest of the population was made up of farm labourers and tradesmen. At a time when such villages were largely self-sufficient these tradesmen included a blacksmith, a wheelwright, a baker, a grocer, a butcher, tailors, carpenters, joiners and cordwainers (shoe makers). There was the odd weaver and even a mason. Anything these tradesmen could not supply would have to be obtained by a six mile trek to the market town of Lough-borough or a journey of twice that distance over rutted and often muddy roads to Nottingham, but as John grew up he could be clothed, shod and fed from the resources of the village. Many villagers rented their land or cottages, but early 18th century poll lists show around 30 freeholders with sufficient property of their own to vote. This meant a significant number of people with a good degree of independence, politically as well as economically, in contrast to West Leake where all but two families were beholden to the manor.

St Mary's church, East Leake

St Mary's Church dominated the scene physically and in many other ways. The committee of principal villagers responsible for running day-to-day affairs met in the vestry. Churchwardens monitored villagers' church attendance and moral conduct. At least twice a year they appeared before the archdeaconry court in Nottingham, reporting any flaws in the fabric or fittings of the church and any failure of the clergy to conduct regular services. They were expected to 'present' any parishioners who failed to attend church or were deemed guilty of immorality. There were often one or two non-church attending dissenters to be presented, notably some members of the Mugg and Wild families; others with nonconformist leanings may have kept up a nominal level of attendance to stay on the right side of the authorities.

The Wight family had strong links with the parish church. They took their turn to be churchwardens and Elizabeth Wight's father was responsible for inscribing the churchwardens' names on a beam in the church roof in the 1630s. However, in 1681 Elizabeth Wight's name appeared among the presentments for a second time as 'standing ex-communicate', probably this time for non-attendance at church, so young John may not have had a strong church upbringing.

The landscape in which John grew up must certainly have influenced his childhood. The countryside surrounding the village was much more open than it is today, with far fewer hedges. Most of the parish consisted of three large fields, named in 18th century documents as Hill, Brickliffe and Woodgate fields, each divided into strips and farmed in rotation with a different crop each year. Probate inventories of the time indicate a rotation typical of north midland clay country. Wheat and barley in one year were followed by a crop of peas the next, then in the third year the field was left fallow, providing pasture for cattle and sheep, before being sown with winter wheat. The hills between East Leake and Bunny and between East and West Leake were well wooded and provided both fuel and building materials. Other poor land on the fringes of the village was unsuitable for the plough and used for rough grazing. Mixed farming was the rule.

Although we have no information about the farm run by John Hopkins, John's uncle by marriage, contemporary inventories suggest that one of the village's main farmers might have 15 or 20 acres of land in each open field, 10 or 20 cows, several score of sheep and a few pigs, as well as the team of horses used for ploughing. Manure from the animals fertilised the arable land and in return the crops fed both animals and humans. In a good year there would be surplus produce to sell at Loughborough market to pay for seed, tools or even the occasional luxury.

The rhythm of the agricultural year governed the life of the whole village, for a typical tradesman was also a 'cottager', keeping a cow or a pig and tending small strips of his own in the open fields. Even children were involved. The open field system required a high level of co-operation. Everyone had to sow at the same time and reap at the same time. Animals could only graze in certain places at certain times and there was a set day after harvest when they were allowed onto the field to forage and to deposit their manure. During August whole families were involved in the harvest, men cutting the corn with their sickles and women raking it together before binding it into stooks using straw ropes made by the children. Young John doubtless played his part in this and possibly the June hay harvest as well. The pace of life was slow but unrelenting and, when the weather was harsh, conditions could become very grim. At such times the village again had to pull together to help the vulnerable. The Poor Rate, largely paid by the wealthier farmers, enabled parish officials to provide basic support, but any failure of the harvest would mean extreme hardship for most in the ensuing winter.

The strip system in the Midland counties ensured fairness, everyone getting a share of the good land and the bad. It also meant that all farmhouses, including that of John Hopkins, were in the core of the village because farmers wanted a central location from which to manage their scattered holdings. Outlying farms appeared in the parish only after 1798, when these holdings were consolidated into individually owned fields under the East Leake Enclosure Act. Later local tradition held that John grew up in the farmhouse now known as 10 Brookside or in an earlier house near the site. This would have been one of the more substantial farmhouses of the time and John Hopkins, a yeoman farmer of reasonable substance, may well have lived in such a place. However it is now thought this particular property was part of Joyce's manor, purchased by rector John Davys in 1676 around the time of his very advantageous marriage into the de Ferrers family, whereas John Hopkins was later recorded as a tenant farmer of Sir Thomas Parkyns who held the other two manors. The Hopkins had at least four children, born between 1674 and 1680, namely their own son John, Mary, Elizabeth and Thomas. So if Elizabeth's son did grow up with this family, he had plenty of other children for company.

John's family evidently wanted him to receive at least a basic schooling. Before he could enter a worthwhile trade he must be able to read and write and needed to master elementary arithmetic. There is no record of a school in East Leake at the time John was growing up, and most local children probably received no education at all. There were schools in some nearby villages, though. John Wild was registered as a schoolmaster in West Leake in 1674 and stayed there for many decades. A local tradition retold by Rev. Sidney Potter in 1934 in the Nottingham Weekly Guardian, stated 'a further tradition says that he [John Bley] was sent daily to a private school at Hoton' and there are records of a schoolmaster in this small village just over the Leicestershire border. For John this would have meant a trudge of four miles over open countryside to school and four miles back again. (See map on page 2.) He may have been accompanied by his cousin John Hopkins whose father, as a substantial yeoman, presumably had the means to pay tuition fees.

The walk was probably more straightforward than today, thanks to the open fields, the most direct route being straight across country past the old Rempstone church, now the deserted site known as St Peter's in the Rushes. In dry weather the youngsters may have continued down to the brook on the Leicestershire county boundary, then up the hill to Hoton. When the brook was in spate it would mean a longer way round by the road. In good weather this could be an enjoyable walk, even exhilarating on a fresh spring morning with the birds singing and wild flowers coming into bloom. In the depths of winter the journey might be very different, not least in the terrible winter of 1685 when John was ten years old. This was the coldest ever recorded in England and was memorably described in R. D. Blackmore's 'Lorna Doone':

> such a frost ensued as we had never dreamed of, neither read in ancient
> books … The kettle by the fire froze, and the crock upon the hearth-

cheeks; many men were killed, and cattle rigid in their headropes. Then I heard that fearful sound, which never I had heard before … the sharp yet solemn sound of trees, burst open by the frost-blow.

And that was in temperate Somerset. The frost lasted for months and there can have been few birds singing when spring belatedly arrived. Perhaps it was then John resolved that if ever he made his fortune he would build his native village a school of its own.

Judging by John's later activities he was highly astute and he was no doubt quick at his lessons. He would not necessarily attend school every day, as he might be needed on the farm for harvest or for bird scaring duties, but he went sufficiently often to get a good grounding. One set of John's business accounts survives, written some 30 years later, and it gives clues to both the extent and limitations of his schooling (see page 218). He learned a neat open hand, very legible and ideally suited to business correspondence. The accounts were copied out neatly, with no crossings out, suggesting much practice at such exercises in the schoolroom. The arithmetic is fully correct, doubtless also the result of copious practice, but the spelling is idiosyncratic. In particular, the words 'bureau' and 'succeeding' are spelt entirely phonetically, rendered as 'bewrow' and 'suckseeding' respectively, which suggests John had never seen these words written down – likely enough if his general education had been confined to a village school, but not if he had been educated at university or was widely read.

Once he had learnt to read, it may not have been long before John's mother asked him to demonstrate his accomplishment by reading aloud letters from her brothers and other relatives in London. For many years the Wight family maintained links with East Leake whilst following apprenticeships and setting up in trade in the capital and elsewhere. Visits from London would involve an arduous journey of several days on atrocious roads, so most news probably travelled by mail. The Wights were not unusual in having London connections; other families in the area with such links included the Price and Quinton families of East Leake, the Wilds of East Leake and Costock and the Birds of West Leake. However, the Wight connections were more extensive than most. (See family tree p.177.)

Elizabeth's oldest brother George lived on the fringe of London. He was described as a yeoman of Charlton, near Woolwich in Kent, when his youngest son was apprenticed in 1701. The Charlton-by-Woolwich St Luke burials for 1702 contain the entry 'George Wight, servant to Sir Wm Langhorn was buryed Aug. 22', Langhorn being a wealthy East India merchant who lived at Charlton House. So George may have acted as bailiff on the Charlton House estate besides farming land of his own, following the example of his uncle who had been bailiff and farmer in East Leake. George's eldest son, another George, requested to be buried anywhere but Charlton! Perhaps father and son had quarrelled. In contrast, a grandson wished to be buried at Charlton 'with a stone pillar' even though he lived in Kensington.

Another of Elizabeth's brothers, Robert Wight, had established himself as a poulterer in Newgate Street, Farringdon, a handy location for such an occupation since Newgate market was the centre of London's meat and poultry trade. His surname was sometimes spelt Wayte, perhaps a reflection on East Leake pronunciation in the ears of Londoners. Robert lived no more than a mile from where John Bley would eventually settle so may have become one source of support in London. However the uncle closest to John over his lifetime was his mother's youngest brother Edward Wight, or Weight as he preferred to spell the name.

Although records of John's financial dealings are fairly sparse, they include two substantial transfers of Bank of England stock to Edward Weight, £200 in 1709 and a further £600 in 1730. Both John and Edward divided their time between East Leake and London. John's correspondence shows Edward living in East Leake in 1718, while we shall see in later chapters that Edward must have spent much time in London when John was there. Uncle Edward lies in East Leake churchyard, with an elegantly carved headstone that stands very close to John's tomb, emphasising their connection. When John needed a father figure in London, it was most likely Edward Weight to whom he would turn.

The next generation, John's cousins, were also starting to follow the Wight tradition of apprenticeships. Uncle George's eldest son George became a cooper in London and his youngest son Edward was apprenticed to Charles Pearce of Hereford to be instructed 'in the managing and converting of timber'. It is unlikely this apprenticeship was completed, as Pearce was bankrupt within five years. Young Edward must have picked up some administrative skills, though, as he later became clerk to a brewer in Southwark. The middle brother, Samuel, took to the sea, first as a waterman, ferrying passengers on the Thames, then as master of a coasting vessel, finally becoming a pilot of Trinity House. As John entered his teens the time fast approached when he, too, needed to be found a trade, a step that would shape the whole of his future. The Wights rallied round, possibly co-ordinated by Uncle Edward who, as far as we know, had no children of his own at the time.

Arranging an apprenticeship in the 17th century could be a protracted process. First the family needed to choose a suitable trade, taking into account their youngster's talents, the long-term prospects and the premium likely to be asked. The surest route to riches lay through apprenticeship to a leading London merchant but this could cost several hundred pounds, which was out of the question for the Wights. A boy might be apprenticed to a menial trade for a few pounds, but would never be likely to make much of a living by this route. To be sure of making his way in the world John needed membership of an incorporated livery company, such as the Poulterers Company to which Uncle Robert belonged, because this would confer citizenship of the City of London and valuable trading privileges.

Elite companies, such as the Mercers, Skinners and Fishmongers, demanded high premiums and their members might well be unhappy about John's background, but there were plenty of newer incorporated companies offering good prospects for a premium of £50 or less. The choice made for John was a shrewd one. The Worshipful Company of Distillers was one of the younger London livery companies, but definitely on the rise. It had obtained its royal charter from Charles I in 1638, had been enrolled in the City in 1658 and had been granted a monopoly of distilled liquor production anywhere within 21 miles of the capital. A rapidly expanding London population meant a rapidly expanding market, so there were excellent prospects for a newcomer to the trade.

The next thing to be found was a master in need of an apprentice. This may not have been easy, as distillers took on fewer apprentices than many other trades and many operated alone. Furthermore, the master needed to be a man of good character and sound reputation, willing both to give his apprentice a thorough grounding in his trade and to oversee his moral welfare. It was here that another of John's Wight relations may have stepped in. Thomas Wight was a 'dissenting teacher' of Essex and, incidentally, the first of many Wight relatives listed 40 years later in John's will. Thomas' own father had been a London feltmaker, so he must have known the London business world, but it is his dissenting contacts in Essex that are of real interest since they may have brought him into contact with the Gilson family.

Thomas Gilson the elder was a puritan clergyman ejected from his living in Little Baddow, near Chelmsford, soon after the restoration of Charles II and later granted a licence to preach to an independent congregation in Brentwood. His younger son Daniel also became a dissenting minister in Essex, but the elder son, another Thomas, was apprenticed to a London distiller. By May 1690 the younger Thomas Gilson, aged 37, was firmly established as a London distiller in his own right. Thomas Wight's exact location in Essex is uncertain but there was a minister of this name at a large dissenting meeting house in Hornchurch in 1698, not so very far from Brentwood. It is likely he knew at least one of the Gilson ministers and this may well have provided the contact between John's uncles and the younger Thomas Gilson, a distiller with a devout background in a position to employ an apprentice.

In his 1747 book 'The London Tradesman' Robert Campbell stated that London distillers might demand an apprenticeship premium of up to £50, but surviving apprenticeship agreements show that the cost might be much lower. Thomas Gilson was not one of the distilling elite and probably asked much less than the maximum, especially if doing a favour for a family friend. Moreover the Distillers' Company records, admittedly incomplete, do not show Gilson engaging any other apprentice over his career, so the arrangement may have been temporary. Once a master in a more substantial line of business could be found, Gilson may have been willing to pass his apprentice on. A fund of £30 to £50 should have been more than enough to convey John to London, buy him his first livery and pay his premium. This was serious money, but surely well within the combined means of a family that had contrived to fund London apprenticeships for the previous generation of Wights, even after the early death of their father.

Accordingly, terms were agreed, a contract was drawn up in the form of a standard City of London apprenticeship indenture and a corresponding entry appeared in the apprenticeship records of the Distillers Company:

> The Thirteenth of May 1690 John Bley Sonn of William Bley Clerke doth put himself Apprentice to Thomas Gilson Cittizen & Distiller of London for seven yeares

In these two documents, the apprenticeship indenture and the register entry, we have at last clinching evidence that the curate William Bleay was indeed John's father. Or, at least, we have clinching evidence that this is what John's mother had told him and what he himself believed. We do not know at what precise point between 1675, when Elizabeth Wight refused to name John's father, and 1690, when John enrolled as an apprentice, the youngster became known as John Bley, but from now on this was the surname he used. Perhaps he had never seen his father's name written down, for he was consistent throughout his life in writing *'Bley'*, whereas the previous generation, Thomas and William, always wrote *'Bleay'*. It is also likely that, with his Nottinghamshire accent, John Bley's pronunciation of the name differed from the modern 'Blay'. While John always wrote his name as 'Bley' clerks frequently recorded it as 'Bly', but never 'Blay', and on one occasion it was misheard as 'Blyth'.

This variation in the name reinforces the evidence that, after his birth, John had no contact with the man he believed to be his father or any other member of the Bleay family. His presumed parents lived completely separate lives and, as his mother's will testifies, she remained 'Elizabeth

Wight …. single woman'. Neither Thomas nor William Bleay made any acknowledgement of Elizabeth or John's existence in their wills. Clearly it was his mother's family who had the motivation, the contacts and the means to give John a start in life. So, in the early summer of 1690, with the aid of the Wights and doubtless with his mother's blessing, the raw youngster of 15 left his home, family and friends in rural Nottinghamshire and set off for a new life in London. He was about to enter an utterly new world.

John Bley's apprenticeship indenture, bearing the arms of the Distillers Company, detailing the reciprocal obligations of master and apprentice and signed by John on 13 May 1690. This copy would have been kept by Thomas Gilson and surrendered to the City authorities when John was granted freedom of the City seven years later. John would have retained a second copy, signed by Gilson.

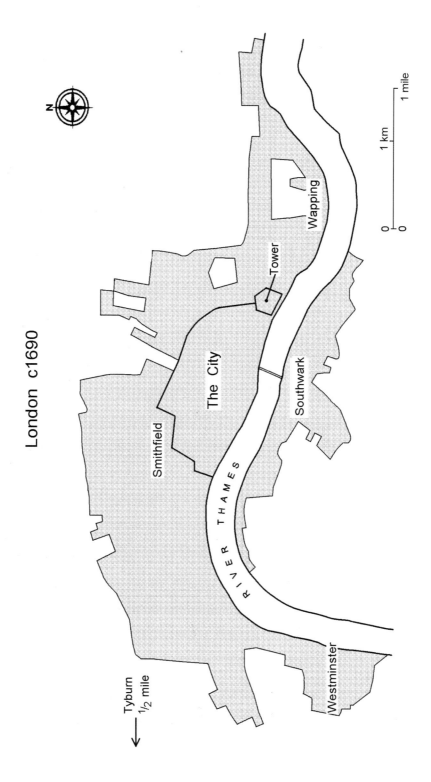

London c1690

Tyburn
1/2 mile

Smithfield

The City

RIVER THAMES

Tower

Wapping

Southwark

Westminster

1 km
1 mile

Chapter 2

'Distiller of London'

London in 1690 could not have been a greater or more bewildering contrast to rural East Leake. With half a million inhabitants, the capital dwarfed every other city in the country. Norwich, the next largest, had a population of just 30,000 while Nottingham held a mere 5000, less than East Leake has today. Twenty-five years after the Great Plague and 24 years after the Great Fire, London was in a ferment of new building and about to overtake Paris as the largest city in Europe. The political and financial centre of the nation, England's capital city was also its principal port and handled more than 75% of the country's trade. It was, too, the main centre of manufacturing and of trades ranging from dyeing and weaving to ironmongery and coach building. Thus the capital dominated the life of the country more completely than in any other period in history. At the same time it was a profoundly unhealthy place. Large-scale migration and international trade combined with crowded and insanitary living conditions to form a storehouse and breeding ground of disease; for every two children born in London at this time one was likely to die before his or her second birthday.

At the heart of the capital, forming its historic core, lay 'The City', then as now the nation's financial centre. Its population of 80,000 had been far outstripped by the rapid growth of sprawling suburbs, but it had lost none of its importance. With narrow cobbled streets festooned with overhanging shop signs, tall buildings and a shroud of smoke, the City was a crowded, noisy, dirty and smelly place and the smelliest, dirtiest, noisiest and most crowded part lay on the north bank of the river around Thames Street. In 17th century theatre the name Thames Street had become a byword for the fruity language of its carmen, or carters, and for its even fruitier stench. A few years later Salmon, in his Survey of London, would write:

> Thames Street ... lies low and wet, and is perpetually throng'd with Carts that carry Goods from the Wharfs on the Thames side into the City, there is not a dirtier or more incommodious Street to walk in in London

This same Thames Street, with its adjoining lanes and alleyways, was to be John Bley's home for the best part of 40 years.

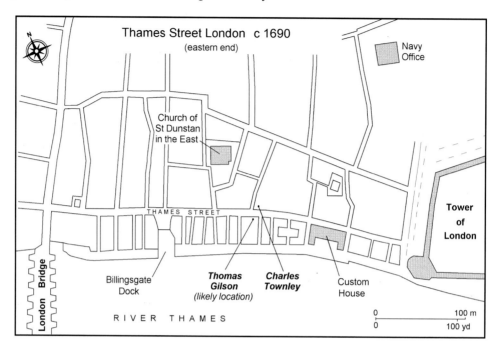

Thames Street London c 1690 (eastern end)

For administrative and taxation purposes, the City was divided into 25 wards, each sub-divided into precincts. The name of John's first master, Thomas Gilson, appeared in the 1693 property tax list under Ralph's Key, one of 12 precincts in Tower Ward. This places his house roughly halfway between the Custom House and London Bridge in, or close to, Thames Street and near the river. The amounts for which Gilson was assessed in 1693, £35 for the rental value of his house and £100 for his stock, suggest a tradesman in a modest but sound line of business. As well as distilling liquor, almost certainly gin, he sold directly to the public – his name appearing on a later list of retailers licensed to sell spirits. So he doubtless expected his apprentice to help in the shop as well as assist with distilling.

Typically, the ground floor of a distiller's home was given over to the shop and business, with domestic accommodation on the floors above. The 1692 tax return and a 1695 survey show that Gilson shared his house with his wife and daughter, both called Mary, a manservant and a maidservant.

It was normal for an apprentice to become part of his master's household and John's apprenticeship agreement promised that Gilson would provide him with 'meat, drink, apparell, lodging, and all other necessaries acording to the custome of ye City of London'. So we can picture John Bley, at the outset of his apprenticeship, living with the Gilson family above a gin shop, his status as an apprentice placing him somewhere between servant and member of the family.

John had much to learn before he could become a distiller in his own right. To begin with, he must learn the names and functions of all the apparatus in his master's still-house. Central to the process of distillation were the still, the worm – a helical tube used to condense spirit vapour boiled off from the still – and the worm-tub in which this tube was immersed to be cooled. There were iron bound tubs, cans and funnels, each with its own name and purpose, pumps, presses, cranes and valencias, flannel bags for straining liquor, fire irons and cooper's tools. Then there were all the ingredients used to produce and flavour spirits, all of which had to be properly preserved and processed.

Stillhouse with small still used for rectification (c1705)

Besides the fetching and carrying expected of any apprentice, John needed to learn the crucial importance of hygiene. All utensils had to be kept spotlessly clean to prevent the spirits from becoming contaminated and scrupulous care had to be taken in assembling and sealing the apparatus before distillation could start. As he grew accustomed to the still-house John's duties were doubtless extended to include operating the hand pump which maintained a flow of cold water through the worm-tub and maintaining the fire beneath the still at just the right temperature to ensure that only pure alcohol was boiled off.

The raw materials used by distillers included fruit and molasses, the latter derived from imported cane sugar, but the commonest raw material was fermented malt produced from grain. The conversion of fermented malt into saleable liquor involved several stages. Two distillations were required to produce 'malt spirits', the 'low wine' produced by the first distillation being left for up to 14 days before the second distillation took place. Juniper berries, or other ingredients, were added to the malt spirits for flavouring and the whole distilled a third time to give the final product. Usually this product was gin which, unlike other spirits, had the great advantage that it could be sold immediately without needing time to mature, but it might also be imitation French brandy or some medicinal draught, such as peppermint water. Generally, the work was split between two different types of distiller. Malt distillers, the elite members of the trade, produced the malt spirits and usually operated on a large scale. These spirits were then sold to the far more numerous compound distillers who made the finished 'compounded' product.

The gin produced by late 17th century stills was very different from modern unsweetened 'dry' gin, being much more full-bodied with a pronounced malty taste and aroma. It had a coarse flavour that had to be masked before it was fit for sale. As part of his apprenticeship, John would therefore learn how to 'dulcify', or sweeten, the distilled liquor and which types of sugar should be used for the purpose with different grades of spirit. To make the final product fit for sale it was clarified, using such substances as alum, and further colouring and flavouring might be added.

Spirits were highly inflammable and the presence of a fire was a constant danger to any distiller in this period, so Gilson would stress safety from the start. In his 'Compleat Body of Distilling' published in 1725, the Kendal distiller George Smith wrote:

> Above all things beware of lighted candles, torches, papers, or other combustible matter being brought too near your Still or any vessel wherein your goods are contained; which are subject to take fire upon very slight occasions: As it is in itself most dreadful, being compar'd to Fire and Gunpowder

Contemporary newspapers frequently carried reports of catastrophic accidents, usually caused when excess pressure caused the head of a still to fly off and inflammable liquid was sprayed over the surroundings. To reduce the risk, distillation normally took place in an outhouse separate from the distiller's main dwelling.

While most of his work lay indoors John doubtless had to run errands, which meant finding his way around London's streets and alleyways. These were very different from the spacious main street of East Leake. The houses in Thames Street towered some 40 feet above the ground, considerably more than the width of the roadway, and the limited strip of sky was obscured not just by the general murk but by numerous signs projecting from the buildings. Dating from an age of widespread illiteracy when written names above shops were of limited use, these illustrated hanging signs were still used to attract customers. Thus the ironmonger's shop on the corner of Thames Street and Harp Lane was identified by a sign in the shape of a giant frying pan. The Bear Key alehouse across the street stood by the lane leading to the riverside quay of the same name, but in the best heraldic tradition of visual puns it displayed a picture of a bear and a key above the heads of passers-by. With so much competition for attention, some of the signs were huge – the leases for one group of buildings in Thames Street specified a weight limit of 300 pounds.

Added to the sense of physical enclosure were the noise and the smell. The clatter of iron-shod hooves and iron-bound cartwheels on cobbles and the oaths of the carmen must have been incessant, at least in daytime, and there was no vegetation to stop the sound reverberating from the tall buildings. There was, too, the all-pervasive stench of putrid fish, rotting fruit, refuse and industrial effluent for which Thames Street was notorious down the centuries. Little wonder, then, if a raw lad from the country felt driven to flee such a claustrophobic environment; fortunately escape, at least temporary escape, was possible. There were open fields within half an hour's walk and, at the risk of being made homesick, John might head there when given time off on a Sunday afternoon. An even quicker way to get out of the narrow streets, though, was to head for the river.

Threading his way past the warehouses that separated Thames Street from the river Thames, John would emerge onto a broad quayside on the stretch of the Thames known as the Pool of London. This was the very heart of the country's trade and a scene to fire the imagination of any youngster with the least sense of adventure. In front, and stretching along the river in either direction, were sea-going ships and the lighters used to ferry goods to and from the shore. Away to the left, stood Christopher Wren's magnificent Custom House, headquarters of the customs service, where all incoming and outgoing goods had to be signed off and duties paid, with the Tower of London in the background beyond. To the right lay London Bridge, the capital's only physical link across the Thames, joining the City to Southwark on the south bank. Rebuilt in stone after the Great Fire of 1666, it was like no other bridge John could ever have seen, with shops and dwellings lining its entire length.

London Bridge from Strype's 'Survey of London' (1720)

Throughout working hours the quay was thronged with porters, purposefully threading their way round piles of goods as they tramped to and from the waterside. Outlandish accents and strange languages could be heard, for the riverside workers were a cosmopolitan bunch. John might pick up names of far-off exotic places from snatches of conversation between sailors, porters, merchants and wharfingers. He might even hear of places much closer to his Nottinghamshire home, because foreign trade was far from the port's only activity. The poor state of England's roads meant that most goods were transported between London and the provinces by ship or barge rather than by wagon. Thus a 'Merchants and Traders Companion' of 1715 listed two wagons per week travelling from London to Nottingham, but a daily shipping service to the same destination. The latter sailed via the east coast and the river Trent and departed, as it happened, from Ralph's Key. Numerous small coasting vessels, such as the Kentish hoys used to transport distillers' grain from the Medway to Bear Key, added to the panorama. The hustle and bustle of the riverside must have made a deep impression on this young apprentice used to nothing more exotic than hay wagons, an impression that may well have had a crucial influence on his future.

Overwhelming though London must have been for a boy fresh from the country, there were factors that made it easier for him to settle. The city was expanding so rapidly that most of the population were, like John, first generation Londoners. Every year some 8000 new apprentices arrived from the country to meet the demand for fresh labour, making John's provincial accent less conspicuous and making it easier for him to blend in. Secondly, there were relatives not far away who might keep an eye on him, making sure he was well treated, properly employed and behaving himself.

It is unlikely the youngster had much pocket money to spend in his leisure hours which was perhaps just as well. The standard warning in John's apprenticeship indenture 'He shall not play at Cards, Dice, Tables, or any other unlawfull games … He shall not haunt Taverns nor Play-houses nor absent himself from his said Masters service day nor night unlawfully' was there for a very good reason. Drinking and gambling were rife and were the ruin of a many a young apprentice. 'Entertainments' such as cock fighting were numerous. John had probably come across this pastime in East Leake, but in London it was organised on a grand scale:

> There has been all this Week a great Cock Match at the new Cock Pit near Gray's Inn: The Gentlemen of Middlesex and Hertford fight

against the Gentlemen of Suffolk and Norfolk; each Cock has five guineas laid on his Head; and the match continues till this Night.

Flying Post, Thursday 14 April 1698

Bull-baiting, bear-baiting, rat-baiting and dog fights all vied for attention and all were scenes of fevered gambling. Free spectacles were provided by the public punishment of criminals. Petty thieves were whipped, forgers' ears were struck off and the greatest highlight of a young apprentice's life was deemed to be a 'Tyburn holiday' – the occasion of public hangings. Condemned criminals were carried by cart over the two miles from Newgate prison to Tyburn, followed by howling mobs who alternately mocked and applauded the hangman's victims then watched eagerly as the condemned men jerked in agony on the ends of their ropes. It says something for the Gilsons and for the oversight of John's London relatives that he did not lose his way in the pleasures of the capital – and says much, perhaps, about the values instilled by his mother.

A Tyburn Execution: William Hogarth's depiction of the fate awaiting any apprentice who went to the bad, from his series 'The Idle Apprentice'

It is unlikely that John saw much, if anything, of his East Leake family and friends during the seven years of his apprenticeship. The round trip from London by stagecoach took at least a week and cost around £5 together with the price of food and lodgings en route. Even if his master could spare him for the couple of weeks needed for a worthwhile visit, the cost was well beyond the means of an unwaged apprentice, so any visit home was probably made in the company of an uncle and limited to the summer. Distillation was a seasonal activity, the summer months being too hot for the purpose, so John could be spared more readily between April and September – a time when, in any case, the roads were at their driest and the journey easiest. So visits to East Leake were possible, but likely to be rare and limited to summer time. Letters, on the other hand, could be conveyed between London and the provinces for a few pence, so John could at least write home. The indications are that Elizabeth Wight was illiterate and therefore relied on relatives or neighbours to read out her son's letters. This would limit the amount of information John received from Leake and the extent to which he might reveal his own feelings. As the years of his apprenticeship went by East Leake must have seemed increasingly remote and it is likely that John came more and more to think of London as home.

At some point in his apprenticeship John Bley changed masters; the Distillers Company records for 1697, when the apprenticeship was completed, give his master's name as Charles Townley, not Thomas Gilson. The precise timing of the switch is uncertain, the best available evidence being the 1692 poll tax return which proves inconclusive on this score. Neither Gilson nor Townley admitted to having an apprentice living with them that year, though apprentices could be described as servants and Townley is recorded as housing a 'nephew' called John – no genuine nephew of that name has yet come to light. Whatever the timing, the changeover was definitely to John's advantage, since Townley had a more substantial business than Gilson and certainly occupied a more senior position in the Distillers Company.

Townley's house stood on the north side of Thames Street, between the signs of the Frying Pan and the Three Tongs and Sugarloaf and thus close

Charles Townley's section of Thames Street, based on 19th century sketches

to the corner of Harp Lane. The house later became known as No. 76 Lower Thames Street. The probate inventory of a later tenant mentioned cellars used for storage and a counting house, which presumably occupied the ground floor. Above this, Charles Townley and his wife would occupy the principal part of the house with their children, and at the top of the building were twin garrets, one front and one rear, which John probably shared with the two servants. Geographically, John's move was a short one, so short in fact that one suspects Gilson and Townley may have had business links. In other respects, however, the transfer represented a significant change in circumstances.

For one thing, there is no record that Townley kept a shop, so John was able to concentrate more fully on learning the process of distillation. As a wholesale distiller, Townley may well have used his position close to the Thames to ship gin around the country, in which case there may have been opportunities for his apprentice to travel. Socially, Charles Townley was well connected, being descended from a Catholic landowning family of Lancashire though himself an Anglican. His father, Nicholas, had frittered away his money in futile attempts to claim a northern estate and left his sons to earn their living from trade, but Charles Townley was well on his way to repairing the family fortunes. As part of his household, John was sure to encounter many prosperous tradesmen and merchants, not least those connected with the drinks trade. Getting known by such people and getting accustomed to their company, would stand John in very good stead in his later career.

Townley's position as an 'Assistant' in the Distillers Company was another important asset. As was normal for a livery company, its affairs were run by a group of 24 distillers, known as the Court. This was chaired by the Master, aided by three Wardens, the other court members being known as Assistants. The chief business of the Court was registering apprenticeships and approving newcomers to the livery. Occasionally it took legal proceedings against people who had infringed the company's rules and it also initiated or responded to parliamentary legislation. It had an important and generally effective lobbying role. The Court met quarterly and held annual elections, a fresh Master being elected each year. As a general rule, the Master chosen was the senior Warden, the other Wardens moved up one place and the next Assistant in order of seniority was elected as a junior Warden. Former Masters reverted to being ordinary Assistants after completing their year of office, such men making up at least half the Court. If an Assistant died, a replacement was elected from the body of the membership. Voting was limited to existing members of the Court, so anyone hoping to become an Assistant needed to be on good terms with the hierarchy. Once voted onto the Court, it was normally only a matter of time before a distiller was elected Warden and then Master.

Some distillers declined the time-consuming higher offices, preferring to pay a nominal fine and concentrate on their own business. Townley appears to have been one of these. By strict order of seniority he should have become Master in 1704 and the records for that time are patchy, but his name does not feature in any of the surviving lists of Masters. He remained a respected member of the Court until his death in 1719, acting as auditor of the company accounts on at least one occasion, a role normally entrusted to former Masters. Charles Townley was clearly a man of some influence and his patronage was much to be valued.

John had arrived in London in 1690 as a raw lad of 15 but by the middle of the decade he was a fully grown man, able to do a man's work. As his apprenticeship neared its end he could expect increasing responsibility and he could also expect to learn the commercial side of his master's business. John needed to learn book-keeping and, at a time when virtually all

London trade was done on credit, the importance of keeping an exact account of all credits and debts. As Daniel Defoe put it, 'If [the books] are not duly posted, and if every thing is not carefully entred in them, the debtors accounts kept even, the cash constantly balanc'd, and the credits all stated, the tradesman is like a ship at sea, steer'd without a helm'. John would also learn the art of buying, how to judge the value of goods by colour and taste, whom to buy from and whom to avoid. Selling, too, could be a subtle art, as George Smith explained in his distilling treatise:

> You must be so prudent as to make a distinction of the persons you have to deal with: What goods you sell (especially fine goods, which always yield a good profit) to Gentlemen for their own use, who require a great deal of attendance, and as much for time of payment, you must take a considerable greater price than of others: What goods you sell to persons where you believe there's a manifest, or at least some hazard of your money, you may safely sell for something more than your common profit: What goods you sell to the poor, especially medicinally, (as many of your goods are saniferous) be as compassionate as the cases require.

John also needed to master all the accepted forms for business correspondence, including orders for goods, bills of parcel, bills of lading, invoices, receipts and letters of credit, learning to express himself clearly and concisely so as to come across as a tradesman who knew his business. From the one sample we have of his customer accounts, he certainly achieved this.

John's apprenticeship duly came to an end and on 13 July 1697 the following customary entry was recorded in the books of the Distillers Company:

> John Bley upon testimony that he served Mr Charles Townley seven years was this day admitted and sworne a member of this company

John was sworn in as a freeman of the City of London, swearing allegiance to the King (William III), the Mayor and the City authorities. This gave him the right to vote in parliamentary and local elections, a right he was to exercise many times over the years, and a number of prized trading privileges, such as freedom from local taxes when trading in the provinces.

As part of the freedom ceremony he was given a copy of 'The Distiller of London', a manual setting out the rules of the company and approved standards for the production of a wide range of variously flavoured spirits.

The recipes included such concoctions as angelica water, clove water, surfeit water, scorbutical water and a rich infusion of herbs in proof spirit known as plague water. The indefatigable George Smith wrote of the latter 'It is called plague-water because of its being a sovereign antidote or remedy against it, as against the cholick, gripes, faintings, ill-digestion, etc. and has a peculiar virtue to dispose one to sleep'. Memories of the Great Plague of 1665 had not faded.

X X V I.

ᴿ Strong proof ſpirit, *Q. S.*
  Juniper berries, ˣ *n.*
Enulacampana Roots, dry, ˣ *y.*
  Calamus aromaticus,
  Gallingall, *ana,* ꙅ *o.*
  Wormwood,
  Spear Mint, *ana,* ꙅ *n'.*
  Red Mint, all dry,
  Caruway, ſeeds, *ana,* ꙅ *n.*
  Angellica
Saſſafras Roots, with the bark,
  White Cynnamon, *ana,* ꙅ *v.*
  Nutmegs,
  Maces, *ana,* ꙅ *y.*
  Ginger,
  Cloves,
  Red poppie flowers, ˣ *o.*
  Anniſeeds, ˣ *n'.*
  Bruiſe them all.
Diſtill them into proof ſpirit.
Dulcifie with white ſugar, ˣ *ys.*

Recipe from 'The Distiller of London' (1698)

Becoming 'free of the Worshipful Company of Distillers' placed a distiller in the most basic rank of membership. The next rank was membership of the livery, which required the approval of the Court and payment of a fee; this sometimes took place at the same Court meeting. There is no record of when John Bley was elected to the livery – records for the period being incomplete, as we have mentioned – but he was certainly elected before 1710 since his name appears in livery lists from that year on.

John was now free to set up business on his own account. As far as one can judge from the limited evidence available it took him a few years to establish a flourishing distilling business, which suggests that his initial resources were limited. Archdeacon Robert Marsden of Rempstone hinted as much in his commonplace book many years later when he stated that

John had started out with no more than £100. This implies that he had enough to rent and stock a shop but not enough to acquire the premises and equipment needed to set up immediately as a distiller in his own right. John might have hoped for more substantial financial support from his family, in particular from his uncle Edward Weight, but there may have been good reasons this was not forthcoming. A document received by the House of Lords just five months before John completed his apprenticeship indicates that Uncle Edward had financial difficulties of his own.

A petition against 'An Act for Relief of Creditors by making Composition with their Debtors' was submitted in 1697 by a certain Edward Weight and two members of the Haberdashers Company, Arthur Marshall and William Buckle, along with other creditors of haberdasher Francis Simkins. The chain of debt may well have led back to the government, as Simkins supplied goods to the army and on more than one occasion had trouble getting paid; in 1693 he had petitioned the Treasury for £821 owed for hats he had supplied to two regiments. The first signature on the 1697 petition is a very good match with two that have survived for Edward Weight of East Leake, so it is likely this was indeed John's uncle. The precise reason for the objection was not stated in writing, but presumably the petitioners were owed money they could not afford to lose and feared the proposed legislation would make full recovery more difficult. As the first signatory, Edward may have been the principal creditor. All this suggests that Edward was in a substantial line of business, probably relating to haberdashery, but that he had recently suffered sizeable bad debts that might stop his advancing a large sum to his nephew.

A gap in surviving taxation records for London means we cannot track John Bley's activities or movements on an annual basis during the first few years of his career, but we can guess the course he most probably took. He could hardly set aside the amount of money he needed to set up as a distiller while just working as a journeyman for Charles Townley, so he is likely to have lost little time in striking out on his own. The cheapest way to do this was to rent a shop in a suitable location, stock it with liquor produced by his old master, and run the shop for a year or two while accumulating enough capital to purchase his own distilling equipment. It was common for masters to support their former apprentices in this way and, as a wholesaler, Townley would stand to benefit from an extra outlet. Moreover, according to one member of the trade, London distillers commonly made a 100% mark-up on their goods, so there was a very large profit margin to share round.

What few records we do have support the idea that John started out by running a shop. The land tax returns from 1697, the year he completed his apprenticeship, to 1702 are missing, but 1703 and later returns show him paying tax on a shop in Thames Street within Bear Key precinct, in other words the stretch of Thames Street between Harp Lane and Water Lane. The term 'shop' could mean workshop as well as retail outlet, but John's name appeared in an October 1701 list for Tower Ward of 'the names and surnames of the inhabitants of the said ward who are willing to take out licences according to the Act of Parliament for retailing of brandy and other distilled liquors'. So John was almost certainly running his own Thames Street liquor shop by 1701, if not earlier.

The combination of tax returns with such other documents as insurance registers enables the location of John's shop to be pinpointed exactly and its position is distinctly interesting. Four lanes or alleys connected the section of Thames Street between Harp Lane and Water Lane to the quayside running along the north bank of the river. Named after the sections of riverside to which they led, these were, from west to east, Little Bear Key, Bear Key, Porter's Key and Custom House Key. On the north side of the street the Townleys' house stood roughly opposite Little Bear Key and the house of Nathaniel Jarvis, a former Townley apprentice some ten years older than John, faced down Bear Key. At the corner of Water Lane, opposite Custom House Key, was the house of distiller Samuel Robinson. All three were prime locations for anyone hoping to attract the custom of riverside workers or tradesmen returning to Thames Street from the waterfront, but there was one obvious gap in the pattern.

A house known by the 'Sign of the Red Cross' faced the entrance gateway leading to Porter's Key and the shop on its ground floor occupied the fourth key location. Charles Townley had once been a tenant of the same landlord, possibly even in the same house, so may have provided the contact that gave John a foothold there. The residential part of the Red Cross was occupied by a Charles Robertson, but he had no need of the shop on the ground floor and John was able to rent it. Thus it was in a shop opposite the entry to Porter's Key and under the sign of the Red Cross that John Bley set out to earn his fortune.

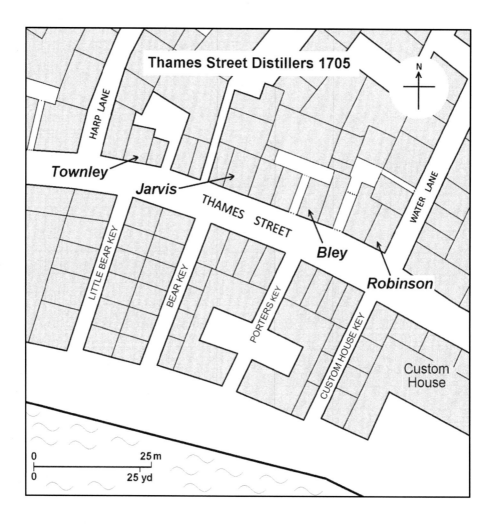

Chapter 3

Wealth

The day in Thames Street began early with the clatter of wheels and horses' hooves, the carmen taking up position in the street with their carts between 5 and 6 a.m. in the summer months and only a couple of hours later in winter. Goods on the quays could be loaded and unloaded from dawn to dusk in winter and from 6 a.m. to 6 p.m. in summer so, except for the very darkest days of winter, merchants and port workers alike were passing John Bley's shop for well over 12 hours a day. Taking full advantage of this passing trade, let alone evening trade, meant long working hours.

With the abundance of customers came a wealth of competition, most of John's neighbours in Thames Street being connected with the drinks trade in one way or another. Many of the premises were licensed to sell alcohol to the public, including the coffee houses of which there were at least five very close to John's shop. Smithers Coffee House stood in the yard behind Samuel Robinson's house on the corner of Water Lane. On the other corner of Water Lane was the King's Arms Coffee House (sometimes also described as an inn), while Sam's Coffee House was opposite Robinson's premises, on the corner of Thames Street and Custom House Key. Also on the south side of the street stood The Garter run by John Gigg, close to the corner of Bear Key, and next to it, nearly opposite John Bley, was Anne Willey's coffee house. This concentration of coffee houses is explained by the proximity of the Custom House, which made them ideal watering holes for the well-to-do merchants and traders who had regular business with the customs service.

A tavern known as the Dolphin adjoined Samuel Robinson's house and in the yard behind John's shop was the Vine tavern, owned by Peter (later Sir Peter) Eaton, and run successively in John's lifetime by Eaton himself, William Green and John Lucas. The tavern attracted some select customers, being chosen for example by the Fishmongers Company, one of the 12 elite livery companies, for one of their annual dinners in preference to any of the fashionable coffee houses.

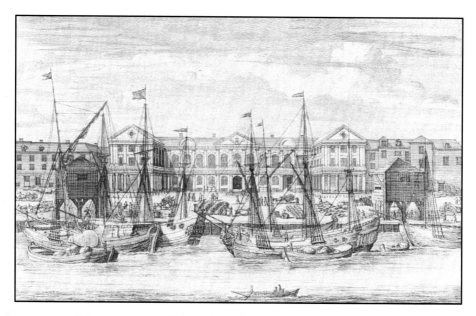

Wren's Custom House from Strype's 'Survey of London'
(published 1720, but showing the building as it was before 1715)

But there was collaboration as well as competition, as the 1701 list of liquor licences shows. The law required two people to stand surety for each licence holder and the 21 licensed liquor sellers of St Dunstan in the East parish accordingly organised themselves in threes. Each member of a threesome then stood surety for the other two. For this purpose, John Bley teamed up with former Townley apprentice Nathaniel Jarvis and a former apprentice of Jarvis called Benjamin Pinkney. The name of Thomas Gilson also appears in this list, teamed up with a fellow distiller and a victualler, but there is no mention of the two most senior Thames Street distillers, Charles Townley and Samuel Robinson, confirming that by this stage in their careers they were operating as wholesalers.

This co-operative approach helps to explain why Townley's two ex-apprentices, and later on two of John Bley's own apprentices, stayed in the short stretch of Thames Street where they had been trained. However, they had an even more important reason for starting a business where they knew, and were known by, all the local tradesmen. This was all to do with the way that City trade was conducted, not so much with cash but through the use of credit and promissory notes. The extent to which the City operated on credit was graphically illustrated by Daniel Defoe in his 'History of the Lives and Exploits of the most remarkable Pirates, Highwaymen, Murderers, Street-robbers, etc', as were the dangers inherent in accepting promissory notes from strangers.

Defoe related how two villains, tiring of their life as highwaymen, arrived in London in search of easy pickings. Forcibly struck by London traders' extensive use of credit, they determined to exploit the practice for their own ends. Pretending to be brothers operating in two widely different trades, they sought out suitable premises to rent. One villain set himself up near the Tower as a Holland merchant, while the other went into business, as it happens, in Thames Street as a corn chandler. To begin with they each bought goods in small quantities, paying with a mixture of cash and promissory notes drawn on the 'brother'. Finding that these notes were always paid promptly, the respective suppliers soon came to trust them for larger and larger sums. The two villains were able to offer good prices because they were not concerned to make a profit and within three months they had built up a large number of customers and suppliers. They then put the final part of their plan into action. Each approached his regular customers saying he would have goods available on a specific date at a special rate in exchange for cash. They then ordered the goods from a range of their usual suppliers, paying with promissory notes drawn on the 'brother' and payable in three days. The customers, told to arrive at separately appointed times to avoid suspicion, duly collected the goods and handed over their cash. Three days later, the suppliers turned up to redeem the promissory notes only to find the premises boarded up, the furniture seized for unpaid rent and the birds flown with a net profit of more than £1600. Operating within a network of local tradesmen they had known for years not only helped the Thames Street distillers obtain ready credit, it also protected them from falling victim to such fraudsters.

The rapidly rising population of London had made it a good time to start in the liquor trade in 1690 and this remained true, but the trading environment was changing. When William of Orange came to the throne in

1689 he was already leader of the Protestant forces fighting France in the Low Countries and was keen to bring England into the war. In line with this policy, he almost immediately banned imports of French brandy and to undermine the demand for foreign spirits he abolished most restrictions on the distillation of spirits in England. The result was an upsurge in the production and consumption of cheap gin in the capital, to the chagrin of the Distillers Company which saw its monopoly being eroded. It campaigned unsuccessfully to retain its control over standards but more successfully over the question of excise duties.

The distillers pointed out the medicinal benefits of their products and their important place in the wider economy. In particular they emphasised the link between distilling and agriculture, a link neatly encapsulated in the sign over Nathaniel Jarvis's shop, the Plough and Still. Distillers' waste products, spent grain and the 'wash' left behind when the spirits had been extracted, provided winter food for the pigs and cattle kept in London over winter to help feed the population. Even more importantly, the Distillers Company said, they supported agricultural prices by consuming malt and grain, especially poorer grain that could not otherwise be sold. This last argument was aimed directly at the 'landed interest', the landowning classes who dominated government and parliament, and it proved highly effective. Until 1729, excise duty on spirits remained negligible and significantly below the duty on beer. The net effect of the removal of controls combined with low duties was a huge increase in gin consumption by London's poor. By the 1720s this would lead to a chorus of protest and even as early as 1695 there may have been some concern. In that year, London's magistrates issued an order that 'vintners, coffee-sellers, alehouse-keepers, victuallers etc. shall not suffer any person to continue in their house tippling and drinking after 10 pm.' It is worth noting, though, that this order was directed at all sales of alcohol, not just gin.

The expanding market for gin among London's poorer classes is well documented, but the population 'of the middling sort' was also growing rapidly and they had more sophisticated tastes. Moreover there was no shortage of prosperous residents in Thames Street itself. Some of John's near neighbours were members of the most prestigious livery companies, including a Grocer, a Merchant Tailor and a couple of Salters. All in all, despite the grime and stench, it was a prosperous area frequented by well-to-do merchants. If he concentrated on selling gin John might make a living from the humbler inhabitants of the district, but if he were to sell more expensive spirits as well there was sure to be no shortage of customers and the profits might be significantly higher. To attract these more affluent customers and bring in really worthwhile profits John needed to broaden his stock.

One alternative to gin was rum imported from the colonies. This was fast becoming popular, whether consumed on its own or used as the basis of the punch which was served in taverns and coffee houses. Direct brandy imports from France had been banned, but brandy from Spain and Portugal was available as a substitute and even the highly sought-after French variety could be obtained quite readily. Although English ships could not trade with France, England's Dutch allies continued to do so, providing one legal route through which French goods could travel. Another legal source lay very close to hand in Thames Street itself, in the form of captured or confiscated brandy auctioned off in large quantities by the authorities. In both 1697 and 1698 several such sales took place at Smithers Coffee House, as this report from the Flying Post of 2 June 1698 demonstrates:

> On Wednesday last the Commissioners of the Prize-Office sold to the value of 3000l [£3000] of Wines, Brandy, etc. at Smithers Coffee-House, and 14 days hence will hold a Sale at the same place.

Illegal French brandy also found its way to London in large quantities, courtesy of a network of smugglers that had sprung up all around the coast to circumvent the import ban. The Kent coast was supplied by numerous French smuggling vessels landing a steady stream of brandy from across the Channel and East Anglia provided many secluded harbours and beaches where smugglers could operate. We know from John Bley's will that he had friends in Great Yarmouth, then a major port and one that developed quite a reputation for smuggling. In his book 'The Romance of Smuggling' a later vicar of Great Yarmouth would write:

I live in a house that was constructed with a view not only of the Yarmouth Roads and the North Sea but a further one of plundering the Revenue, and with the definite object of conveniences for this peculiar work. Beneath my feet as I write are large and roomy cellars, once used for the storage of imported goods, and until a few years ago a subterranean passage connected these with a landing stage by the water-side; and, let the full truth be told, the designer of all was the vicar of the parish and this house was, and is still the vicarage.

So John's acquaintance with Great Yarmouth may have brought him into contact with the smuggling 'trade'. Smugglers used major ports as well as secluded coves; officials searching for illegal arms at the port of Leith near Edinburgh in 1711 found casks of smuggled brandy hidden beneath a cargo of timber from Norway, and, as we shall see in a later chapter, the same could happen in London. What is more, we shall find a direct link between John's Great Yarmouth friends and the Norwegian smuggling route. So there were many means, legal or otherwise, by which French brandy, still the luxury tipple of choice for many Englishmen, might be added to the range of stock in John Bley's shop and help to swell his income.

John almost certainly lived in lodgings during the early part of his career, but by 1705 his business had become established sufficiently well that he could afford a house of his own. When Charles Robertson vacated the house above John's shop that year the young distiller took over the tenancy and, apart from one dramatic interruption, the house known by the sign of the Red Cross was to remain his home for the next 20 years. John's first rental agreement has not been found, but a surviving later renewal of his lease gives the history of the property. The freehold of the site belonged to a charitable trust for the parish of St Dunstan in the East and they leased it to Thomas and Elizabeth Burdett. Prior to the Great Fire of 1666 the Burdetts had four houses on the site, including a very substantial house with 12 hearths where they lived and three smaller dwellings that they let out. After the 1666 fire had destroyed the property the Burdetts built three new houses on the same plot, one of which was the tavern known initially as the Nag's Head. In due course the property passed to their son and daughter and it was from them, or their successors, that John Bley leased the most easterly house in the group.

The house was a substantial brick-built dwelling – the whole area had been rebuilt in brick since 1666 as a precaution against fire – and almost certainly had four storeys, together with a cellar. Besides specifying what building materials might be used, the regulations brought in after the Great Fire required each of the main floors to be around 10 feet high, further adding to the overall height of the building. Attached to its neighbours on both sides, the building had a street frontage of 22 feet and measured 34 feet from front to back. It was thus much taller and narrower than John's house that still stands in East Leake, but was typical of London and of this part of Thames Street. John's house and the one adjoining it on the west were mirror images, save that while his was adorned with a red cross the latter bore the sign of 'The Sugarloaf and Tobacco Roll'. The upper floors of the two houses met over an entrance passage leading to a yard at the back and to the tavern, which was now called 'The Vine'. The house being similar in size to neighbouring properties for which we have rental figures, John's rent must have been around £40 to £50 per annum.

In December 1705, soon after buying his house, John took the precaution of insuring it against fire for the sum of £300. A number of fire insurance companies had sprung up in London since the Great Fire, but John chose 'The Amicable Contributors for Insuring against Loss by Fire', more commonly known as the Hand-In-Hand Insurance Company, after its distinctive emblem of two clasped hands under a crown. This pioneering mutual company had been founded on a very small scale in a coffee house in 1696, but despite limiting its activities to London had grown rapidly, its mutual basis enabling it to undercut rival premiums and still pay annual dividends to members. John's policy was the 9633rd to be issued, though seemingly the first on this stretch of Thames Street. The company was far more than a provider of insurance. With public provision against fire in the hands of ineffective parish authorities, all insurance companies retained their own teams of fire fighters. Insured buildings had to display the

*The firemark on John Bley's
London house (reconstructed)*

company emblem to identify them to the Hand-in-Hand firemen who were directed to threatened properties by paid watchers. The Hand-in-Hand even employed a team of builders to effect repairs. The company sent surveyors to measure up properties and check their construction before agreeing to insure them (any timber-framed houses paid double) and we are indebted to the Hand-in-Hand property registers for many of the details of John Bley's house given above.

Once John was established in his Thames Street home, his fortunes blossomed. Almost at once, he started looking around for an apprentice of his own and on 25 January 1706 the Distillers Company recorded his choice in its register of apprenticeships:

> Henry Saunders, son of Robert Saunders deceased, apprenticed to John Bley for seven years

The youngster came from a seafaring family but, unlike his brothers, preferred a career on dry land. John chose well. Not only was Henry destined to have a long and successful career as a distiller but he would also become a valuable friend to John and his family. More immediately he provided his master with an extra pair of hands and, once he was able to mind the shop on his own, he freed John to look around for fresh opportunities. John did this with such startling success that by 1709 he was putting away over £1000 a year in surplus profits, more money than any East Leake farmer could hope to accumulate in a lifetime. It seems that John was distilling his own liquor by this time, rather than relying on Charles Townley as a source, since he was able to train Henry so effectively that in due time the latter rose to be Master of the Distillers Company. Also, as we have seen, John had access to other spirits to swell his sales. But this hardly explains such a rapid accumulation of wealth. Starting in trade from nothing and making such a fortune certainly did happen, but it was rare; almost all successful London tradesmen in the 18th century started with family money behind them.

So what was John's secret? For one thing, building a successful business from scratch required determination and self-discipline, which were qualities that John may have developed to a high degree to compensate for the social handicap of his illegitimacy. James Lackington, a successful 18th century entrepreneur who invented cut-price bookselling, claimed that self-discipline was crucial and expanded on the issue in his memoirs:

> I have for many years expended two thirds of the profits of my trade; which proportion of my expenditure I never exceeded. In the beginning, I opened and shut my own shop, and welcomed a friend by a shake of the hand. About a year after I beckoned across the way for a pot of good porter. A few years after that, I sometimes invited my friends to dinner and provided them a roasted fillet of veal; in progressive course the ham was introduced, and a pudding was the next addition made to the feast. For some time a glass of brandy and water was a luxury; a glass of Mr Beaufoy's raison wine succeeded; and as soon as two thirds of my profits enabled me to afford good red port, it immediately appeared

Though written near the end of the 18th century, this might almost be a blueprint for John Bley's own early career. But there was more to Lackington's business success than living well within his means, important though this was. A crucial factor in his case was that by selling at a discount he did something radically different from his fellow booksellers. John was not quite in Lackington's league, but his accumulation of wealth between 1709 and 1712 was much more rapid than one might expect from a conventional independent distiller, no matter how self-disciplined or determined; so in John's case too there must have been a 'something different' that marked him out.

Daniel Defoe, ever ready with advice for the aspiring tradesman, warned against early marriage as a serious impediment to business success. John certainly avoided this pitfall; indeed as far as we can ascertain he never married at all, whether by choice or through the social stigma of illegitimacy. This must have helped to minimise his outgoings and avoid distractions from his work, but it hardly marks him out as exceptional. Instead we must turn to the minutes of Her Majesty's Treasury to find the special factor that explains how John made his fortune.

For each of the years 1711, 1713 and 1714 the Treasury minutes list some 20 or 30 people licensed to make post entry (retrospective) payments of import duties on Spanish and Portuguese brandy and West Indian rum. Then, as now, spirits destined for export were carried in concentrated form and then diluted before sale, thus saving transport costs. However, such 'overproof' spirits were subject to double the normal rate of duty despite being only 20% over strength. The concession minuted by the Treasury allowed named persons to land their imported spirits then reduce them to normal strength by the addition of water before paying duty at the single rate, thus saving a significant amount of money. The importers were merchants who specialised in buying rum or brandy abroad and arranging for it to be shipped to London and sold at a suitably generous profit to wholesalers and retailers. Only one name in these lists belonged to a member of the Distillers' Company and that name was John Bley.

This indeed indicates a radical break from the normal activities of a distiller and at last provides a convincing explanation for John's unusual success. By cutting out the middlemen, he could keep a much greater share of the profits for himself. No longer limited by what he could sell in his own shop, he could greatly expand his business by selling imported spirits on to other traders.

This development suggests that John was not working alone, as it required a whole new set of skills. An importer had either to travel abroad to purchase his wares or to employ an agent sufficiently skilled to select high quality goods, assess their value and negotiate a good price. Shipping had to be organised to bring the goods to London and fees paid for 'lighterage (bringing the goods ashore), craneage and wharfage'. Before taking possession of his goods the merchant had to visit the Custom House to pay customs and excise duties and complete his paperwork. This involved making seven copies of his bill of entry, listing the quantities of goods and the duties payable, taking them round a succession of clerks who recorded payment of the different duties and obtaining the document that allowed the goods to be released. John was unlikely to learn all this without a mentor; a number of possibilities suggest themselves.

The Long Room in the Custom House where paperwork for imported goods had to be completed (pictured in 1808)

Charles Townley may have provided some of the relevant training and contacts while John was his apprentice. Townley's son, Charles Townley junior, was now married with young children of his own and had embarked on a highly successful career as a merchant. Moreover, the name 'Charles Townley' appeared in the post entry licence list in 1715, the year after the last entry for John Bley. So John may have been in partnership with the Townleys. A second possible partner was Nathaniel Jarvis. He had co-operated with John over liquor licences a few years earlier and appeared in the land tax records as 'Captain Jarvis' for several years, more likely a

R U L E S

FOR THE

Port of *London* :

OR, THE

Water-fide Practice.

Wherein is fhewn,

The Method to Compute the CUSTOMS by the *Book of Rates.* Likewife the Manner of making Entries, paying Cuftom, Free, or by Certificate. Penalties in feveral Acts of Parliament, relating to Imports and Exports. The Tares and Draughts allowed by the King to the Merchants. With the Fees due to the Officers. And many other Things, neceffary in *Cuftomhoufe* Difpatches.

Title page of 125 page book of London port rules

nautical rather than military designation. It is even possible they were all in business together. Another possible partner was the cooper John Bird, an acquaintance from back home in Nottinghamshire. John Bird came from an established West Leake farming family and had close ties with John Bley, whose later correspondence describes how they travelled together when visiting the Leake area (see chapter 5).

Whatever the details, the discovery that he acted as a rum or brandy merchant goes far to explain John's sudden prosperity.

It may also explain a newspaper advertisement from the end of his career which suggests that his distilling equipment was adapted for the production of molasses spirit. If carefully distilled, this spirit was purer and less pungent than malt spirit and with appropriate colouring and flavouring it could be used to mimic foreign brandy. The first edition of Encyclopaedia Britannica, published later in the century, described the widespread use of molasses spirit to eke out genuine brandy and thereby increase a distiller's profits.

By the year 1709 John's success had given him a novel problem; his trading activities were generating far more income than he could plough back into the business and he needed somewhere to put his money. Earlier generations had little option but to invest in property, either by outright purchase or by advancing money in the form of mortgages, but the scope for investment had been transformed in the years since John's arrival in London. Nothing less than a financial revolution was taking place, initially brought about by the government's need for money but now creating the financial engine that would eventually drive the world's first industrial revolution. The protracted wars against France, begun by William of Orange soon after his succession in 1689 and resumed under Queen Anne, had to be paid for. Initially King William's parliament raised money by poll and property taxes – not least the land tax that has provided us with such useful information. The reformed customs and excise services made an increasing contribution, public lotteries were used, but still there was not enough. Then, in 1694, the Bank of England was founded.

The purpose of 'The Bank', as it soon became known, was simple: to raise money for the state. In return for the guarantee of an assured income, backed by future tax revenues, City investors bought £1.5 million of Bank of England stock within the first fortnight of the bank's launch and the National Debt had, in effect, been born. Interest-bearing exchequer bills, another form of government debt, were first issued by the Treasury in 1696 and soon became an accepted part of the financial scene. Like Bank stock, they traded readily as an alternative to money or private promissory notes. While all this was going on, a thriving stock market had developed in the City, complete with brokers and stock jobbers, enabling people to invest in private companies. The range of possible investments had become huge.

Grocers Hall, home to the Bank of England 1694 to 1734
from William Maitland's History of London 1756

Exchequer notes may have been one of John Bley's first investments; he is known to have had two such notes in his possession some years later, of value £100 each and both issued in June 1709. What we do know for certain is that later in that year he began buying Bank of England stock. On 16 November John bought an initial £230 of this stock and by the following August he had accumulated £1500 worth in his own name and transferred a further £200 worth to Edward Weight. Given the quoted prices for 'Bank stock', 120 in November 1709 falling to around 110 at a time of financial crisis in August 1710, John must have paid close on £2000 for these investments.

The launch of the South Sea Company in June 1711 was another landmark in the financial revolution and gave John an opportunity to diversify. The company had been established by a Tory administration partly as a counterpart to the Whig-dominated Bank of England, with the promise of a monopoly on South Atlantic trade (essentially the slave trade) in return for taking on £9 million of short-term government debt. John Bley was one of the earliest investors in this company; in June 1712, just before the first anniversary of the company's launch, his name appeared in a list of more than 2000 shareholders entitled to vote at the first annual general meeting. Voting was restricted to investors with a least £1000 worth of stock while those with £3000 worth were given two votes. John had one vote, so it follows that within the space of three years he had invested around £2000 in the Bank of England and between £1000 and £3000 in the South Sea Company. His business was certainly flourishing!

Meticulous in money matters, John renewed his house insurance for a second seven year term in 1712, several days before it was due to run out. Not content with this, he seems to have persuaded his neighbours to insure their property with the same company, so that their whole section of Thames Street would become a priority for the Hand-in-Hand firemen if fire did break out. His next door neighbour Daniel Lampden signed up in April 1706, within four months of John, and by 1710 the majority of houses along the north side of the street from Harp Lane to Water Lane displayed the emblem of the Hand-in-Hand. This included seven of the nine properties east of Wycherley's Yard, stretching from Nathaniel Jarvis's house to Robinson's (now Mackley's) on the corner of Water Lane. It also included the two largest, the Vine Tavern and Smithers Coffee House. John's policy number was the oldest and his house was at the group's centre, making it highly likely he was the instigator. The remaining two properties in John's vicinity may have been insured elsewhere, particularly Benjamin Beard's Dolphin alehouse since Beard had taken the trouble to insure his goods with the recently founded Sun insurance company. John had taken every step possible to protect his property.

The renewal of John Bley's house insurance in 1712 (dimensions of the house, before and after 1715 rebuilding, in left-hand margin, 1715 note of insurance increase to £400 on right)

While John Bley was making investments and securing his property, his assistant Henry Saunders was nearing the end of his apprenticeship. The seven year term ended in January 1713 and Henry moved to premises just east of Water Lane, though he may have continued working for John for the time being. When the opportunity arose in 1715 Henry moved to within three doors of John and, as we shall see, the two men stayed in close contact. On 19 February 1714 a new apprentice, William Green 'son of William Green, gent', was appointed to take Henry's place. Coincidentally, a different William Green was now landlord of the Vine, but there was no connection between the two. John charged a premium of £60 for his new apprentice, a high figure for a member of the Distillers Company and a reflection of the position he had now established for himself.

Another new face appeared briefly at the Red Cross around this time; in the 1713 land tax return the payment for the property was split between John Bley and a cornfactor called Robert Godfrey. Intriguingly, Charles Townley junior, son of John's old mentor, took over the premises recently vacated by Robert near Seething Lane, suggesting possible business or social links between the three of them. By the following year the cornfactor had moved on, appearing as the sole occupant of a house on St Dunstan's Hill and leaving John Bley alone as before, but a long-lasting link between the two men had been formed. Their backgrounds were very different, with Robert belonging to a landowning family from Hampshire, but it was to Robert that John would shortly turn in a crisis and Robert's four children would be remembered in John's will.

Initially the South Sea investment proved a disappointment, as the shares slumped, but John hung onto them and in the longer term they recovered. By contrast, Bank of England stock held up well and by 1715 John had increased his holding to a face value of £2200 and a market value around £2900. In addition to all this he may, of course, have made other investments for which we have no record. Business must have been doing well; since the Treaty of Utrecht in 1713 and the signing of peace with France, trading conditions had never been more favourable. As the reign of Queen Anne drew to a close and John Bley's 40th birthday approached, the fatherless youngster from East Leake had become a successful man with a highly profitable and established business and several thousand pounds in the bank. Prospects could hardly have seemed better; no-one could have foreseen that troubles were looming.

One indirect cause of the impending crisis in John's life was a seemingly innocuous piece of legislation passed in July 1714, the last month of Queen

Anne's reign. Ironically, it was legislation designed to further the interest of British merchants. The country's future prosperity was so dependent on trade that the lack of an accurate and reliable way of establishing the positions of ships at sea had become a serious problem. The Longitude Act established a large fund to encourage scientists and inventors to come up with a solution and there were many contenders for the prize. One leading candidate was the eminent scientist and mathematician William Whiston, formerly Lucasian Professor of Mathematics at Cambridge in succession to Sir Isaac Newton. Whiston's scheme involved stationing a series of ships at fixed points across the ocean and firing star shells thousands of feet into the air to be detonated at precise times. By observing the detonations and measuring the time taken for sound to reach an observer, Whiston claimed, passing vessels should be able to determine their position.

In the autumn of 1714, Whiston carried out a series of experiments to further his scheme and entrusted the manufacture of the exploding shells to Charles Walker, a near neighbour of John Bley. Walker sold oil and gunpowder from a small shop at the sign of the Hand and Gun on Bear Key, next to the Bear Key alehouse and just off Thames Street. An acknowledged expert in the field of rockets and explosives, he was in the words of one chronicler 'esteemed by the ingenious to be an expert Ingenier and was therefore look'd upon as the most properest person to be employ'd in such an Undertaking'. This may have been welcome work for Charles Walker but, as the next chapter will show, it was to prove a fateful undertaking for John Bley and his other neighbours.

Chapter 4

1715 Fire, ice and rebellion

The death of Queen Anne on 1 August 1714 marked a watershed in British history. It brought the House of Hanover to the throne, ended the grip of Tory ministers on government and ushered in a prolonged period of political dominance for the Whig party. As a staunch Whig voter, John Bley must have welcomed the shift in power, but the change was far from popular with Londoners in general and there was mounting unrest.

The root of the political problem lay in religion. James II had been expelled in 1689 essentially because of his Catholicism and his son, James Stuart, was still recognised as the rightful British monarch by the king of France and by many sympathisers – Jacobites – in Britain itself. The new king, George I, was the nearest surviving Protestant relative of the dead queen, but was so distant a relation that many questioned his legitimacy. Furthermore the London mob distrusted the Whigs, associating them with religious nonconformity and thus with the bleak Puritanism of the commonwealth period. The reserved, German-speaking king did little to endear himself to his new subjects and, as the months went by and the Whigs entrenched themselves in power, support for James Stuart grew.

Faced with rising discontent, the government determined to bolster the King's popularity by declaring a public holiday. They proclaimed that Thursday 20 January 1715 was to be a day of general thanksgiving for the succession of King George, a day of fireworks and celebration. Preparations for a grand firework display were put in place and men were set to work making squibs and rockets. One of these was reported to be the explosives expert Charles Walker, based some 40 yards from John Bley's house, just round the corner in Bear Key alleyway. The fireworks display, coming on top of Walker's longitude work for Whiston, meant there was an unusually large stock of gunpowder at the sign of the Hand and Gun that January.

Contemporary accounts combine to give a vivid picture of what happened on Thursday 13 January. The most detailed report states that Walker was away from London that afternoon and, with only a week left before the fireworks display, his apprentice was hard at work packing gunpowder into rockets. By five o'clock it was becoming very dark and it is presumed the youngster lit a lamp in order to continue working. The lamp may have been knocked over, or it may simply have been moved too near the gunpowder. Whatever the exact chain of events, the powder ignited and exploded, with a blast so violent that it destroyed both Walker's house and much of the alehouse next door, killing most of the occupants and setting the surroundings ablaze. Channelled by the narrow street and high buildings, the blast was powerful enough to kill ironmonger's apprentice John Smith as he stood at the door of the Frying Pan, just along Thames Street. Such an explosion must have shattered every window in the vicinity and brought everyone, John Bley included, rushing into the street.

In calmer weather the damage might have been limited to the immediate area, but a near gale was blowing. Flames leapt to the warehouses across the narrow Bear Key alleyway – warehouses packed with inflammable export goods awaiting transport and imports awaiting customs clearance. They were soon burning fiercely. The fire spread to other houses nearby, then, carried by the strong south-westerly wind, drove northwards across Thames Street to where Nathaniel Jarvis' house stood. From Cuxon's 'Full and Particular Account' of the fire it seems Nathaniel and his family had very little time to get out; indeed, Mrs Jarvis was lucky to escape alive:

> At the Stillers next ... to where the fire began they was forced to take the Woman of it out of a Window up two pair of Stairs by a Ladder.

Further along the street John Bley and his immediate neighbours just had time to rescue their most prized possessions before they, too, were driven out by the advancing flames. At the Vine tavern, just behind John's house, William and Elizabeth Green gathered their young children together and prepared to flee along with their most precious belongings, including a collection of coins, medals and valuable rings in a japanned box and a bundle of down pillows and lace garments tied up in a flaxen sheet marked with William Green's initials. Both box and bundle were lost in the confusion. Unhampered by children, John may have been able to move more of his belongings to safety, but it is unlikely he was able to do much about his distilling equipment. The Garter Coffee House and the other buildings on the south side of Thames Street were directly in the path of the fire and must have been destroyed early on. On the north side too, the flames marched inexorably along the line of houses towards the junction with Water Lane. John Bley's home was engulfed.

All was noise and confusion. Fire fighters and onlookers rushed to the scene, as did merchants frantic about their goods. Residents fled in the opposite direction, shepherding their families and carrying their valuables. This made it hard for the fire fighters to force a way through and engage the flames. The warehouses south of Thames Street burnt so fiercely that the southern edge of the fire was able to edge slowly against the wind towards the river. There was pandemonium on the quayside as desperate efforts were made to evacuate goods across the water. Looters and pickpockets helped themselves to anything they could, taking full advantage of the darkness, smoke and confusion. Large quantities of merchandise were lost or ruined in the panic.

As the insurers of most properties lining the north side of Thames Street, the Hand-in-Hand had a major interest in fighting the fire and rushed all 28 of its available firemen to join others at the scene. Their main weapons against the flames were water buckets and hand pumps which were of limited use against a major fire; nevertheless, for a while, they seemed to have some effect. By midnight, the flames were subsiding and the fire fighters thought they had gained the upper hand. They may have become complacent and some may even have left the scene; certainly the Hand-in-Hand directors were far from satisfied with the conduct of their men and later issued formal reprimands. In the early hours the fire flared up again and, driven by the strong wind which had swung round towards the south, worked its way steadily up the west side of Water Lane and through the warehouses behind Thames Street towards Tower Street to the north. Trinity House, headquarters of the Thames pilots, was destroyed. The inflammable nature of the merchandise stored in the warehouses, not least the spirits, meant that once these buildings were well alight it became impossible to dowse them.

By noon on Friday the fire had reached Tower Street and threatened to leap across into Mark Lane, with its opulent merchants' houses. The Lord Mayor, in his capacity as chief magistrate, had taken personal charge of operations, assisted by one of the sheriffs, and decided it was imperative to prevent the fire spreading further north and repeating the destruction of 1666. He ordered seven houses on Tower Street to be blown up to create a fire break. This checked the spread of the fire but at the cost of several lives. The southern end of the conflagration had now reached the river and had worked its way as far east as the Custom House, threatening it with imminent destruction, along with the loss of several hundred thousand pounds worth of goods. The Mayor and Sheriff called for the Custom House to be saved, one of the Customs Commissioners promised a reward and a bold army lieutenant leapt into action, blowing up Sam's Coffee House and the houses immediately adjoining the Custom House.

There were many individual acts of heroism in the fight to stem the fire, many injuries and further deaths, not least from the use of gunpowder to demolish houses standing in the path of the flames. At least one fire fighter was killed outright and several others were injured, including three employed by the Hand-in-Hand. The spread of the fire was finally halted by mid-afternoon on Friday though the last of the flames were not extinguished until the following day. Only then could the residents, merchants and authorities begin to take stock of the losses.

Initial newspaper reports of 200 houses destroyed and 50 deaths were much exaggerated, but the truth was grim enough as the subsequent report from the City magistrates made clear:

> upon the thirteenth day of January last past there happened a sudden and dreadful fire in Thames Street, Tower Street and other parts in the parish of St Dunstan in the East in the said city of London which in three days time burnt down utterly consumed and destroyed to the ground upwards of fifty dwelling houses besides a great number of warehouses and vaults full of merchandizes of the said petitioners which were utterly consumed many of the said petitioners narrowly escaping the flames not having time to save any of their goods and

merchandizes but lost all their whole substance by this sad and calamitous accident and that the said petitioners who before lived in a reputable manner are now reduced to extream want and poverty and that both they and their families must inevitably perish unless timely relieved by the charity of well disposed persons and that the said poor sufferers have hitherto been preserved from starving by private charities.

This report was prefixed with the names of 60 petitioners, a mixture of residents with traders who had lost their goods. It mentioned others who had been left widows and orphans and ended with an appeal to the Lord Chancellor to allow the collection of alms to relieve the suffering.

The devastated area extended northwards from the river to Tower Street. To the east it reached the Custom House but did not cross Water Lane. To the west it stretched just past Nathaniel Jarvis's house on Thames Street and affected the backs of some properties on Harp Lane. The latter included the house of John Bley's friend William Parker, who had shown the foresight to insure his goods with the Sun insurance company as well as insuring his house with the Hand-in-Hand. Trinity House was the most substantial building burnt to the ground and Bakers Hall, close to Charles Townley's house, was damaged. Initial reports said that Wren's Custom House had been saved, but it turned out to be so badly damaged that it had to be pulled down and replaced. John Bley, James Wyke next door, the Green family at the Vine Tavern and Nathaniel Jarvis all lost their homes, as did John Mackley, Samuel Robinson's son-in-law and successor as distiller on the corner of Water Lane, Benjamin Beard at the Dolphin alehouse, the Giggs at the Garter coffee house and everyone else living on the stretch of Thames Street between Bear Key and the Custom House.

The board of the Hand-in-Hand responded to the loss with impressive speed. Not waiting for their regular meeting scheduled for the Tuesday, the directors all assembled on the morning of Monday 17th to inspect the damage in person, accompanied by a team of surveyors. The latter were instructed to waste no time in preparing an assessment of the likely cost in time for the board meeting on the following day. The directors must have been taken aback by the extent of the damage, for when they reconvened in the afternoon their discussion focused largely on what losses they might avoid paying. They agreed they should not pay for internal door locks or 'leaking glass plates in frames or doores' in partially damaged property, but could not agree on payment for lead downpipes that had been melted by the heat, postponing this part of the discussion until the next day.

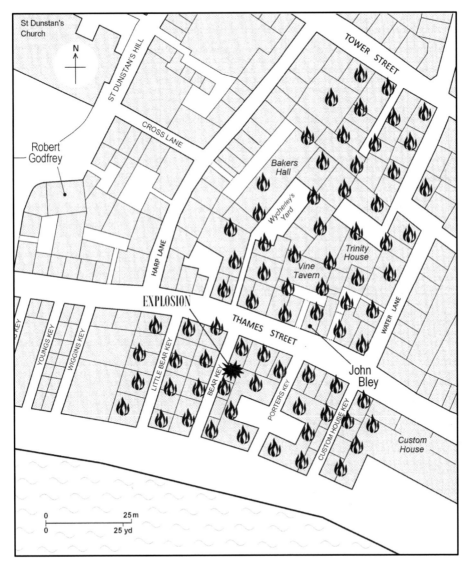

The extent of the Thames Street fire 13-15 January 1715

On Tuesday 18th the first claims were heard. The distillers John Mackley and Nathaniel Jarvis both appeared before the board and it was at once agreed that, since their houses had been completely destroyed, they should be paid the full amount insured (£300 and £400 respectively) and this should be handed over the following Monday. A few of the assessments on less badly damaged properties were disputed by the owners, including William Parker who eventually settled for £12 5s 6d, but settlement was agreed promptly and in full on all houses completely destroyed.

When the board met again the following Saturday another batch of claimants appeared including William Green's landlord Peter Eaton, who claimed £800 as the owner of the Vine tavern, and John Bley:

> Mr John Bley appearing at the Board in relation to his house burnt down at the aforesaid Fire No 6933 insured in this office at £300 Ordered that the Treasurer pay him this sum on Saturday the 29th Instant he allowing the usual discount for prompt payment.

So John received his payout just two weeks after the fire and was free to begin clearing the site and planning a rebuild. This could not necessarily start at once however, as he had party walls and neighbours to consider, and it was to be eight or nine months before rebuilding was complete and he could move back into his Thames Street home.

Within days of the fire, all the main insurance companies were advertising for claimants and competing to show how quickly they could respond. On 28 January the Friendly Insurance Society reported that repairs on 16 indemnified houses were almost complete. By March they were advertising that they had paid out £3000 to the Fishmongers Company for houses and warehouses destroyed by the fire and £1500 to the Corporation of Trinity House, whose headquarters had been destroyed. Not to be outdone, the Hand-In-Hand Company announced that it had paid out a total of more than £9000 for the fire in Thames Street together with one in Houndsditch the previous July. The relatively young Sun insurance company (founded in 1710) could not compete directly with these figures but published the names of 13 people who had received pay-outs, William Parker and Benjamin Beard among them. So most buildings in the area were probably insured and the owners compensated, but relatively few had insured their goods.

In the case of the warehouses, the contents were far more valuable than the buildings that housed them and total losses were officially estimated at £500,000, a huge sum for the time. There was limited compensation available, either through an appeal fund raised by the civic authorities or from the government. The July petition to the Lord Chancellor was accompanied by a list of losses claimed by the 60 petitioners amounting to a total of £7639. Two of the largest claims were recorded by Nathaniel Jarvis and by John Bley's next door neighbour James Wyke, £433 12s 6d and £515 10s respectively. Elizabeth Gigg of the Garter claimed £103 12s 6d and Benjamin Beard of the Dolphin £73 5s – presumably for losses over and above the compensation he received from the Sun insurance company for goods destroyed. The name John Bley did not appear on the petition, which may mean he had time to organise the removal of his goods or that they were separately insured. They were not insured with the Sun, though, since John's name does not appear on the 1714 list of Sun policyholders and the Hand-in-Hand insured buildings only. Some other groups of merchants petitioned parliament for relief and eventually received compensation from the Treasury. One of these groups was led by Thomas Coleman, the proprietor of Smithers Coffee House.

Evidence of looting became increasingly apparent in the days following the fire. Newspaper advertisements began to appear, offering rewards for the return of pocket books and letter cases containing valuables 'lost at the late fire'. Other notices mentioned goods carried off while owners had been trying to rescue their property. These included the Greens' japanned box and bundle of linen, one merchant's 11 casks of white Barbados ginger 'thought to have been carried away by boat', another's casks of sugar and a third merchant's bales of cloth. In one case it is clear an abandoned house in Thames Street had been looted, the choice pickings including silverware, silk clothing and barrels of anchovies. All this suggests the work of organised gangs as well as casual pilferers. Some bystanders, though, were far more public spirited. Seven days after the fire, the Weekly Review reported that a merchant had been sitting in Garraway's Coffee House, ruing his losses, when a gentleman approached and handed him a bag containing 500 guineas in gold 'which the other in a Fright had put into his hands at the Fire'. The merchant had no idea to whom he had given the money and had been convinced he would never see it again.

Looting apart, some people profited from the conflagration quite legitimately. Builders and newspaper proprietors stood to gain – then, as now, sensational news sold papers. J. Cuxon published the story of the fire in the pamphlet which has been quoted above. It bore the unwieldy but informative title 'A Full and Particular Account of that Sad and Deplorable Fire, Which happen'd on Thursday the 13th of January 1714/15, about 6 a clock, at Bear-Key, between the Custom-House and Billingsgate, with a True and Exact List of all the Persons who were Kill'd and Wounded, as also their Names and Places of Abode; Likewise the Number of Houses which were Burnt, Blown up and Damag'd.' and sold at one penny a copy.

Cuxon's pamphlet is the most detailed account to have survived and must have been written within days of the fire, as it speaks of people still trapped under the rubble. Among the dead he listed three members of the Bond household at the Bear Key alehouse, several other local residents and many people with homes outside the immediate area. The latter may have been there on business, may have come to rescue goods in the warehouses or were perhaps just curious bystanders who got too close to the action. Although the insurance companies lost money in the form of payouts, they may also have benefited in the longer term; by advertising their payouts they doubtless hoped to attract fresh business. John Bley's friend Robert Godfrey, for example, insured his property on St Dunstan's Hill with the Hand-in-Hand just days after the fire. London preachers found the fire a fruitful subject for their sermons and were not above cashing in. By the end of the month it was possible to buy a sermon on the theme of the fire by Mr John Evans for four pennies or 'A Call to Repentance by Jonathan Owen, Minister of the Gospel', based on the fire, for just three pence.

Recriminations began almost before the embers had cooled, with the directors of the Hand-in-Hand interrogating their fire fighters, dismissing half a dozen, demoting others and reorganising their fire fighting teams. The City magistrates held their own inquiry to establish the facts and count the cost. Many people asked why no lessons appeared to have been learnt from the Great Fire of 1666 and a lengthy letter to the Daily Courant from a Dutch merchant drew very unfavourable comparisons between the orderly way fires were dealt with in Amsterdam and 'the great confusion and impertinent crowd there always is at a fire in London; no body governs, no body will obey, very few will work, and the many, the very many only look on and incumber the ground'.

But it was the residents of the burnt-out area who had to deal with the aftermath. For tradesmen who had lost their premises the loss of business must have been a huge setback. It might mean months without any income and it might also result in the permanent loss of customers. A few houses were rebuilt with remarkable speed, but most were still unoccupied when that year's land tax assessment was signed off in October. John Bley and his neighbours had to find alternative accommodation for several months, not just for families but, if at all possible, for their business activities and for this they fell back on friends and relatives.

William and Elizabeth Green and their children sought refuge with Elizabeth's father in Smithfield – it was from here they advertised the loss of their property and a £10 reward for its recovery. So the Greens had help supporting their family, but they had to wait many months before they could reopen the Vine tavern and resume business. John Bley found a base on St Dunstan's Hill, this being the address he gave in August that year. It was very likely the home of his friend Robert Godfrey who had substantial premises on the south side of the street facing the church. Robert had insured this property for £800 in the wake of the fire, so must have had a considerable amount of space; he may even have been able to furnish John with room to carry on at least the import side of his business.

To judge by the land tax return, John was back in Thames Street by October, ahead of most other residents and in time for the winter distilling season. Meanwhile the re-establishment of his home and business made inevitable inroads into his savings. Re-equipping a still house could set him back hundreds of pounds and the £300, less discount, that he had received from the insurers must have been more than used up in restoring the dwelling house. In December John increased the insurance on his house to £400, a sign that he had not stinted himself and had spent significantly more than the insurance money on rebuilding. John and his neighbours probably took the opportunity to adopt the latest building style; this section of Thames Street, 'that part of it that has been rebuilt since the fire, anno 1714[/15]', stood out as particularly 'well-built' in a survey of 1731. Almost certainly they incorporated the newly fashionable tall multi-paned windows that we now associate with the Georgian period. As we shall see in a later chapter, such windows still exist in the house that John was having built in East Leake at roughly the same time.

St Dunstan's Hill & Church from Thames Street (Cooke 1834)

One part of Thames Street that was reconstructed far more quickly than the rest was the block of five properties between John Bley's house and Water Lane owned by the Fishmongers Company. Whereas work on the St Dunstan's Charity land was not finished until the autumn, the Fishmongers' block was restored within two months. Added to close similarities in the details of construction, this suggests that rebuilding was organised by the principal tenant, though paid for by his five sub-tenants. By March, leases for the 'newly built' houses were being drawn up. Distiller John Mackley signed a new lease for his house on the corner of Water Lane, but then decided to move his home and business to Clerkenwell. This created an opening that John's ex-apprentice Henry Saunders was quick to exploit, moving into the premises at the end of March and then negotiating a fresh 21 year lease with an option to extend it for a further 21 years. In the event, Henry remained at this address, subsequently known as 62 Lower Thames Street, for the rest of his life. He worked there as a distiller until his death in 1771 at the ripe old age of 80.

The details of Henry Saunders' lease, together with a much later sale notice, give a good picture of his style of living and indirectly indicate how John Bley himself now lived. John's Thames Street home, valued at the same amount as Henry's by the land tax assessors, being the same size and insured for the same amount, must have been broadly similar, apart from being in the middle of a row rather than on a street corner. Henry's house was brick-built with its main entrance on Thames Street and a side door opening onto Water Lane. On the ground floor he had a warehouse and counting house, with a still house at the back. The living quarters occupied the upper floors, with a dining room, kitchen, five bedrooms and various closets, arranged three rooms to a floor. There was full-height deal panelling in all the main rooms, 'chair high' panelling on the stairs and in the kitchen and crown glass in all the windows. The latter were secured by 26 window bars. There were four marble fireplaces, those in the kitchen and the room above being of Purbeck marble while those in the dining room and the room over it were set with 'gally tiles'. The roof was covered with lead. Henry was responsible for all maintenance, including the adjoining pavements on both streets, and had to insure the building for at least £400 against fire. The two houses between Henry Saunders and John Bley, let out by the same person, had almost identical descriptions. Smart on the outside with their Flemish bond brickwork and elegant windows, these houses were no doubt equally fashionable inside, with the latest style in furniture complementing tastefully painted panelling.

A spacious house needed staff as much as it needed furniture and John would lose no time in finding suitable people. Besides his apprentice, William Green, John's household required servants to cook, wash and clean and for at least some of these it is very likely he looked to his native village.

There were several advantages in bringing staff from East Leake: John would know their family and personal backgrounds and they would owe their chief loyalty to him, not anyone else in London; they were less likely than locals to gossip about his affairs to alehouse cronies or to steal his valuables, as they could hardly return home to East Leake denounced as thieves. John may also have wanted to help deserving youngsters from his home village by providing employment. Certainly the servants named in John's will 15 years later were all linked to East Leake families.

Although there may have been external architectural improvements, the north side of Thames Street essentially retained its previous layout with houses rebuilt on their previous foundations and overhanging signs reinstated. These signs included the Red Cross on John Bley's house, mentioned when John extended his lease a couple of years later, and probably the Sugarloaf and Tobacco Roll on the other side of the re-established gateway to the Vine tavern. One sign did not reappear, though, for Nathaniel Jarvis had decided to move out of the area. His house was sold to someone unconnected with distilling and when the new owner's name was inserted in the insurance register the phrase 'the Plough and Still' was crossed out and a new sign name written in. On the opposite side of the street, however, the picture was different. Sea-borne trade had boomed in recent years and storage space for goods was at a premium. Although the south side of Thames Street itself was lined with rebuilt shops and coffee houses, there were none on the alleyways leading down to the river. The whole area between Thames Street and the river was now devoted to warehousing. When the Custom House was eventually rebuilt Wren's concept of a 'Long Room' was retained but the building was significantly enlarged, acquiring an extra storey and extending westward over ground previously occupied by a row of business premises. Maps of the period, while not wholly reliable, appear to show fewer but larger premises on the section of street facing John Bley's house.

A quite separate event took place shortly after the fire, just possibly throwing light on the activities of John's Uncle Edward. On 7 February 1715 a Treasury minute noted an application by a certain Edward Weight to be readmitted to the post of deputy searcher to the excise service at Gravesend, a position he had held since 1700. The application was successful and on 25th a warrant was issued allowing him to be resworn into office. Although the salary for the searchership at Gravesend was modest, just £10 a year, the rewards could be considerable. Searchers collected fees from all ships sailing from London, ranging from ten shillings for ships bound for the East Indies to four pence for coastal vessels, together with six pence a time from passengers. They searched the ships for contraband and kept a substantial share of any money raised from the sale of confiscated goods. Such searcherships, along with other customs and excise posts, were commonly given as sinecures to those in favour at Court, while deputies were paid to do the actual work.

Ripley's Custom House that replaced the one damaged in 1715

This is radically different from the haberdashery interests mentioned in the second chapter, so we cannot be totally sure this Edward Weight was John's uncle, but it would link him to Gravesend. Four years later, at Rochester cathedral, an 'Edward Waite' married Eleanor Archer of Milton near Gravesend and we know from his will that Uncle Edward married relatively late in life and that his wife was called Eleanor Archer.

Furthermore, if Edward had business that took him to the Thames Street headquarters of the Customs and Excise, he could keep in regular touch with John Bley and get to know Henry Saunders well. In the event, he became such friends with Henry that 13 years later he made the latter executor of his will. From John's point of view as an importer of spirits, having a close relative working for the excise could not fail to be useful.

While the residents of Thames Street were absorbed in their own troubles for much of 1715, public affairs were taking an ominous turn. The unrest following King George's accession had steadily increased. Jacobite activists seized every opportunity to stir up trouble, even proclaiming the Thames Street fire as a portent from heaven. The anniversary of Queen Anne's coronation on 23 April was the pretext for riots in London. Further royal anniversaries in May and June were marked by more rioting up and down the country as well as further disturbances in the capital. Dissenting meeting houses were particularly targeted, along with the residences of leading Whig merchants and politicians. By July the situation was so bad that draconian measures were called for and the newly elected Whig government passed the famous, or infamous, Riot Act. This enabled magistrates to disperse crowds without having to wait, as previously, for trouble to start. They simply had to read out the proclamation:

> Our Sovereign Lord the King chargeth and commandeth all persons, being assembled, immediately to disperse themselves, and peaceably to depart to their habitations, or to their lawful business, upon the pains contained in the act made in the first year of King George, for preventing tumults and riotous assemblies. God Save the King!

The crowd then had one hour to disperse before force was used against it. This let magistrates take action before a mob could build up to an uncontrollable size. The Act also made it a capital offence for anyone 'riotously assembled' to cause serious damage to 'places of religious worship, houses, barns, and stables'. Although passed as an emergency measure, the Riot Act proved so useful that it was kept on the statute books and used to tackle civil unrest throughout the next two centuries.

While this emergency legislation may have deterred some of the mob violence, it did little to reduce the very real threat of a Jacobite uprising. Plots to place James Stuart on the throne were discovered, imagined and real, and leading Tory politicians known to sympathise with the Jacobite cause were arrested or fled abroad. Rumours of impending rebellion were rife. In August, members of the Whig party drew up lists of people they suspected of disloyalty so that their houses could be searched. Roman Catholics were automatically included and even being a staunch Tory may have been enough to warrant inclusion. Some 61 houses were listed for Tower Ward, including the homes of Charles Townley senior of Thames Street, his son Charles Townley junior of Tower Hill and John Bley's next door neighbour James Wyke. The inclusion of the Townleys is not surprising. Although they had abandoned the religion of their ancestors they had made no secret of their allegiance to the House of Stuart, each naming his two eldest sons Charles and James.

As a staunch Whig, John's loyalties were not in question and he had nothing to fear personally from these searches, but there were other threats to his peace of mind. In August he was still coping with running what business he could from temporary premises, overseeing the rebuilding of his house and probably dealing with the building of his house in East Leake all at the same time. This was hardly the best time to suffer a new financial blow. However, the following advertisement appeared in the Daily Courant of 27 August and was repeated in at least two other papers:

> Lost the 26th instant, between the Tower and Fenchurch-street, two Exchequer Notes of 100 l. each, No 12514 and 12519, both dated the 28th of June 1709, interest paid at the Exchequer to the 25th of March 1714; whoever brings them to Mr Tho. Maddocks of the Bank of England, shall have 5 l. Reward. Payment being stopt.

Such advertisements for lost, or more likely stolen, property were quite common, though seldom involving as much as £200. Although the notes had been issued by the Exchequer in Whitehall, interest payments were managed by the Bank of England, which explains the bank's involvement.

A second version of the advertisement that appeared a few days later makes it clear the owner of the notes was John Bley:

> Lost the 26th of August last between the Tower and Fenchurch-street, Two Exchequer Notes of 100 l. each, No. 12514, and 12519, both dated the 28th of June 1709, interest paid at the Exchequer to the 25th of March 1714; whoever brings them to Mr Tho. Maddocks of the Bank of England, or to Mr. John Bley on St. Dunstan's-Hill, Tower-street, shall have 20 Guineas reward, and no Questions ask'd. Payment being stopt.

Evidently the first notice had not achieved an immediate result and John was anxious to get his money back – far too anxious to wait. He may even not have bothered consulting Thomas Maddocks before raising the reward to 20 guineas; both versions of the advertisement appeared in the same edition of the London Gazette on 30 August, though on different pages. The final outcome is uncertain. There is no record of these notes in the Bank of England's lost or stolen list, so they may indeed have been retrieved, but there is no positive confirmation. The incident does show that John was dealing with substantial sums of money that August, perhaps in connection with rebuilding, but we can only guess what exact errand caused him to carry such valuable notes through dangerous streets – streets that were less safe than ever that summer because of the worsening political situation.

In September open rebellion broke out in Scotland and an invasion of England was anticipated at any time. A dangerous uprising in the West Country was narrowly averted by the arrest of its key leaders and arrests continued in London, Oxford and elsewhere. As autumn wore on, further news trickled through to London. There were rumours of an uprising in Lancashire and reports of rebel advances and setbacks in Scotland. Any news from the north was many days out of date by the time it reached the capital and this added to the uncertainty. A Jacobite force crossed the border from Scotland on 1 November, but it was a further seven days before the Daily Courant and other London papers reported that this group of rebels had entered England and was heading for Kendal. Further reports followed, as the 1500 strong rebel army moved south via Lancaster to meet up with its Lancashire sympathisers and government forces converged to intercept them. Then on 18 November the London Gazette announced a comprehensive rebel defeat at Preston. At the same time news of an inconclusive engagement between the main rebel army and government troops at Dunblane reminded the authorities in London that the danger was not yet over. They decided to administer an oath of loyalty to all persons suspected of 'treasonable practices', thus anyone on the lists drawn up in August. Both John and his friend Robert Godfrey were named among the 18 commissioners chosen to supervise the administration of this oath in Tower Ward, so John may have found himself in the embarrassing position of overseeing the swearing of oaths by his former master and by his next door neighbour.

Fortunately for King George and for the Whig government, the rebellion was badly managed. James Stuart did not arrive in Scotland until December, by which time the uprising had lost its momentum and his forces were in retreat. The death of Louis XIV of France on 1 September had deprived James of his most important supporter and the Regent acting for the under-age Louis XV, beset by debt, failed to provide any troops. By February 1716 James was heading back to France and the rebel army dispersed, many of its leaders being captured and brought to London for trial, others following James into exile. One of the captives was Charles Townley's distant cousin, Richard Towneley of Towneley Hall in Lancashire, who was put on trial for treason and lucky to be acquitted. Richard's younger brother Francis was to be less fortunate 30 years later when he was executed for taking up arms in support of James Stuart's son, Bonnie Prince Charlie. King George and his government were safe, but they were still far from popular with the citizenry of London and intermittent unrest continued for some time. On James Stuart's next birthday, 10 June 1716, the government was sufficiently edgy to order troops onto the streets and these patrolled with drawn swords to forestall any repetition of the previous year's rioting.

Fate had one final twist in store for John Bley and his fellow Londoners as this momentous year drew to a close, but not this time through human action; it came in the form of the weather. In December an exceptionally hard frost set in and the Thames above London Bridge, protected from inflowing tides by the bridge's narrow arches, froze over completely. Ice-floes further downstream made navigation impossible, the waterborne trade on which much of John's business depended came to a complete standstill and riverside labourers were thrown out of work. The freeze lasted for two months and by mid-January the ice was so thick that it supported an extensive frost fair with stalls, wrestling matches and other entertainments set up on the ice. One line of tents was dubbed 'Thames Street' and doubtless featured plenty of liquor stalls. According to Dawks' News-Letter of 14 January:

> The Thames seems now a solid rock of ice; and booths for the sale of brandy, wine, ale and other exhilarating liquors, have been for some time fixed thereon; but now it is in a manner like a town: thousands of people cross it, and with wonder view the mountainous heaps of water, that now lie congealed into ice. On Thursday, a great cook's shop was erected, and gentlemen went as frequently to dine there, as at any Ordinary.

Printing presses were set up on the frozen river to turn out commemorative cards, the theatres were abandoned in favour of the ice and the Court turned out in force to view the scene. On 21 January Dawks reported:

> his Royal Highness the Prince of Wales attended by several of the Nobility, crossed the River upon the Ice to see the Curiosities there; on which Day there was such an extraordinary Spring Tide that it over-flowed Palace Yard, and filled most of the Cellars thereabouts; and notwithstanding the Ice was raised several Foot perpendicular, it gave no interruption to the Diversions on the Thames.

No doubt the fair was an unforgettable experience for local children, and for John's young apprentice William Green. It might also be enjoyed as a novelty by those adults who had sufficient fuel and food to cope with the cold and no urgent need to earn a living. John Bley's enjoyment, though, must have been tempered by the thought that this was yet another unexpected interruption to trade, just when his life had got back to normal.

A frost fair on the Thames, showing booths, carriages, bull and bear baiting and other activities on the ice, with London Bridge in the background

In due time, however, the great freeze ended, political unrest subsided and normality did indeed return for the residents of Thames Street. We have no means of knowing if John Bley saw the year 1715, and particularly the Thames Street fire, as a pivotal time in his life, or if it made him rethink his priorities. To the biographer, however, it forms a very clear watershed. Before 1715 all the evidence points to a man making his way in the world and building his fortune. After 1715 the emphasis is very much on John Bley enjoying and sharing the fruits of his labour, establishing a position in society, in both London and East Leake, and leaving his mark on posterity. It is now time to leave London, to find out what was happening back in East Leake and to learn what we can glean about John Bley from his correspondence with arguably the most important man of his acquaintance.

Chapter 5

'Devotedly your faithful servant' – the Bley-Parkyns relationship

Amongst all the various official and semi-official records of John Bley's life there is, apart from his will, only one group of papers which comes to us directly from the hand of John himself. Most fortunately we are able to read a series of four letters plus several notes, receipts and accounts written by him and including his signature. These are the product of the relationship between John and his near neighbour in Nottinghamshire, Sir Thomas Parkyns, Bart, Lord of the Manor of Bunny. What remains of the Parkyns family archive has been maintained at the Manuscripts and Special Collections Department at Nottingham University. The extracts quoted below are not in chronological order but are treated thematically. References are as listed in the catalogue, starting 'Pa' for Parkyn's papers. The documents cover the period from 1690 to the death of Sir Thomas in 1741, but nearly all of the references to John Bley come in the very brief period from 1717 to 1718. What we get, therefore, is a snapshot in some detail of a relationship which was already well established and which probably continued well after these dates.

It is unusual in any early period to find such a close personal relationship between an aristocrat, however lowly or recently ennobled, and a commoner – and an illegitimate one at that – who is neither a relative nor an employee. Such a friendship was uncommon at this time because the late 17th and early 18th centuries saw the beginnings of the landed gentry's outspoken fear of the rise of wealthy parvenus of whom John Bley was utterly typical. To try to understand the nature of this relationship it is necessary first to outline Sir Thomas' remarkable life and achievements.

Sir Thomas Parkyns of Bunny and the Parkyns Papers

Bunny is a small village some four miles to the north-east of East Leake. As with its near neighbour Bradmore it now lies on the main A60 route between Nottingham and Loughborough/Leicester. In 1674 this road took the carriers from Nottingham to Leicester and London via the village of Costock. From here a minor road connects to East Leake.

Sir Thomas Parkyns (1662–1741) was the grandson of a Royalist colonel and governor of Ashby Castle whose son was given a baronetcy for his father's services to the crown during the Civil War. Thomas was educated first at Westminster School and then at Trinity College Cambridge where he was much impressed by Isaac Newton. Back in Bunny he became a magistrate and did much for the village including repairs to the church and the rebuilding of many farmhouses and of Bunny Hall itself at a cost of £12,000. His major work was Bunny School which he designed and built in 1700 on behalf of his mother Lady Anne Parkyns at a cost of £400. Together and with great foresight they endowed it securely with £10 p.a. from a £16 rent on land in

Sir Thomas Parkyns' memorial in Bunny Church: 'Cornish Hugg' pose

Thorpe-in-the-Glebe four miles away. The school was to be free to every child in Bunny and Bradmore (the adjacent village) after an entry payment of 1s. The children of wealthy parents would have to pay 6d quarterly. A local architectural gem, the school still stands on the main road in Bunny. It seems to have become a model for John Bley's own later investment in free schooling. Further bequests by Sir Thomas supported the poor and the widows of the two parishes of Bunny and Bradmore.

Sir Thomas pursued some rather unusual personal interests including 'Cornish-Hugg' (sic) wrestling, on which he wrote an entertaining book (he was known as 'The Wrestling Baronet'). He wrote a Latin primer intended for his grandson and in 1721 published a treatise on how to stabilise labourers' wages by establishing fixed wage bands – but without acknow-ledging any right of negotiation. Sir Thomas was a generous and lively country gentleman with many aristocratic friends including the Dukes of Newcastle and Rutland and Lords Mansfield, Middleton and Chesterfield whose son later gained fame as politician and writer of letters. According to Ellis Flack, his most reliable biographer, Sir Thomas was 'shrewd in business, and certainly not to be trifled with … a genial squire' with a 'rugged and eccentric personality'. His social status is best described as one of the 'mere-gentry', Trevor-Roper's phrase, whose family had benefited from both the Tudor religious upheavals and the 1660 Restoration.

Bunny Hall in the 18th century (Thoroton Society Transactions 1945)

Most of Sir Thomas' wealth came through a succession of marriages, first to Elizabeth Sampson who left him after she had borne him two sons one of whom was named Sampson after his mother. She, though, eloped to London and after agreeing to a separation did him a favour by dying in 1727. His second wife, Jane the daughter of Alderman Barnatt (or Barratt according to some accounts) of York, had three children. But his first two sons had died by 1713 leaving him with a much younger grandson, Thomas, as his only heir at the time, plus various nephews and nieces to be supported. Over time his family life became complicated and tiresome. The 'wrestling baronet' was a fortunate and eccentric benefactor with an extensive family network to support. Thus by the time of the Bley-Parkyns correspondence, Sir Thomas had only one heir and, because of the estrangement of his wife, no chance of a second marriage and further sons.

Sir Thomas began to take a close interest in East Leake during the process of extending his land holdings in the surrounding villages plus, again according to Ellis Flack, 'a manor and estate in East Leake, including Shirley's manor and Coxby's [sic] manor and some lands of Joyce's manor and certain small freeholds'. The Parkyns papers give a list of East Leake tenants' payments at Lady Day from 1701–3 worth nearly £90 per year (Pa M 32) while another document lists fines collected in 1705 (Pa M 33). These accounts include £9 for the half-year rent from John Hopkins 'for his farm' and other land. Rent would probably have been paid to Bunny Hall via a steward or bailiff, so Sir Thomas's familiarity with these lands and income would have led him to build relationships with people in East Leake.

In about 1700 Sir Thomas built 'Leake House' for his son Sampson at what is thought to be Shirley's Manor, to the west of the church. Sampson died at the house in 1713 and his inventory lists many horses, foxhounds and other hunting paraphernalia including 'six otter spears'. Clearly the family had a major presence in the village and such activity would have aroused much interest amongst the existing tenants and landholders. Perhaps Sir Thomas and John Bley's family had met at some point during this ambitious acquisition process.

In 1711 Sir Thomas had been appointed a county magistrate, operating from Nottingham, and as such had responsibility for all legal matters and civil disputes to the south of the county including of course East Leake. By 1718 he was sitting on the local Highways Board. He was therefore the most powerful political figure as far as the Wight family was concerned and so was in a strong position to protect their interests in the area. Thus

Parkyns was not only Lord of the Manor, principal landowner and principal employer in East Leake, he was a very active magistrate. If John Bley ever needed a local friend who would oversee his work in his home village then Sir Thomas was his man.

The precise origin of John Bley's relationship with Sir Thomas is difficult to date. The earliest firm evidence we have of any contact between them is a set of accounts and associated receipts dated 1717. Sir Thomas was of course 12 years older than John Bley and was probably already at school in London when John was born. Whether or not Sir Thomas knew or knew of John as a young lad, it seems most likely that the two began a closer relationship after John was established in London and began to make return journeys to East Leake. Sir Thomas might have asked him to undertake some personal task en route or perhaps convey a message or make an inquiry at the Inns of Court, the country's main legal institution, on Sir Thomas' behalf. Two further reasons for Sir Thomas' close interest in London followed the death of his son Sampson in 1713. Five years later the grandson and heir to the Parkyns estate, also called Thomas, who was born in 1709 was sent to Westminster School under the Headmaster Dr Freind (or Friend). Here he was lodged with a Mrs Tollett while Sir Thomas' mother Lady Anne (nee Cressy) was living in nearby Tufton. It is testimony to Sir Thomas' faith in John Bley that he now invited him to act as custodian to his grandson and heir while in London.

The years from 1713 to 1719 were also a time of financial crisis in the Parkyns family. So another possible trigger for the close relationship with Bley was Sir Thomas' threatened bankruptcy in 1717. The case against him went to court in Nottingham but, supported by no less a person than the Archbishop of York, he managed to avoid embarrassment after a meeting with creditors in the Bishop's Palace in Nottingham. It is entirely possible that at this critical time Sir Thomas looked to a reputedly reliable neighbour from East Leake for help in organising his affairs, a neighbour who then became in effect his agent in London. Perhaps in return for all John's support, it was agreed that Sir Thomas would look after John's own mother in East Leake – two of the letters do refer to her in passing.

So the two had mutually supportive family interests at either end of the roads to London, but how did their political and religious allegiances compare? Political loyalties were rather loosely held at that time, but two broad groups were beginning to appear after 1660. Historians usually refer to these as Town (= commercial, more liberal and 'modern') and Country (= more honest, established landed gentry). These groupings were further developed if not cemented after the 1688 'Glorious Revolution' whereby the Catholic Stuart King James II was replaced by the protestant monarchs William III and Mary Stuart, sister of the deposed king, from the Dutch Republic. Those openly supporting the very successful 'revolution' called themselves Whigs and by way of contrast called their traditionalist, 'Jacobite' opponents by the derisory nickname, 'Tories'. We know that John Bley voted Whig in the Parliamentary, City (mayor, sheriff, chamberlain) and Ward elections in London at this time. His commercial interests would have led him towards the 'Town' rather than to 'Country' groups both politically and socially. By contrast the Parkyns family had held long-established royalist and traditional land-holding affiliations which would have placed them firmly in the broadly Tory political camp. In 1702 Sir Thomas was appointed Deputy Lieutenant for the county and this would have brought him into contact with the local landowning nobility. However he seems to have looked both ways when he began to interest himself in national politics. According to Myrtle he voted for one Whig candidate (Lord Howe) and one Tory (Sir Thomas Willoughby) in 1710. This suggests that he was putting self-interest and local connections ahead of any family tradition. By 1717 the most important man to keep in with in Nottinghamshire was the Duke of Newcastle, the most powerful landowner, a major political player and a very active Whig election 'fixer'. Sir Thomas did go on to vote for both Nottinghamshire Whig candidates in the parliamentary election of 1722. So it does not look as though there would be any serious party political difference between him and John Bley. Difference of outlook (town v country) is another matter and may have led to some interesting discussions – though even here there were mutual interests, with the distillers dependent on the 'landed interest' for support, as we saw in Chapter 3. In terms of religious affiliation John seems to have expressed no religious views though, as we shall see, some distant family members appear to have had dissenting connections. Parkyns, we know, remained a strong supporter of his local church.

The most useful of the Parkyns Papers are the letters written between 1718 and 1719. There must have been written by John in a strong, confident and open handwriting other letters before these, and probably more afterwards too, and we do not know why this other correspondence has not survived. We cannot therefore place the letters accurately in context. Even after 300 years the effect is that of opening a door into another room and breaking into the middle of a private conversation between close friends.

The letters to Bunny were written clearly and carefully with modern spelling and punctuation suggesting a good education:

John Bley's handwriting: extract from a letter to
Sir Thomas Parkyns August 1718 PaC 47

On the reverse side of two of them, sometimes in the margins, we have Sir Thomas' rather poorly crafted replies:

Sir Thomas Parkyns' handwriting: extract from reply on the
back of a letter from John Bley June 1718 PaC 46

There are also numerous associated bills, receipts and accounts between the two of them. Most of these papers were taken on William Lacey's 'Mansfield Carrier' between Mansfield and London via Nottingham and Bunny. The letters give interesting detail of the postal system then in use. 'The Carriers Cosmography' of 1633 notes hundreds of such carriers transporting goods and letters across the counties. From 1635 this haphazard postal non-system was made illegal and only official carriers could be used, but this restriction was clearly impossible to police and casual practice continued throughout the 1700s. The vehicles themselves were unsprung wagons which travelled at about 4 m.p.h. at best and thus the Mansfield Carrier normally took three days to reach London from Nottingham. Safe transportation of persons or goods could not be guaranteed of course. An early stage coach was available and this was quicker but also more expensive and less frequent.

The address is written on the reverse of the letters which are then folded but not sealed. There is no reference to payment for postage. At Bunny on the way down either Mr Wellings or Mr Weddall accepted the letters, sometimes enclosing large sums of paper money, addressed to Mr John Bley of Thames Street, London. The wagon reached either the George or the Bull Inn in West Smithfield, London at 10.00 a.m. each Sunday morning and set out again the next day (Meadows, Gilliver and Clarke, 1738). This service operated from 1681 to 1738. In return the carrier picked up John Bley's letters, packets and cases at the same depot for return to 'Sir Thomas Parkyns, Bunny' with no reference to Nottingham or the county.

Social chatter

The letters give us the only windows into John Bley's social life in London and East Leake. The references are few and give little detail but we can reconstruct some idea of what must have been a wide circle of friends and other contacts made during a busy life.

First in June 1718 Thomas wrote to John that he had called in to East Leake on his way home from his work as highways magistrate in Loughborough. Here he comments on a visit to John's new house:

On Friday last, being at Loughbrow at an Highways session, I made use of the opportunity of visiting Mr Wight and your Mother. I saw your house so well finished and handsomely furnished that I am fearful some will be unwilling to depart in peace and make way for you and yours.

We will make further reference to this extract later in the chapter. Sir Thomas then went on to ask a favour:

Advise I desire you send me one half of a dozen or more Mackerell by Nottingham Stage Coach which sets out early on Friday morning, cut off their heads and embowel them put them in a thin basket or my [box] with store of fresh straw or hay they must be delivered early on Thursday night.

By 'embowel them' Sir Thomas probably meant disembowel or, as we now say, 'gut them'. This may have been an attempt to reduce their deterioration. We know the stage coach would have taken three days for the journey to Bunny, thus arriving on Sunday evening at the earliest. Mackerel being what they are then as now, one wonders what condition they would have been in after three days on the road, in June. Perhaps the lucky diners had them well spiced!

Then there was a short letter from 1 September 1718:

[Sir,]

Yours with a kind invitation to myself and friends for tomorrow I received. But Mr Bird is at Barrow and so fatigued with his journey that I don't expect to see him till the latter end of the week at soonest. Shall have time enough to settle our short account, therefore request you'll not deprive yourself on our account, which with humble service is the needful. From your obliged humble servant.

John Bley

(modernised spelling)

John Bird, we know, was a modestly placed gentleman from London, now living in Barrow but whose family were established freeholders in West Leake. He was almost certainly weary from travelling to London for business with his relation Thomas Bird, a cooper and eventually one of John Bley's legatees. The letter implies that he and other of John's friends have been invited to Bunny Hall for some kind of celebration, possibly a duck shooting party. This may have been a regular event since there is chat about Sir Thomas's duck decoy in a letter of January 1719 (PaC56)

I am glad you had so good sport at your decoy. I have also received your three pair ducks by the Leeds carrier, two pair I sent to Mr Edwards, two pair to Mr Thomas Banks who desires me to present his humble service and return you hearty thanks. Another two pair I and friends made merry with, frequently drinking to the doner's [Parkyn's] health. They [the ducks] proved fat and excellent good and I return many thanks for 'em

(modernised spelling)

Purchasing agent

Most of the other material in the correspondence concerns purchases by John in London on Sir Thomas' behalf and the consequent transfer of goods and payment usually 'in large money' or notes. One very large document (PaA64) refers to the whole account for the period October 1717 to August 1718, presented by John to Sir Thomas on 22 September 1718. This appears to be a copy of one complete page from John's account books. His handwriting here is extremely neat and the whole account very carefully set out. It gives us our first direct insight into John's qualities as a businessman and as keeper of his own accounts. Nearly 40 separate expenditures are listed and dated, including several luxury items:

Chocolate box and porter

French brandy and runlet ([a small wine barrel]

Thomas Plampin [wigmaker of Thames Street in the City] for 2 wigs

John also itemised separate cash payments of £91 13s and £1,000 to Carew Weekes, the former 'in acc' and two more cash payments, for £166 11s and £132 4s, to Mr Madden, goldsmith, plus the costs of the carrier himself. These were very large sums indeed to be paid on trust and on account. On the 'Creditor' side there are bills paid by Mr Sam Smith for £1,200, £200, £100 and over £55. Samuel Smith was the owner of Smith's bank in Nottingham, claimed to be the earliest regional bank in the country. Then there is cash carried down by the Mansfield carrier for £160 (presumably what John was paid for some of the silverware: see below) for which we already have Sir Thomas' covering letter and John's receipt. There are then two records of John taking the profit of £24 from two half year's dividends on an investment by Sir Thomas consisting of one fifth portion of 'an adventurer's share in the New River Waters', a new water company. Perhaps these investments had been made by John on Sir Thomas' account with a formal agreement for the dividends to be sent to John on Thames Street. With his ready knowledge of and contact with the rapidly developing financial world in the City John might well have advised Sir Thomas about these investments. Finally there is the intriguing entry 'By cash to Mother at Leak … £5'. This must have been a payment to John's own mother Elizabeth Wight and suggests that Sir Thomas might have helped look after her financial affairs during John's absences in London.

From the variety of bills and receipts in the Parkyns Papers we can see that over six months between February and August 1718 John made six major purchases on behalf of his friend costing nearly £400 or about £40,000 today. These included 18 silver plates and four small dishes plus engraving and unspecified pewter in a deal box on 4 August 1718, for which Sir Thomas had already given John £160 'in large money received of friends and servants' at the George Inn, Smithfield one month earlier. Then John bought six large silver dishes specially engraved and in another deal box on 11 August (PaA58) and finally a large engraved silver dish 'to hold water' and gravy, in another deal box, two weeks later. Sir Thomas also bought '100' of grained tin (one hundredweight of high quality tin in powder form) from John. This could be used for 'tinning' kitchen utensils or for adding to bronze alloy. But why Sir Thomas would want a hundredweight of it is something of a mystery.

John seems to have been operating as a purchasing agent for goods which would not have been readily available in Nottingham and certainly not in Bunny. As creditor for Sir Thomas he records payments to himself in cash and/or notes. On 19 July he claimed 6d for a 'porter to assist me to bring ye money from Mansfield Carrier' – possibly a trunk of coins too heavy for one man to carry without bringing attention to himself. On the same day he records receiving the £1000 for Carew Weekes and the four bills 'on Saml Smith' for £55 9s 8d, £100, £200 and £1200. Perhaps he employed other 'porters' as personal bodyguards! The accounts for this year might have been preserved at Bunny Hall because of the need to present them at some stage during Sir Thomas' bankruptcy proceedings in the same year (1718).

The accounts also make it clear that it was John who was paying the necessary cash for the grandson's education. It is those items that enable us now to reconstruct the start of the young man's school life at Westminster.

To Westminster School

It is ironic that John, who as far as we know had no children of his own, was now spending time helping his friend to deal with the latter's only male heir in London. Three generations of Parkyns – father Sir Thomas, son Sampson and grandson Thomas – attended this prestigious and expensive school.

Westminster School hall in the early 19th century

Westminster was later recognised as one of a handful of 'great' or what we now call public schools. The school was situated right at the heart of government and was also convenient for the Inns of Court where Sir Thomas had extended his own education and training. He was so keen for his grandson to succeed at school that he wrote a new Latin grammar guide to help him.

This was published in Nottingham and begins with a preface deriding the current efforts of teachers of Latin: '... it's generally to be fear'd that most teachers will go on in their old beaten and thread-bare road, without so much as looking on, or at least considering, to render their tasks more easy and profitable...' On a visit to Bunny School in 1902 members of the Thoroton Society thought the book rather amateurish and unlikely to have been used by Thomas's headteacher Dr Freind at Westminster.

It was usual for boys from the provinces to live in boarding houses in the vicinity of Westminster School run by 'dames' and it seems that the Mrs

Tollett mentioned above was one of these. In Sergeaunt's 'Annals of Westminster School' he states that 'About 1718 William Murray, afterwards Lord Mansfield, was at Tollett's in Dean's Yard'. Young Thomas was well placed with Mrs T. for a certain George Tollett had been the second master at the school but had died in 1714. The new second master (or 'Under Master') was John Nichols who is mentioned elsewhere in the accounts.

Among John's accounts is one large page for 12 August 1718 listing at least 13 items for the school including 'stockens', gloves, a quire of paper, candles, for the barber, for 'sweeping the church' and for 'a seat in the church'. Elsewhere John says he himself paid 34s (£1.70 or £170 today) for a 'bewrow' at Westminster School. Also in the archive are careful and very detailed accounts of Sir Thomas' annual expenditure for

A
PRACTICAL
AND
Grammatical Introduction
TO THE
LATIN TONGUE.
BY
Sr. *THOMAS PARKYNS*
OF
BUNNY, Bart.
For the Ufe of His
GRAND-SON
AND OF
BUNNY-SCHOOL.

The *SECOND* Edition, with many Additions.

NOTTINGHAM:
Printed by *William Ayfcough* in *Bridle-fmithgate.* 1716.

Parkyns' Grammar title page

the grandson which alone would explain the comment of V. A. Marshall, one of his biographers, that he had 'caused much grief to his grandfather as well as being a heavy drain on his finances'.

From the Record of Old Westminster scholars we know that grandson Thomas started there in January 1718 (1717 on the old calendar). He seems to have reached London for the first time on 18 January 1718, for on that day John claimed 3s 1d for 'expenses at Inn with Mr Carter'. This is thought to have been the proprietor of the Bull Inn at Smithfield, the London terminus for the coaches and carriers from Nottingham. From other items accounted for in that period we can probably reconstruct the eight-year old's arrival for his first term.

The youngster apparently travelled to London by coach, possibly accompanied by a servant for the two or three day journey. If they arrived late in the day they may have stayed at the Bull Inn overnight – this would explain payments to Mr Carter as well as the Nottingham coachman. John Bley collected young Thomas from the inn on Saturday 18 January, using a hired coach, and took him the two miles to Mrs Tollett's house in Dean's Yard Westminster. The fact that Bley paid for the return journey to Mr Carter's may indicate that there was a servant who needed to be taken back to the inn in readiness for the return to Bunny. Then on Monday 20th John went back to Westminster to pay a five guinea deposit to Mrs Tollett and a further six guineas to the teaching staff, Dr Freind (three guineas), Mr Nichols the deputy or Under Master (two guineas), and 'ye Usher' or boarding-house tutor (one guinea). Such direct payments to the headmaster and staff were quite normal, although the sums involved here do seem to be extravagant. There were also payments to Mrs Tollett of five guineas for the half-year from January, and a further £5 12s 11d for 'quarters board' with another £6 1s 10d from July.

Over the following few weeks we see the purchase of various clothing requirements for the youngster at school, such as a gown, shoes, gloves, a hat and lace, neckcloths, handkerchiefs, hose, three shirts (plus 6d portage from Smithfield) and 'ribbon for shirt sleeves'. Then there was a tailor's bill for £1 11s. Other items are not easy to interpret: two types of cloth, 'Drugett and Shalloon,' at £1, and 'Peck [two gallons or about a bucketful of] Chesnuts bag and porter' at 3s 9d.

John is here acting as a sort of distant family friend or guardian as well as paying the young man's landlady or housekeeper for the costs of upkeep. In February John bought 'a Box of Petters pills' (apparently a patent medicine) and 1s 6d for 'potrige' or porterage of an unknown quantity 'of ye Verjuice from ye carriers to Mrs Tollett'. Verjuice was crabapple juice which was probably sent from the Bunny estate. As for Petter's Pills, Mrs T. seems to have been expected to dose the youngster with extra medicines against the winter chills on the river Thames. Evidently Sir Thomas approved of Mrs T.'s hospitality, for John also gave her 10 shillings 'to drink Lord Chesterfield's health', though why that good Lord should require such recognition is not known. The Mr Blake also mentioned may have been a school tutor or even the bursar.

Another letter (dated 3 January 1718 but actually 1719 due to calendar difference) ends with news of the boy's first days at Mrs Tollett's in the following year:

> Sunday last designing to give him his first airing in the park but was prevented by a shower of rain. He's in good health and continues to grow tall [and] is but little marked with the smallpox. I shall give Mrs Tollet's sister and Mr Blake as you direct

John's concern for his ward's health and mention of smallpox reminds us of the ever-present dangers of life in the metropolis. The smallpox suggestion might well refer to a less pernicious form of the disease, possibly chicken-pox. The lad survived well enough, at any rate, but was to predecease Sir Thomas at a later date. In June John recounts what must have been quite an exciting expedition down the Thames:

> The latter part of Whitsun week the young esquire and I made a voyage into Essex and the Monday night following I conducted him safe to Mrs Tollets. He's in a perfect state of health and very much grown at least half a head.

In August he visited the boy again 'and delivered him his shirts. He continues in a perfect state of health which is needful at present.'

As we shall see in a later chapter it was probably during this year, 1718, that John began his plans for building a school of his own in East Leake. One wonders whether John's interest in the young Parkyns boy's school helped to prompt this development.

Family advisor

By far the greater part of the text in the longest letters concerns Sir Thomas' family and legal business. The flavour of this communication is perhaps best demonstrated by quoting the following short letter (PaC 47) again using modernised English:

Sir,   London Augt the 5 1718

By the Mansfield carrier this week comes the plate undermentioned. The rest will be ready against next Monday. Expect the hollow dish for fish and the conveniency for sauce but when I see the pewter models packed in the case for your approbation, if I mistake not, Mr Maddon is mistaken in the model for sauce. I understood you designed it double for hot water to keep sauce warm. But however if you like the form it may be made double in the form. The pewter models are packed in one square deal case. I thought it more advisable to send it at twice [i.e. twice the normal cost] least any accident should happen. Yesterday my Lady Parkyns sent her servant to enquire where Mr Carew Weeks might be found and also a letter received from Mrs Lane [Parkyn's niece Rawleigh, married to Matthew Lane] for me to read wherein she sets forth that her husband had contracted such debts that he could not appear and she feared everything would be seized. Therefore now she finds herself ruined, begs Lady's advice though she would take none to prevent it...

From your humble servant
John Bley

Attached to this letter was a detailed account for the silver plate and pewter dish, plus a receipt for these and for half a year's dividend on shares in the New River water company. This combination of financial settlement, purchase and conveyance of goods, contact with Sir Thomas' mother and the problems of her friends and family, and updates on his grandson at school in Westminster, is typical of the longer letters.

The crux of the correspondence concerned problems of inheritance faced by Sir Thomas and his family, and it may well be the legal content is the real reason why this correspondence has been preserved. At the beginning of the longest letter Sir Thomas tells us that Bley's letter has 'raised a heap of obligations' which 'I cannot tell how to answer'. His problems were typical of the time. Basically, for anyone with property at that time there was the constant problem of married women's legal inability to inherit in their own right. To protect their daughters' future livelihoods therefore, parents went to great lengths to settle money on their daughters and their successors by trust or deed. However, matters could become difficult for grandchildren if a daughter died before her parents – as here, where their mother Katherine had died before their grandmother Lady Anne. This was Parkyns' first problem. Secondly, the situation was complicated by the fact that before modern Land Registry searches etc., buying land or houses did not always give the new owner unencumbered title to the property. Although land ownership was always vested in an individual, because of historical family settlements or entails, other family members or even relatives of previous owners could have continuing rightful interests in the property. To counter this limitation on new owners, lawyers had devised a number of ways of dealing with the problem by for instance 'barring the entail'. This technical device could be used to assure the buyer's final rights and the whole process was settled in court by lawyers – at, naturally, great expense to the new owner and to the financial benefit of the lawyers themselves. The plots of many famous English novels centred on these same issues of dependent daughters and disputed inheritance, from Jane Austen's 'Pride and Prejudice' to Dickens' 'Bleak House'. Sir Thomas Parkyns seems to have been very aware of his own difficulties but was equally unsure of how to proceed. John Bley stepped into the breach and acted as his London agent to speed up the process for him.

The twin problems of entails and the inheritance rights of women centred upon Sir Thomas' underage relatives. His nephew Carew Weekes Jnr and his two nieces Ann, who had married Thomas Jury, and Rawleigh who was married to Matthew Lane, all had disputed claims on earlier settlements made on them by their grandmother Lady Anne. (The Weekes were direct descendants of Sir Walter Raleigh, no less). By 1718 they were all short of ready cash. Jury and Weekes both lived in London, Jury had married young, and both were desperate to make good their shares in the Parkyns' settlements. Lady Anne had promised to give each of her grandchildren (rather than their husbands) £91 on attaining their majority and they were now keen to discover whether they were entitled to any more from an old land settlement. The financial plight of Rawleigh and her husband Matthew Lane was becoming acute indeed: shortly afterwards, in the London Gazette of 16 September 1718, Matthew was in fact declared bankrupt. We have already seen that Sir Thomas was on the verge of bankruptcy at this point: the Parkyns family do not seem to have been very careful in managing their financial affairs!

Faced with this pressure on his own time and resources Sir Thomas had written to his trusted friend John Bley to ask for advice.

John's letter of 17 June 1718 is a reply to the question of what monies Sir Thomas' nephew and niece were entitled to. Jury and Weekes were claiming the larger inheritance of their aunt's land at Highfield in Costock which had an entail managed by William Leeke of Wymeswold and Henry Cropper of Costock, who were the trustees of the original owners. John Bley said he thought that the terms of the original settlement made any direct gift impossible, but 'being but little experienced in affairs of this nature' he had asked Sergeant-at-law Hooper at the Inns of Court for his legal opinion. Sir Thomas would, he thought, have to disentail the inheritance from the original settlement, which would involve a bureaucratic legal procedure (a 'foot of fine') at some cost which must be done within a fixed time limit. As things stood, Sir Thomas' mother Lady Anne had had no claim on Highfield. 'If she hath', said John, 'I am wrong in a parallel case of a purchase I have made and would be glad to have this question answered I being yet within time limited in the deeds to have a fine at any cost.'

In the meantime John now reported that he had spoken to Lady Anne about all of this and had tried to show her the deed, but she seems to have been still grief-stricken about her other son Beaumont's death three years before and did not seem to understand what John was trying to say. V. A. Marshall in 2000 claimed that she was suffering from dementia at the time. Bley then spoke to Mr Weekes about the problem, showed him the deed and 'at the same time took the liberty to advise him to frugality and to think of ways and means to advance himself of his own diligence and merit'. Or as we would say today, 'Get yourself a job'. John closes the letter with apologies for being so uncertain about the case, reports some minor financial exchanges and ends with an enigmatic footnote 'I believe it will be Monday before anything will be done.'

Sir Thomas' reply is written on the back. It summarises his position, and then suggests that John might also have problems of property ownership and inheritance (a 'parallel case') and advises him to deal with the matter immediately or he would have much to lose. This might well refer to John's own purchase of land in 'The Nook' in East Leake which will be discussed in a later chapter.

Meanwhile poor John had been pestered in turn by the nephews. Thomas Jury had just married Ann (on 8 May according to one letter), had bought a house and wanted to stock it with goods in order to set up as a shop or storekeeper. His new wife was under age and, having been baptised outside her parish of birth had difficulty in establishing her rights. Here is Thomas Jury writing to his wife's uncle, Sir Thomas, in Bunny on 13 November 1718 asking for her share of £91 13s 4d. He has already been promised £400 from Sir Thomas, but wants more (his rather wayward spelling is retained but modern punctuation has been added for clarity):

Honoured Sir,

This is to sattisfie you conserning the housis i rott to you abought. The whoman that had the deposing of them had a mind to sell tham butt since is upon the pick of being married and since thinks nott to sell them. So Mr Bly [sic] brought me the deed of purchace to look over to see hoe i like itt and i think itt very well made on both sides. Conserning the £400 wich shall be desposed in to any hands as you shall think proper butt i think the government [Bank of England annuities] the best till wee can heare of something worth the buying. For conserning the £91:13:4d wich you rott to me lay in Mr Bly hands ...He was this day att my house and i mention itt to him because i am to mufe into one of those houses i menshooned i have taken a lease of and i was talking abought Mrs Lane and Carew [two other relatives in a similar position] drawing his mony ... for i am to movfe in a weeks time to a larg house next dore wich will coste a grate deele of mony fitting upon wich the good trade i have & hope to doas well as any sittizen in London...   [PaC 50]

He thanks his wife's uncle, sends news of Sir Thomas' mother and signs off. A week later he writes again to Sir Thomas to say that he has consulted John again over what best to do with his £400:

I reed your letter and to your desire went to Mr Bly this morning conserning the £400 and Mr Bly and I consulted wich was best to buy South Sea stock or Lottery newiteys butt we think Lottery newiteys the best butt eather of them will come to more mony wich I will lay out myself...

Here John is acting in the role of financial advisor to Sir Thomas' family in the new business of investment options – but Mr Jury has clearly misheard the latest term 'annuities'!

So now John was acting as the go-between over the disputed inheritance purchase. Fourteen months later the issue was still unresolved so Mr Jury wrote a third letter to his wife's uncle Thomas (spelling modernised):

I am ashamed I should trouble you with another letter ... My lady rec'd your letter this Tuesday last and desired me to show it to Mr Bley which accordingly I went to his house this morning and he read his part of your letter over to me wherein he desired me to acquaint you that he thinks it most proper for your deed and bond of Aunt Annie's legacy of the £91. 13s. 4d. and upon the executing of that deed and bond he will pay the money but not till he has full satisfaction how and where you will please to have the deed and bond drawn. He has forgot the terms of the other deeds and the only person he could confide in is dead so that he is unacquainted in that affair we both. [PaC 59]

Was John stalling? Or was there a genuine problem with the legal status of the details of the original settlement? In November 1718 he found himself offering advice to young Rawleigh Weekes, Sir Thomas' other niece, on a similar purchase of a house. From other sources we know that over a period of 12 years from 1717 children of Carew and his wife Catherine 'were constantly badgering their uncle over money matters ... Sir Thomas must have experienced a trying time during the last years of his life'. One cannot help but feel very sorry for John who most likely had to field all the flak for this personal onslaught. We cannot know how willing he was to take on this extra work, or how fruitfully it turned out. Sir Thomas considered that in going to these lengths to help his nephews and nieces he was fulfilling his duties: in his will he bequeathed them just enough for mourning rings and no more.

Mutual benefits – deference and reciprocity

John's payment of £1,000 to Carew Weekes and Sir Thomas' payment of £1,200 via Samuel Smith clearly suggest that both of them had access to large deposits in Smith's bank in Nottingham. This well-established regional bank issued its own notes as well as dealing with Bank of England notes. Unfortunately the bank's accounts have not survived for this period so we cannot run a check on the size of their deposits or the extent of their business. One result of the financial revolution of the late 17th century had been the increasing reliability of promissory notes, now called bank notes. Carrying large amounts of gold coin was no longer necessary – between trusted colleagues. By 1718 other banks, in London and elsewhere, had sprung up to support and encourage the retail trade so there was no real need to use the Bank of England. It thus became much easier for commercial activity to take place on trust between respected colleagues and friends especially when separated by a three or four day journey.

A similar approach was used when financial or legal advice was required. Beyond the capital, lawyers were expensive and not always dependable or available. Within the City they were very expensive, and also not necessarily reliable. Lawyers were trained at the Inns of Court but modern professional standards and safeguards were rare and for another couple of hundred years most lawyers were happy to act privately and largely for their own convenience and benefit, as readers of Dickens will recognise. Personal recommendation was all that clients could use for guiding their choice of lawyer, with personal or family loyalty at a premium. Thus family tradition and personal relationships became then and still continue today to be a strong factor in patterns of service. This is even more true with the offer or sale of financial advice. Someone like John Bley was thus invaluable to Sir Thomas Parkyns. Bley was a known contact with local ties and responsibilities. He had personal knowledge of Sir Thomas' own family relationships and responsibilities and crucially of his recent financial difficulties. An astute businessman and financially sound himself by 1715, he knew at first hand the workings of the newly emerging commercial and financial world in London. He knew about the Bank and other investment resources, and was increasingly familiar with problems of inheritance and the purchase of property. He had that most valuable commodity in a shifting and developing environment – contacts. John was thus in an ideal position to act as Sir Thomas' agent in London which was where, after all, Sir Thomas' mother and other relatives had set up homes and businesses. And finally, John was in a position to make occasional visits to his own and Sir Thomas' village for, no doubt, much discussion and exchange of news and opinion. He was trustworthy, skilled and available. It is no wonder Sir Thomas came to rely on him so much at a crucial time in his family and personal history.

It is a little more difficult to answer the question of what John himself got out of the relationship. We have no way of knowing whether John was receiving a salary or retainer, or even one-off payments, which have not been recorded or retained within the Parkyns archive. But there were many other benefits of a less than material nature. Sir Thomas, as we have seen, was socially the most influential figure in the area and politically was by far the most powerful individual. John's assiduous cultivation of Sir Thomas, child minding and errand running and so on, seems a small price to pay for such a guarantee of social acceptance in an area where his origins must be known. Sir Thomas was on hand in almost the next village possibly keeping an eye on John's mother and his house (the first letter mentions just such a visit) and other personal and family interests. But one would like to think that there was more to it than that. John might have been very flattered, of course, to have been considered a friend and confidant of the local lord and the wealthiest man in the area. He might perhaps have used Sir Thomas' name and title to increase his standing in the London social and commercial world. Perhaps the title alone sufficed – a letter of introduction to the Bank of England, for example, would have helped to establish John's credibility and financial solvency. But there is no evidence of any repayment, and John seems never to have taken out a significant loan from any source. The correspondence itself speaks of a close and personal friendship between equals with no hint of debts to be repaid or guilt to be assuaged. Nor is there any sign of resentment on John's behalf for the time he must have spent helping the younger Parkyns or purchasing so many goods of such high value. This was all done without profit or other financial benefit, so far as we can tell. We are left with the simple sense of mutual respect based on interlocking interests. And occasionally John was entertained at Bunny Hall and was able to enjoy the ducks and the duck hunting.

The relationship with Parkyns probably lasted throughout John's life. From the mid-1720s Samuel Sterropp of Nottingham was the most important lawyer in the county town and was employed by Sir Thomas to advise him there and in London. In 1727 Parkyns used both Sterropp and Bley as witnesses to his settlement with his second wife Jane Barnatt, and Sterropp later acted as one of the executors of John Bley's will. They trusted each other's friendship and judgement to the end.

Throughout this chapter we have seen the two worlds of metropolitan commoner and landed gentry meeting and interlocking. On the one hand we have an illegitimate tradesman, a distiller and minor shipping merchant, and on the other sat the landowner, benefactor, Lord of the Manor, magistrate and friend of two Lords (Middleton and Chesterfield) and two Dukes (Newcastle and Rutland), not to mention the Archbishop of York. During the Middle Ages, a couple of hundred years earlier, such a relationship would have been rare if not unthinkable. During the Tudor period it was quite common for the wealthy to act as patron to young and talented protégés. Such was the support given to Shakespeare by Lord Southampton. From the 17th century onwards though, the landed aristocracy had increasingly tried to sustain their social distance from the common folk by, for instance, relocating houses and even whole villages out of sight of their new stately homes. At the same time social distances had been narrowed somewhat by the Civil War conflict: Lord Fairfax fought for Parliament alongside the commoner Oliver Cromwell. It was becoming not at all unusual for minor gentry to develop friendships with well-established commoners from a professional or a trade background. And soon it became quite common for younger sons of even senior gentry to be set up in trade which was an important factor in the generation of investment for what became the 'industrial revolution' of the 18th century.

As far as we know Parkyns was no patron, and John was not a protégé. In John's will there is no acknowledgement of any role played by Parkyns in the former's rise to commercial success. But there is clear evidence that the relationship continued for at least a decade after the surviving correspondence. Bley and the Nottingham lawyer Samuel Sterropp were joint trustees of Parkyns' Ruddington estates in 1727. The fact that the estates were then valued at £13000 makes John's appointment as trustee the more remarkable. This alone showed considerable faith in John's probity and in his awareness of Parkyns' family situation.

One insight into the reality of the social pecking order here in south Nottinghamshire may be gleaned from a reconstruction of the story of the exchange of luxury goods between our two correspondents. Lord Chesterfield, the leading aristocrat, gave his friend Sir Thomas a whole deer as part of a 'standing commission' for venison. Sir Thomas, county gentleman, then passed on a part of this beast to John Bley's uncle who in turn had venison pie made for John's mother. *Noblesse oblige* all the way down the social order. Near the bottom of this little local hierarchy John Bley, distiller, was given three 'pair of fatt ducks'. Meanwhile Sir Thomas paid John ten shillings and sixpence for his one gallon of brandy.

So just how close were they? At the end of his life John made no mention of Sir Thomas in his will. But that is not surprising; it would have been both inappropriate and embarrassing for the Lord of the Manor to have received a legacy from a commoner. And anyway, at this time, kinship mattered more than friendship when it came to matters of inheritance. Their letters tell us more. While Thomas Jury, admittedly in a pleading letter, addressed his wife's uncle 'The Honourable Sir T. Parkyns' and 'Honourable Sir', John writing to the baronet simply began 'Sir' and ended 'Your humble servant'. For himself, Sir Thomas signed off:

I would have you that I am devotedly your faithful servant ...

Were these anything more than the contemporary formalities? We will never know whether they really became friends as we understand the term today. And it is extremely unlikely that this ever developed into a relationship of equals. The social divide between the commoner businessman and the 'mere-gentry' had certainly narrowed, but was it ever crossed?

Chapter 6

'Charity in his lifetime' – an East Leake interlude

One of the Parkyns letters confirms that John must have visited his home village from time to time. Most likely he came home to receive local news and to reassure his mother at regular intervals. He probably brought her sufficient cash funds to maintain or enhance her lifestyle. At that time most London gentlemen and businessmen left the city in the hot summer season to spend time in the country, either 'back home' or in their newly acquired country houses. It would have taken John at least three days to make the journey by horse or even longer by covered wagon, later by coach, and this would have been a tiring and not inexpensive journey especially in winter. In this he might well have been accompanied by a group of fellow travellers from the local area, for safety as well as company. He may have visited at Christmas, too, when the weather allowed.

Unfortunately there is precious little evidence to show how often he made the journey from London. As far as we know the only will he witnessed in East Leake was that of Thomas Hopkins in 1730 and no Churchwardens' or Constables' accounts have survived for this period. We have no correspondence between John and family members such as Uncle Edward and it would seem that his mother might well have been illiterate as she witnessed the will of Luke Hallam in 1709 by simply making her mark. The most obvious reflection of John's impact on the village, therefore, lies in two important new buildings – his house and his school.

Before John was born there were no really impressive houses in the village. The Hearth Tax return for 1674, for example, shows only three out of 63 houses with four hearths, whereas the manor house at West Leake had 12 hearths and the rectory had five. Costock, Bunny and Gotham all had houses with between five and ten hearths. But the late 17th century saw the start of a spate of secular brick house building in the region, beginning here with the Armstrong family's rebuilding of Cosby's manor house. From an old drawing we can see that this was a twin-gabled brick house fronting onto Main Street. At about the same time a smaller manor house, now called Old Hall Farm, was put up next to the church. The third was Parkyns' house behind the church, built for his son Sampson at the turn of the century. Unfortunately we have no pictures of the house itself but judging by the inventories for Sampson (who died in 1713) and for his wife (1719) there were at least eight main rooms with cupboards, pantry and 'closet' plus servants' rooms and a cellar. Sir Thomas had built several farmhouses in Bunny and Bradmore but this was considerably larger and cost, he said, £3,000. Sampson also benefited from several substantial out-buildings including a coach house, stabling for nine horses and kennels for '18 couples of fox hounds'. Apparently the house was abandoned in about 1734 and the materials robbed out. It is said that the rather oddly shaped stonework set in the East Leake churchyard walls and in the pinfold are all that remains of Sampson's building. There may have been others but the next two new modern brick buildings that we know of for certain were those of John Bley himself. Thus by 1715 the workmen of East Leake and district had experience of building several properties in the modern style. They had probably accumulated the knowledge of design, resources and execution and the skills and techniques to be able to set up on site without too much fuss and oversight by their employers. The busy period for labourers, bricklayers, carpenters and decorators was about to be extended further.

Family ties

Given the circumstances of John's birth and upbringing it would be entirely understandable to us, now, if he had turned his back on his village and become a London merchant pure and simple. But John owed so much to family and village, and he knew it. Many of his friends and acquaintances were from home and he carried the debt of his apprenticeship costs with him into his burgeoning career. While John was developing his skills in the London bear-garden he kept a close watch on developments in his much quieter home village. There was always his mother's welfare to be considered. In 1715 she was 66 years old, had never married and must have had some difficulty maintaining herself in comfort. She would probably have been supported by other members of the Wight family especially her brother Edward, the established London businessman.

We suspect that Elizabeth Wight may have been living on the future site of John's new house in 1709 as it was next door to what we think was the site of the Hallam smithy. Elizabeth witnessed blacksmith Luke Hallam's will that year, a job sometimes done by neighbours. This was probably a traditional timber-framed cottage on an average-sized plot on the north side of the main street, quite close to the church and the brook. No record of the land purchase can be found and there is no contemporary map of the plot. As with all the older plots in the village it carried some rights in the open fields, but this would not usually amount to more than three or four acres plus grazing rights. Nearly 100 years later it came to be associated with Joyce's Manor.

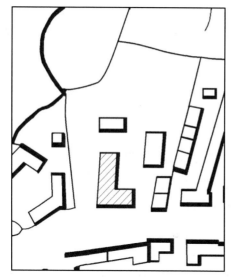

*John Bley's house as shown
on the 1830 parish map*

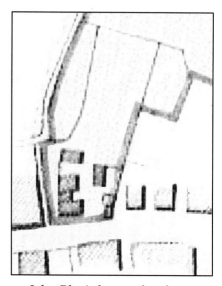

*John Bley's house plot shown
outlined on the 1874 title deed*

By 1715 John had amassed sufficient funds in London to consider investing in a new and much more substantial property for himself and his mother. But who to design the new house; who to build it? Although he had had his London house rebuilt after the fire, he could hardly leave his business for the many months it would require to supervise the construction. However, in Bunny and Bradmore Sir Thomas Parkyns had taken a close interest in architecture and for a number of years had been designing and building farmhouses and other properties for farmers and husbandmen in the two villages. It is entirely feasible that John looked to him for advice and possibly more. However, Parkyns' houses were based on an older tradition of stone quoins on corners and stone dressings around doors and windows, which in turn were wide rather than tall. John's house with its use of chequered Flemish bond brickwork and tall windows was typical of current building practice in London and probably similar in these respects to his new house in Thames Street. This was in the full 'Georgian' style, and was built in what is known as the classic 'double pile' style.

John Bley's house in 1715

John's house was to be symmetrical in appearance with a large rectangular window each side of a central door on the ground floor and three aligned windows of the same size and design in the floor above. This frontage was matched at the rear. The walls would be in patterned red and blackened brick with two three-brick stringers breaking up the rather formal appearance. Solid and stately, it spoke of the Georgian values of honest but unadorned grandeur.

At first glance the house appears to have been built in two separate but matching sections, each a rectangular block with steep roofing parallel to the road. This idea is raised by the dates in the brickwork on the east gable

The earliest photograph of John Bley's house with Victorian porch

111

end, 'IB 1715' in large bold black letters towards the front, while on the rear section is the equivalent 'IB 1728':

Close inspection of that wall shows no break in the brickwork however, though the opposite, west end wall does suggest that it was built in two phases, for the brickwork is slightly out of line all the way up to the gables. Internal examination at the time of a recent restoration confirms the 'single build' theory. The internal wall was revealed as very roughly constructed with no breaks for doors or windows. As to the dates, '1715' would tally with a possible start date for such houses normally took between two and three years to build. But the '1728', 13 years later, remains a mystery. It is surely most unlikely that it took 13 years to build the house, and the external brickwork certainly suggests a single construction. John gave his address as East Leake when voting in a 1727 election in London, so must have moved his main residence there before 1728, while his mother had died in 1727. We have to remember that house dates were not always, as now, intended to record the completion or the opening of buildings, and may have denoted a purely personal event, perhaps even the whim of the owner or builders. But why would anyone add a date 12 or so years in the future? According to the English authority on this style of large house, Maurice Barley, 'double-pile' houses were all built as one unit, the double design made necessary by the maximum length of the internal oak beams then available. This view has been confirmed by Geoff Turner, former Architect to Nottinghamshire County Council, and responsible for all listed buildings in the county. Finally, an earlier completion date is suggested by documentation. As we saw in the previous chapter, in 1718 Sir Thomas Parkyns wrote to John Bley (in London):

> On Friday last... I made use of the opportunity of visiting Mr Wight and your Mother. I saw your house so well finished and handsomely furnished that I am fearful some will be unwilling to depart in peace and make way for you and yours.

The meaning of this last phrase is difficult to interpret. John's mother was perhaps now well established in the house, and Sir Thomas meant that she and her brother Edward were so comfortable that they would be reluctant to let John himself plus his own servants ('you and yours') settle in.

It is interesting to consider where the materials could have come from. We estimate that the building would have required more than 50,000 bricks which would have been made locally. Throughout the midlands there is a widespread scattering of claypits some of which are still recalled in local street names: 'Brickhouse Lane', 'Claypit Road' and so on. Until very recently (2010) there was a large brickworks operating between East Leake and Bunny and there is an old claypit on one of the back roads to West Leake. One of these old pits may well have been used in 1715. At that time the traditional construction method was to make a large 'clamp' or kiln of 'green' or fresh clay. R. W. Brunskill states that 'traditionally clay was dug in the autumn, weathered in the winter, tempered in the early spring and made into bricks in the late spring, summer and early autumn to suit the building season of the Middle Ages and later'. The clamp was built either at the claypit or, more usually, was located on-site for a one-off job. It would have been fuelled by wood, charcoal or turf, and burned for two or three weeks or even longer. A single clamp would provide 30–45,000 bricks at least. Some ends of these were overburnt to a deep blue or grey-blue colour allowing a decorative 'diaper' pattern such as those on the gable ends of Bley's house.

Viewed from the outside the house appears to be symmetrical – almost. Along the front and back and along one side are two stringing lines. The foundations are of limestone although these are now obscured at the front by the raised ground level. There are no original side windows although there is one small modern opening to the east side plus the remnants of one small rounded window on each floor to the front of the east side; these are rather crudely bricked in suggesting a hasty infill in response to the despised Window Taxes then in operation. The front roof was found recently to be of handmade clay tiles which may be original and may have originated from Loughborough brickworks. The other roof is in local slate, probably from Swithland ten miles across the River Soar in Leicestershire. There are four large chimneys suggesting many hearths. The brickwork was repointed in 2005 as part of extensive restoration.

The rear yard is laid out with three layers of cobbles. Outside the back door is a stone-lined well which at over eight metres is unusually deep with a small stream running through the bottom. A recent inspection revealed that, apart from the modernisation to the front, the interior layout itself retains its 1715 outline. There were four rooms on each floor with two sets of staircases, one to the front door and entrance hall and the other to the back door and kitchen suggesting its use by servants. Each staircase is quite wide and of carved oak. Given the date of the house there should be a cellar which a 20th century modernisation at the front may now conceal.

Following the contemporary style the ground floor was given over to servicing the house. There was a rear entrance hall with a tiled floor, a kitchen with bread oven, a dairy or scullery with a flagged floor 20 cm below the present floor, and a barrelled coolroom. To the rear of the dairy was a reception room with a large arched fireplace. The family's main living space was on the next floor, up one of the two carved oak staircases. Here there was a low-ceilinged room with a lime-screed and reed floor which perhaps served as a store or servants' quarters. It may have been partitioned. Three further rooms seem to have been rather better furnished. One of these is still panelled in its traditionally painted Baltic pine rather than oak as was first thought, and would have acted as the main reception room.

The room opposite shows no signs of such panelling but it does have one distinctive feature. One of the two cupboards to each side of the fireplace has a large secret cupboard or hidey-hole under the floor with stairs for access. This suggests a design based on 16th or 17th century priest holes, or perhaps simply a safe area for family treasures.

In the front roof space there were slightly wider stairs leading to two pairs of servants' quarters each side, two with and two without fireplaces. None now has an original window. These rooms appear to have been generous for the household servants although we cannot really tell how much of the overall roof space was allocated to individuals.

John Bley's house in the year 2012

It would be unusual for such a large house to have been built for one person, John Bley's mother Elizabeth Wight. She lived here until her death in 1727 while her brother Edward may have occupied the house from that point until his own death in 1734. But John may well have planned to use it himself, possibly as a retirement home at a later stage in his career.

Elizabeth and/or John would have employed several servants; John himself mentioned four servants in his will, though we do not know how many of them lived in. We do know of a comparable local example: Lady Catherine Wheler, wife of Rev. Granville Wheler, moved into West Leake rectory in 1738 accompanied by 'only' four maidservants.

Nearly 300 years later the house, now a Grade II Listed Building, is still the most dominant and probably the largest in the village.

The Bley School

According to East Leake's first historian Rev. S. P. Potter, as a schoolboy John Bley 'vowed that if ever he were a rich man he would build a school for his native village'. Potter offered no evidence for this claim though, and he was probably citing local tradition. He may have been correct of course but we also need to consider whether Bley was responding to wider historical influences; he was certainly brought up at an interesting time for education.

For many years there had been a scattering of grammar schools across the country. The nearest were a new (1717) school at Barrow and Lough-borough Grammar School which was flourishing. But such schools usually only took boys of course, outsiders were required to pay fees, and grammar schools were supposed to offer the classics, Latin and Greek, for the sons of the wealthy. Such a curriculum was now increasingly seen as outdated and irrelevant for the children of farmers and tradespeople. The demands for more useful schooling were widespread during the late 17th century.

Although it is notoriously difficult to be certain about literacy rates at this time, it is generally accepted that that there were far fewer literate people in villages than in towns – perhaps only 30% compared with 70% in London. Literacy rates had always correlated with levels of wealth and power and especially with religious interests. Ever since the Middle Ages there had been individual priests who were able to teach small numbers of children, and adults, to read and write in English, French (rarely) and Latin. Outside the church a teacher would have needed a bishop's licence to undertake this work. The licensing system enabled the church to retain its control of education and so for some time access to literacy at all levels of society continued to be carefully regulated – in theory. Gradually a scattering of (licensed) lay teachers were paid through charitable donations but permanent schools, as such, were less common even by 1600. The more ambitious schools sought recognition as grammar schools with the intention of teaching the classics to older boys. During the Civil War we then find the Puritans demanding more open access to literacy for social, religious and political reasons. By 1720 education had become a significant requirement for social or economic advancement especially for would-be public officials and budding entrepreneurs. More widely there was a growing recognition of the need for an educated class of people to exploit the trading opportunities presented by wealth and empire. Provincial newspapers were now beginning to advertise new books for sale. Two local Nottinghamshire newspapers, the Mercury and the Weekly Courant, carried the occasional advertisement for and about such schools: in 1725 a 'regular Boarding School for the education of young Ladies and Gentlemen' was to be opened in Nottingham while a house sale in Dronfield boasted that 'NB There is the convenience of a Free Grammar School'.

Political events provided further incentives for action. By the Toleration Act of 1689 protestant nonconformists – except Unitarians – were granted freedom of worship as a reward for their support in the Glorious Revolution of 1688. In theory all teachers still needed a Bishop's licence but the long-established penalties against unlicensed teaching, though unrepealed, were mostly overlooked. Many individuals – and some groups – from varied backgrounds established Charity schools funded from ad hoc endowments. The result was a loose patchwork of schools including some free provision for the poor. They taught reading and writing, sometimes a little arithmetic but not the classics. Fearing that these changes would allow organised schooling to slip out of the hands of the established church, priests tried to insist that the new schools were denominational in character and governance.

Over the next two centuries both Anglicans and dissenters struggled to establish their hold on the new more universal education by forming well

organised voluntary bodies which took advantage of growing state spon-
sorship. John Bley's school on the other hand was somewhat exceptional
both nationally and locally in that it was to begin life as a non-
denominational institution.

John was by no means the first to consider the importance of education
in the far south of Nottinghamshire. Within six miles of East Leake there
were several attempts to establish schooling before and during his lifetime.
In 1641 a school for boys had been set up in Ruddington by bequest and
this was followed by a Bluecoat (i.e. Anglican) school in 1706. From about
1660 there had been intermittent schooling of some kind for a few,
probably fee-paying pupils at Hoton but nothing for the children of the
poor. This was where Bley was taught, according to Potter. Down the road
in Prestwold the local lord built a small school in the churchyard. To the
north, Bunny Free School dates from 1700 with a formal foundation nine
years later. Here Lady Anne Parkyns' charity school was an Anglican
foundation established to 'provide training for poor children in the
knowledge of God and to teach them to read and write, cast accounts and
so much trigonometry related to the mechanical and useful parts of
mathematics'. In 1714 a school for infants first opened in Sutton Bonington.
Four years later a group of wealthier people in the area together raised the
finance to establish the Infant School on a proper basis, to teach children to
'read, write and cast accounts and the Latin tongue'. While it might be
thought inappropriate to teach Latin to young village children in 1718, the
requirement for the children of Bunny and Sutton Bonington to be taught
to 'cast accounts' is a significant development for the country's commercial
future. Unusually Sutton Bonington's foundation was a communal
investment in which the five rectors of the villages bordering Sutton
Bonington (but excluding East Leake) raised most of the finance and were
its trustees. It is significant that the land was given by Charles Parkyns,
kinsman of Sir Thomas Parkyns of Bunny. Again the emphasis is on the
Anglican nature of the teaching. The teacher was probably one Richard
James who married a local girl in 1716 and then, as we shall see, moved to
East Leake. The last of all the local initiatives was Wymeswold in 1730,

conforming to the Anglican pattern with the school built, like the one at Prestwold, in the churchyard.

Thus we can say that by 1720 the villages of Hoton, Prestwold, Sutton Bonington, Ruddington, Gotham and Bunny all had some sort of schooling but Kingston-on-Soar, Rempstone, Costock and East Leake almost certainly did not. There remains the possibility that someone was operating as a teacher or tutor in West Leake at this time. A John Wild had been licensed to teach since 1674 and his name appears in archdeaconry visitation returns of 1693 and 1694. In 1703 he wrote one of the first books proposing the adoption of a more consistent system of spelling in English. We think he was still active in 1719, but West Leake had fewer than 30 families in 1700. As a private tutor he probably charged a fee so it is very unlikely that he taught more than a handful of children at any one time. On balance therefore it seems very possible there was indeed some teaching available in the two Leakes around 1720 but we have no real information as to its form, popularity or value. The history of education is littered with similar examples of small, temporary 'schools' taught by more or less well-educated 'amateurs' at this time. We can only assume that if there was such an establishment then John Bley himself considered it to be inadequate or at least worth supplementing with something more significant, more permanent and more convenient.

We cannot be certain of the full sequence of events leading up to the opening of John Bley's school in 1724. Thanks to Potter we have a Victorian photograph showing older schoolchildren and possibly their usher. Potter added a note of the inscription over the main door: 'This School was built in the year 1724 by Mr. John Bley.' Enlargements of this section of the photograph do not reveal any such inscription.

We now think that Bley bought the land for the school shortly after his house was completed, between 1718 and, say, 1720. We do have a document dated 10 June 1723 confirming a transfer or sale of property in the village costing £60. This may be the source of Bley's 'parallel case' of a property claim in his 1718 letter to Sir Thomas Parkyns. Five years later we find Bley and John Woodroffe applying to obtain exactly such an 'assurance of title' or confirmation by Chancery that together they were now the new and unencumbered owners of the property. Such claims could be made for up to five years after the actual purchase, so working back from

John Bley's School, a Victorian photograph

1723 gives us 1718 at the earliest. The properties concerned are listed as: '2 messuages 2 orchards 7 acres of land 2 acres meadow 2 acres pasture and common pasture for all beasts in Greatleake alias Eastleake'. In making their claim the two Johns (Bley and Woodroffe) were acting in concert while there were three female vendors, also acting together and closely related to each other: Mary Woodroffe (married to Anthony Woodroffe, John's brother), Dorothy Smith nee Patchett, and Sara Patchett. This was not uncommon at the time: females in the family were sometimes grouped together to inherit when there was no surviving male heir. The two Woodroffe brothers were possibly the children of the same Daniel Woodroffe who we met earlier as the churchwarden recording Elizabeth Wight's excommunication in 1681. So this was partly a complex family transaction between the Woodroffes and the Patchetts, designed perhaps to bring income to the widows should that be necessary. At the same time the arrangement created an opportunity for our John Bley as co-purchaser of a school building site in the centre of the village.

We cannot identify with any certainty the location of what appear to be the plots of the two messuages. But as with the land for John's new house we can refer to a detail from a later map showing the layout of the land for the new school.

Almost certainly this would have been unchanged over the following 76 years. The plot covers approximately 1120 square metres and might well have included an orchard to the rear. We know that the school plot backed onto at least one orchard so the other 11 acres would have consisted of strips in the open fields somewhere else in the village. Judging by the later enclosure map there was a frontage of approximately 16 metres or twice that of other adjacent plots that we know are of the same date or earlier (one is

Bley school plot (hatched) shown on 1798 enclosure map

now known as 'Honeypot Cottage'). This double frontage would have been necessary in order to accommodate a school with master's house. The extra length of the adjacent plot, jutting out into the open field, could easily have encompassed another orchard. The following map shows how the location of the new school relates to his house and to the village centre.

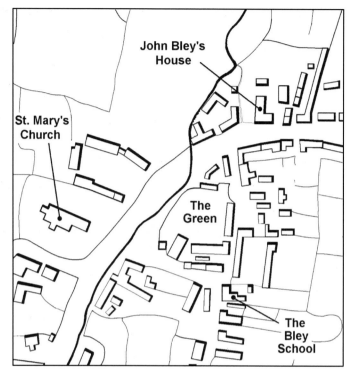

Centre of East Leake as shown on 1830 map

It is possible John purchased land for the school about the time that his house was finished. It could well be that he simply invited the workmen to switch to the new project across the road. The site chosen lay at the centre of the village directly opposite the church, at the beginning of a path south to Loughborough. This area of land was already much settled with at least two timber-framed houses which have survived to this day. The lane is now known as the Nook. The Victorian photograph shows a building of similar size and design to John's house but with more windows on each floor, for extra light, and three dormer windows which may in fact be later additions for the teacher to live in, rent-free. Patterned brick seems to have been used, with stepped gables and asymmetrical chimneys on the end walls. Unlike the house, stonework was used for the corners and window frames, but other features are, so far as we can see, identical. This was another substantial construction which would have aroused much interest amongst the villagers and dominated the view from the church.

Whether or not the church supported this development is open to question. There is no record of anyone applying for a Bishop's licence to teach in the village either then or at any other time in the school's life, but such records are incomplete for the period. The Rector, Michael Stanhope, had been in post since 1717. He was a major national figure within the Church of England and spent much if not most of his time in London on church business. According to Potter he preached the sermon at Whitehall in 1708 and addressed the House of Commons in 1723, when John Bley was building his school. A year earlier he had been in open dispute with his own Archdeacon Robert Marsden over a theological point in a public sermon in Nottingham. Over the years since his appointment at Leake, Foden writes, he 'had been regularly neglecting his duties and rarely even slept at the Rectory at West Leake'. More recently he had become rather withdrawn and stubborn and was described by Marsden as 'contumacious' in a later dispute over the building of a music gallery in his own church. But Bley could have looked elsewhere for official support should it be needed: we have much evidence about Marsden's own close personal interest in education. Stanhope might well have had something to say about Bley's latest project but probably knew little about it and perhaps just did not bother to investigate too closely. East Leake's churchwardens on the other hand may well have welcomed the idea, for one of them, John Woodroffe, had after all been instrumental in the purchase of the school site.

Almost immediately after the purchase of the land for a school, we have evidence of the school itself – or at least of someone doing the teaching. The Norman family were then living in the village (they moved to Costock much later on), and over the following century they carefully preserved some 20 schoolbooks from the John Bley school. The first book is signed by John Norman and is clearly dated 1723 inside both front and rear covers. It therefore predates the formal opening of the Bley School in 1724. It is quite small, measuring 190 x 145mm, of paper in card boards. The writing is very bold and legible, done in quill and ink, and seems to consist of fair copies of exercises set by the teacher who made no comments, marks or corrections in the book. Like most of the series this is what we would now call an exercise book for arithmetic, with two pages of problems for each of a sequence of increasingly difficult arithmetical processes: addition, subtraction, multiplication, division, reduction etc. Included are problems relating to commercial activities such as liquid measure, long and cloth measure, time and 'Single Fellowship' (joint ownership and profit sharing). Typically the problems are given a commercial context:

A piece of cloth costs ...

A factor bought...

A Draper bought 242 yards of broad cloth...

One problem shows the survival of an antique term for money-lending:

A certain Usurer put out £75 for 12 months and received principle and interest £81. I demand what rate percent he received interest.

A few pages show young John Norman working on other matters. There is a page of neat notes on how to make black and red ink, probably dictated by his teacher, while the last page is full of doodles of elaborate lettering, fantastic creatures and ladies' hairstyles – probably *not* dictated by the teacher! And one page has a pasted-in and hand-coloured picture showing that someone at some time had his mind on other things entirely:

It is notable that, in an age when schooling was commensurate with religious instruction in Anglican beliefs and usually required church attendance, John Norman's arithmetical work and the handwriting aphorisms use biblical examples, including creationist references (the age of Adam, 'since the creation' etc.) but no catechistic formulae. Most of the examples are of more practical use in what later became known as utilitarian purposes. The later Norman schoolbooks reflect a similar outlook and are consistent with the work and curriculum of the Dissenting Academies which were set up by nonconformists specifically to offer an alternative and more commercially relevant form of education altogether.

One outstanding problem with this and other books in the series is that we do not know for certain how old the students were at the time. The first book seems to contain problems suitable for an older child, possibly nine or ten years old – by our modern standards of course. He could certainly write well and had good basic arithmetical knowledge. And that then leads to the question of when he first learned these skills, and where. It suggests either that when about five or six years old he went to another school or teacher possibly at West Leake, Bunny or Sutton Bonington, in 1718/19, or that a teacher had already set up a school of his own in East Leake well before John Bley became involved. The latter is, we think, more likely. If so, John would have already identified his teacher, a number of pupils and a house or room from which to operate some time before the school itself was built.

So who was the teacher? We know that Richard James had been living at Normanton and may have been working at the Infant School at Sutton Bonington from its foundation. Unfortunately the 1718 endowment of that school does not mention the teacher or his salary. In John Bley's will of 1731 we find this same Richard James in post at East Leake. So it seems very probable that John, or a friend in the village, enticed Richard to move his growing family to what must have been a larger establishment. Richard James gave formal evidence to the ecclesiastical authorities in early 1733: he said that he had been living in East Leake for 13 years which would make his appointment in 1720. And this would be just right for the first Norman schoolbook. But the exact sequence of events is unknown.

The school seems to have been an immediate success and five years later we have a tantalising detail of some of the children who attended. The

Commonplace Book of Rev. Robert Marsden of Rempstone, about a mile away, has an entry on page 8 noting the cost of sending his village children to school:

the Boys at school   6

£2. 02s. 00d

Marsden's note is undated but from the sequence of other dated pages was written some time in 1728. So six children were costing someone seven shillings each, probably per annum which would have been a considerable sum for any middling parent. Perhaps Marsden was paying for them himself; with a salary of £190 p.a. supplemented by a further £80 4s 6d for his work as Prebendary and Archdeacon, he could certainly afford it. On page 43 he makes a more detailed and rather paternal statement:

May 19th 1729

My scholars at Leake

Boot Anne	Rayner Hannah
Garton	Sotherw. Eliz
Wm. Harris. Peg [?]	Stocks Tho
Hayward Mary	Morris Joh. 2.
Selby. 2.	Sarson. 2.
Wait. 2.	

The numbers here are consistent with having sent 'six boys' a year earlier. It is extremely unusual to find a list of names of pupils attending such a school at this time. Using the Rempstone baptism records we can identify the ages of most of them. Hannah Rayner and Elizabeth Southerwood were born in 1717 making them the oldest at 11 or 12 years, while ten of the others were aged four to nine. Several children are over the age when they could well have been required to work at home or in the fields. Having seen what schooling could do for their boys, were the parents persuaded to pay for their girls, too, in the following year? Or did Marsden pay for all of 'his children', as in the previous year? Rempstone then had 46 families, said Marsden, and the parish register lists 43 born between 1717 and 1726, so his 15 or 16 children of whatever age would seem to be rather a low proportion of the whole. On the other hand infant mortality was high at that time; perhaps most of the surviving children were indeed sent to the school.

An entry of 1730 lists 14 ('reputed') charity schools in the county with their annual fees including:

Page 79 of Rev. Robert Marsden's Commonplace Book (1730)

The entries on this page are difficult to interpret; the final column seems to record the number of children attending for free. Thus Sutton Bonington had a land endowment worth £10 to pay the costs of 60 children, while Gotham was free to all the poorest: 'all ye poor children contribs ... 0.' 'Bunny free to Bunny and Bradmore ... 14 [pounds or shillings] a yeare' suggests that their children's schooling was also free. But does 'Great Leake for ye town 14s a year – 0' record the fees collected, or the cost to the owner John Bley? The 0 in the last column suggests that there was no charitable provision for poor children at the Bley School prior to JB's death – i.e. no endowment for them. This does not necessarily mean they were not taught there; John may have paid for them out of his own pocket or simply made teaching them a condition of Richard James' employment.

If, as seems likely, John based his school on local examples especially Bunny, then from the outset therefore John Bley's school would have offered free education for the poor children of East Leake and to those of other villages such as Rempstone for a small fee. We will see that this principle was to be carried through in Bley's will and was consistent with the terms of the school's eventual foundation document. Unfortunately we have no more formal record of John's intentions regarding the school, its funding, management, curriculum or ethos during his own lifetime.

If the school had been founded as a formal Charity School then it almost certainly would have been given a religious ethos and curriculum and would have been open to inspection by the Charity Commissioners. But the law on charities could hardly apply to philanthropic giving by an individual. The first indisputable documentary evidence for the school comes, therefore, in John's will, about six years after it is claimed that the school was built. So the building and its practical use came first, and the formal foundation several years later. As we have seen at Bunny and Sutton Bonington such a sequence was not at all unusual at that time. It is possible that John did not see any need to formalise the conditions under which a schoolhouse could have operated. Perhaps he ran the school and paid the master's salary and expenses himself, or by proxy from London and through a trusted friend or relation. Uncle Edward would have been an obvious candidate for this task. However ad hoc these arrangements were the school seemed to be prospering when John wrote his will, for there is no indication therein that he was in any way dissatisfied with current arrangements. John Bley's Free School was to survive him by well over a hundred years.

....

John Bley and his family were able to benefit from the fact that East Leake was an open village which allowed unrestricted exchanges of property free from the control of a single landlord or Lord of the Manor. Nor did the rector wield as much influence as he might; from 1667 East Leake had a neglectful incumbent in the person of John Davys and after 1717 it had an absentee one in Michael Stanhope.

John's investments do not seem to have incurred any hostility or jealousy for he was able to draw upon the support of important players in village life and governance – Sir Thomas Parkyns obviously, the Rector of Rempstone and Archdeacon, the churchwardens, the Nottingham lawyer Samuel Sterropp and significant landowning families like the Woodroffes.

In the ten years from 1715 John Bley staked a major claim in the life of his village. The Wight family was now well established both in London and in the south Nottinghamshire village. John's mother was able to enjoy a relatively comfortable dotage in a large, modern house in a centrally convenient location in her village. John's school, meanwhile, was now the second secular institution in the village, the first being the Town Lands Trust formed in 1637. Its relationship to the church's own educational role and function was uncertain however. With no religious management clause for guidance the school may have stood as a challenge and an embarrassment to ecclesiastical dominance. The school's management was yet to be secured however and John had apparently made little financial provision, a weakness that was only to be made good through endowments in his will. When the time came to refound the school on a proper formal basis, the new trustees would take the opportunity to reaffirm religious values with a vengeance.

During his lifetime John Bley brought money into the village through his two building projects. He created employment thereby which must have helped stimulate the local economy. He instigated its first educational institution and employed the obviously talented teacher Richard James who became a regular witness of wills and other transactions. The schoolchildren from surrounding hamlets and villages must have brought life and delight to the inhabitants. The school's evident success lent weight to East Leake's position as leader in local social life. Bley was now a major figure in village life and local people had much to be thankful for.

Chapter 7

'Citizen of London'

Though established with a home in East Leake John Bley still planned a long-term future in London, demonstrating as much in June 1717 by the pains he took to extend his tenure of the house in Thames Street. His lease from the Burdett family could not be lengthened beyond 1750, when the Burdetts' own lease was due to expire and the property was set to revert to the freeholders. Undeterred, John went to these freeholders, the St Dunstan's charity trustees, and negotiated a lease directly from them, to run for 21 years from the expiry of the Burdetts' contract.

With his tenure secure until 1771, John was now effectively sure of possession for the rest of his life. Charles Townley was the first trustee named in the document and may have been instrumental in obtaining the lease. The rent of £15 per annum was what might be expected for the ground rent; as stated in the document, Townley and his fellow trustees took full account of the fact that John had rebuilt the house at his own expense. This was probably the last favour the now elderly Charles Townley performed for John Bley; he died just over two years later.

The opening of John Bley's 1717 lease

The years of peace after the upheavals of 1715 made for profitable trade and London business was flourishing. John's base in Thames Street was now thoroughly secure, his household was well established and his assets were safely invested. With life so well organised, he could afford to devote more time to pleasure. His correspondence mentions a convivial dinner and speaks of a boat trip down the river and there were many other pleasurable ways for prosperous citizens to spend their leisure hours. There was a broad range of entertainments on hand. In May 1717, for example, theatre-goers could choose between Handel's opera Rinaldo at the King's Theatre in the Haymarket, Shakespeare's Henry IV at the Theatre Royal in Drury Lane and Colley Cibber performing restoration comedies at the same theatre. For those with less refined tastes, more robust forms of entertainment were available elsewhere in the West End:

> At the Desire of several Persons of Quality. At the Boarded House in Marybone Fields, the backside of Soho Square, on Tuesday next the 21st instant, there will be a very large African TYGER, Baited with six Bull Dogs and Bear Dogs for 100l. [£100] There will be also a young Mad Bull to be baited with Fire Works all over his Body. Likewise a Wild Bear from Muscovy, to be baited with Fire Works after the same manner. Also a very good Hat to be play'd for by six young men at Blunts, he that breaks most Heads in six bouts wins the Hat: With other variety of Bull-baiting and Bear-baiting as usual; all to be performed upon a Stage four foot high from the Ground. There is but 30 half Guinea Tickets, which are to be had at Rich. Perry's in Channel Row, Westminster. There will be 100 Tickets at 5s. 2s. 6d. 2s. and 1s. each, to be had at the aforesaid Place.

> *Post Man and the Historical Account Thursday 16 May 1717*

The most likely place to find John Bley in his hours of leisure, though, was not the West End, but one of the coffee houses much closer to his City home. The likeliest of these, perhaps, was the Garter Coffee House where he eventually lived. When John first moved in at the Sign of the Red Cross back in 1705 the Garter had been run by John Gigg. Shortly before the 1715 fire Gigg was succeeded by his widow Elizabeth and on her death a few years later daughter Mary Gigg took over. A site plan from later in the century shows the Garter as it had been rebuilt after the fire, with a ground floor 30 feet square consisting essentially of one large room, no doubt furnished with benches and tables for the use of customers. One corner was partitioned off, forming a small room where food and drink could be prepared, and a staircase up against one wall gave access to living accommodation on the upper floors. John was actually living at the Garter when he signed his will in 1730 and his substantial bequests to Mary Gigg 'daughter of John Gigg' and her sister Sarah Gigg suggest a long-standing connection with the establishment and knowledge of the family.

Inside a London coffee house around the beginning of the 18th century

Coffee houses in the 18th century were much more than up-market watering places serving fashionable beverages. Some, such as St James's and the Cocoa Tree were centres of political gossip and intrigue, others, like Lloyds and Garraways, were homes of stock and commodity trading and insurance schemes. They hosted auctions and supplied meeting places for livery companies and business organisations such as the East India and Royal African companies. They also offered individuals the equivalent of postal box numbers; innumerable advertisements gave the names of coffee houses as places where messages could be left. Coffee houses near the Custom House, such as the Garter, catered for traders and merchants by providing customs-entry forms, price lists, auction notices and a variety of foreign and domestic newspapers carrying news of shipping arrivals and political events likely to affect trade. In addition to all this, a coffee house could be an individual's place of work – some brokers advertised regular hours when they were available at a given coffee house to transact business. Even if John Bley preferred to do business in his own counting house across the road, he could use the Garter to talk to other tradesmen and keep his finger on the pulse of the commercial world.

The Garter was also somewhere John could relax with his friends; his correspondence with Sir Thomas Parkyns, discussed in an earlier chapter, tells us he was not averse to a good carouse. John's will suggests the identity of several of these friends, including cornfactor Robert Godfrey who not only lived in the vicinity but also owned part shares in warehouses standing in Wycherley's Yard, very near John's house. The cooper John Bird lived a short way to the east of John Bley in London, probably in Bear Lane where his son was located a few years later. A second cooper, William Parker, lived close by in Harp Lane, as we have seen, and then there was salter Thomas Garrett, living on Thames Street close to London Bridge, and Richard Fendall, a Southwark grazier. The friends

The entrance to the former Wycherley's Yard (by J P Emslie 1886)

may have been joined in time by Bird's son Thomas, also a cooper, and by John's ex-apprentice Henry Saunders. Most members of the group were in related trades, but they also shared political views, views which were public knowledge because secret voting was unknown in the 18th century. Complaints of bribery and corruption meant that results of local and parliamentary elections were frequently challenged and complete lists of the votes cast were published so they could be checked for fraud. Enough of these lists have survived to give us a clear picture of the political sympathies of John and his friends.

Although parliamentary elections occurred only every seven years or so, local elections took place more often. The City was governed by the Court of Aldermen, consisting of one alderman from each of the 25 wards together with the Mayor and Sheriffs, and the Common Council. The latter contained anywhere between four and 16 representatives from each ward, depending on population. Tower Ward, for example, was one of the more populous and elected 12 Common Councilmen. All these representatives were directly elected by the citizens and most elections were keenly contested, so polls were frequent. From the poll lists that survive, we can see that John Bley voted consistently for Whig candidates in a variety of local and parliamentary elections in the years 1710, 1713, 1717, 1722, 1724 and 1727 and that the pattern of his votes was echoed by the friends mentioned above, or at least by those who were citizens and were thus entitled to vote.

One original handwritten poll list for Tower Ward survives. It shows that John Bley and Henry Saunders went together to record their votes in the closely fought election of three Common Council representatives for the ward in December 1717 and both voted for the three Whig candidates. The election, as usual, took place over several days and lists of votes were recorded in two locations in the order that people arrived. Given the predominance of Whig votes in one list and Tory votes in the other, these polling stations may have been the headquarters of the two parties. The names and occupations of the two distillers were written next to each other, interestingly on the list dominated by their Tory opponents. The overall result was extremely close, with the first three candidates polling 204, 200 and 199 votes respectively; one Tory and two Whigs were elected.

Although Henry Saunders had moved into a house of his own he had clearly maintained his ties with John Bley; after all, the two men were only three doors apart. As well as being close socially, Henry may well have continued working for John, for it was only in July 1720 that he paid £13 6s 8d to be admitted to the livery of the Distillers Company. It was a little unusual for this to occur as much as seven years after a distiller completed his apprenticeship. Henry could afford the lease of his house on the corner of Water Lane, so the cost of joining the livery is unlikely to have been an issue; it is more likely that 1720 marks the time that he began to trade in his own right. He had started a family by this time, having married into the well-to-do Burroughs family of Gloucester and London.

The Worshipful Company of Distillers continued to act as guardians of distillers' interests, especially those of the primary or 'malt' distillers. One issue exercising the minds of the Court of Assistants at this time was the threat to their trade presented by smuggling. Although the ban on French brandy imports had ended after the 1713 Treaty of Utrecht, it had been followed by the imposition of swingeing customs and excise duties on imported brandy, amounting to more than £80 per ton. This simply intensified the level of smuggling to a point at which it alarmed parliament as well as the distillers. In October 1717 the Court of Assistants agreed to 'endeavour to prevent the running of Foreign French Brandy' and by the following December this had turned into a determination to get a bill through Parliament imposing greater penalties for anyone found with illicit goods. In due course they succeeded and in July 1720 they 'agreed to print one thousand of the late Act to prevent the running of brandy as to such part thereof as concerns all distillers and dealers in brandy'. The Thames Street distillers doubtless received copies and took due note.

The Distillers Company had other reasons to lobby parliament. From an annual figure of half a million gallons in the mid-1680s, London gin production and consumption had increased many times over and would reach 6.5 million gallons a year by the mid-1730s. The resultant drunkenness and disorder brought ever more strident calls for big increases in excise duties on domestically distilled liquor to curb consumption and the distillers had to exert all their influence to resist the rising clamour. They argued that the proper solution to the problem was a return to control by the Distillers Company, but this did not find favour with landowners concerned for their grain sales. It was the end of the decade before duties were increased and much longer before really effective controls were put in place, by which time the social evils associated with gin drinking were to become even worse.

The Distillers' Court of Assistants continued to process applications for membership. Thus Henry Saunders' successor at the Red Cross, William Green, completed his apprenticeship at the end of his seven year term, was sworn in by the Court in April 1721 and was made free 'upon testimony given by his master, John Bley'. In contrast to Henry, he immediately joined the livery, having 'paid as usuall'. William lost no time in engaging an apprentice of his own, registering Richard Howitt at the Court in July 1721. He also moved into Charles Townley's old premises near the corner of Harp Lane and opened his own shop. Such young and inexperienced shopkeepers could be seen as fair game by some and William fell victim in the autumn of 1722 when a local customer helped herself to his coat while his back was turned. Spotted on the way out, Barthia Fisher was arrested, brought to trial at the Old Bailey and sentenced to transportation, a novel form of punishment introduced just four years earlier as an alternative to the death penalty – previously such a thief might have been hanged.

However carefully they watched their customers by day and bolted their doors at night, the traders of Thames Street could still fall prey to thieves, as Mary Gigg of the Garter Coffee House knew only too well. The Old Bailey minutes for 25 May 1721 recorded how, 17 days previously, her servant John Jones had stolen 'Half a Pound of Coffee, 2 ounces of Bohee Tea, a piece of Garlick Holland, 8 quire of Paper, a Handkerchief and an Iron Key, in all to the value of 10s. the Goods of Mary Gigg'. Mary had become suspicious, searched the man's trunk and discovered the stolen hoard. Found guilty, Jones too was sentenced to be transported to the American colonies. Not that shopkeepers always appeared in court as the victims of crime. In 1724 William Green's next door neighbour at the Three Tongs and Sugarloaf, Joseph Taylor, was sentenced to spend a day in the pillory followed by a year in prison after purchasing tobacco 'stolen from the keys'. Short of murder, crimes against property were normally treated more seriously than crimes against the person. Thieves often went un-detected, but when they were caught retribution was swift and severe.

William Green's imminent departure would create a vacancy at the Red Cross, so John Bley engaged a third apprentice, Gustavus Brooke, son of a victualler and innkeeper of Coleshill in Warwickshire. Brooke was sworn in on 10 November 1720, three months before Green's apprenticeship was completed. This may have been done so Green could show the new youngster the ropes and thereby reduce the drain on his master's time. For John's business interests stretched well beyond Thames Street and must have involved travel. The Rev. Mr Marsden's comment 'he never mix'd his brandy but sold it as it came to him' suggests John was selling his wares as far afield as Nottinghamshire; it also shows that he avoided the widespread London practice of diluting full strength spirits before sending them to the provinces. It is worth noting, too, that he charged Sir Thomas Parkyns of Bunny 10s 6d for a gallon of French brandy in October 1717, another indication that John was selling in his home area and confirmation that he was dealing in imported spirits not just selling the produce of his own still.

Another likely outlet for John's spirits was Norfolk. In his 1722 'Tour through the Eastern Counties of England' Daniel Defoe described Norfolk as prosperous and densely populated and its people as highly industrious – an ideal market for French brandy and other up-market spirits. John's will indicates a long-standing relationship with the Killett family of Gorleston, a town that adjoined the major port of Great Yarmouth and stood at the gateway to England's second largest city of Norwich. The Killetts had a long-established brewery in Gorleston, so may have had a local distribution network that could be used for John's goods, the more so because these goods complemented the product of their brewery rather than directly competing. The family also had extensive shipping interests, so were eminently capable of transporting John's spirits from London to Great Yarmouth for local sale or for further transport up the river Yare to Norwich. According to Defoe the Killetts should have been ideal business partners for 'the merchants, and even the generality of traders of Yarmouth, have a very good reputation in trade as well abroad as at home for men of fair and honourable dealing, punctual and just in their performing their engagements and in discharging commissions'.

The harbour at Great Yarmouth from The Ports, Harbours, Watering-places and Picturesque Scenery of Great Britain Vol.1 (William Finden 1837)

When he was not travelling, John's London life would revolve very much around the small 80 yard section of Thames Street between Harp Lane and Water Lane where his home and business lay. Though it was a prosperous area, the parish registers provide grim reminders that it remained profoundly unhealthy, especially for young children. Soon after the south side of Thames Street had been rebuilt following the 1715 fire, cornfactor Francis Gillow moved into premises just across the road from John Bley and Henry Saunders, doubtless attracted by the proximity of the corn market on Bear Key. Between 1719 and 1728 Gillow's wife Ann had eight children of whom only the first and last lived to adulthood; of the remaining six one was stillborn and the other five died before their first birthday. Several other families in the vicinity had multiple infant burials, while Henry and Mary Saunders buried a young son in the parish churchyard in 1722 – at least this is much the most likely explanation of the bald entry 'Henry Saunders' in the burial register for that year, as there is ample evidence for the continued existence of the adult Henry.

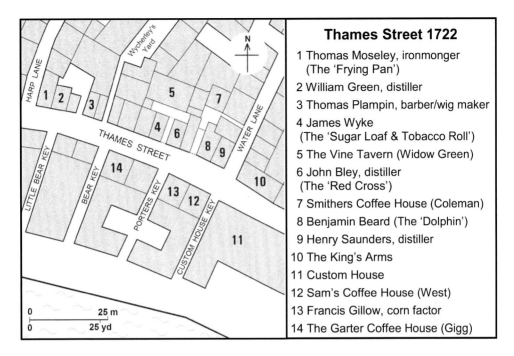

Thames Street 1722

1 Thomas Moseley, ironmonger (The 'Frying Pan')

2 William Green, distiller

3 Thomas Plampin, barber/wig maker

4 James Wyke (The 'Sugar Loaf & Tobacco Roll')

5 The Vine Tavern (Widow Green)

6 John Bley, distiller (The 'Red Cross')

7 Smithers Coffee House (Coleman)

8 Benjamin Beard (The 'Dolphin')

9 Henry Saunders, distiller

10 The King's Arms

11 Custom House

12 Sam's Coffee House (West)

13 Francis Gillow, corn factor

14 The Garter Coffee House (Gigg)

So the street was no healthier than it had been in John Bley's youth, nor was it any quieter. On the contrary, it was busier than ever and the carmen were no less raucous and annoying than when John had first set foot in the area. The 'Rules for the Port of London' published in 1722 set out at length the regulations governing carmen's conduct 'these being very insolent noisy fellows, and think thereby to baffle and run down young merchants, or their servants, who are not much acquainted with the waterside business'. These rules were as detailed as any modern traffic regulations. Carmen were never to ride on their carts, but must lead their horses by the head, not allowing them to trot. Each cart had to carry a brass plate marked with its licence number and there were strict limits on how many could be stationed in any one place. Only two carts were allowed to wait on the section of Thames Street between the Custom House and Porter's Key and another two between Porter's Key and Little Bear Key, though up to six could stand on Harp Lane. On Thames Street they must stand on the south side of the roadway only and must not take up position before five in the morning in summer or seven o'clock in winter. There were strict limits on the size and loading of carts, on the charges that could be levied and the

139

routes that could be taken. Nevertheless, carmen still contrived to annoy and to generate persistent complaints of insolence and overcharging.

As a long established resident John must have taken all the Thames Street bustle in his stride; in fact, he probably missed it when he was away. With a former apprentice installed at either end of his small section of street, he was now a senior figure in the area. We know from his Parkyns correspondence that John inspired trust and that his advice was respected, so his views on both business and personal matters must have been valued by his neighbours. These fellow residents were likely to see plenty of 'Mr Bley' as he went about his affairs in an area that could furnish almost all his day-to-day needs. He could buy snuff from the Three Tongs and Sugarloaf, next to William Green's shop, and his wigs from Thomas Plampin the barber next door but one to William; Sir Thomas Parkyns was apparently so impressed by Plampin's wigs that he commissioned John to buy him two. Within yards of his door, John could find a different place to dine for every day of the week. So whether he was going about business, leisure or civic duties, it is likely that John could generally be found close to home.

As a citizen, John was expected to take an active part in City affairs and accordingly he took his turn with the duties that this involved. He served as one of the land tax assessors for Tower Ward from 1715 to 1725, a role in which he was eventually joined by two of his friends, Robert Godfrey and William Parker.

*John Bley's signature on the
1724 land tax assessment*

The Distillers Company, too, made its demands on John's time. Each April, the Court of Assistants appointed three distillers from the ordinary membership to act as Stewards for the following year, monitoring adherence to company rules. This was not a particularly popular duty and could be avoided by paying a £25 fine, although this might have reper-cussions if a distiller sought higher office later on – in the modern Company no-one is allowed to become an Assistant without first serving a turn as Steward. John Bley's turn to be elected Steward duly came round in April 1720, but he paid the £25 fine rather than be sidetracked from his own business, or indeed from more pleasurable activities.

With the aid of John Bley's will we have already identified one group of friends and his correspondence with Sir Thomas Parkyns reveals another dining companion. Thomas Banks lived a little way to the west along the north side of Thames Street, two doors past the St Mary's Hill junction, in front of the Salutation tavern. He had a large house with a total ground floor area of 1500 square feet, which he insured for £750, and belonged to the Bakers Company, although he traded as a cheesemonger. Intriguingly, when John's mother made her will it was Thomas Banks whom she named as her residual legatee. Through Robert Godfrey, John may have come to know some very influential City figures. Robert's executors included wealthy merchant Sir John Thompson, owner of much warehousing around Thames Street, and banker Henry Hankey – both future aldermen.

John's will gives further clues to the company he kept in his later years when it mentions three bequests to buy mourning. It is no surprise that the first of these bequests was to Uncle Edward and his wife, since John maintained contact with his uncle throughout his adult life. The last recorded occasion was the £600 transfer of Bank of England stock to his uncle in the summer of 1730. The second bequest was to Mary Sterropp of Nottingham, sister of his executor. Like John's uncle, the lawyer Samuel Sterropp bridged the worlds of Nottinghamshire and London. He and John acted together in Nottinghamshire as joint trustees for Sir Thomas Parkyns' marriage settlement in 1727. Sterropp was in London in June 1728 when he witnessed and probably drafted Robert Godfrey's will, was there again at the signing of John's will in October 1730 and was on hand to record an inventory of John's goods and prove the will the day after John's death the following spring.

The third payment for mourning was to John's 'cousin Nutt', the brewer Joseph Nutt of Wapping. John Bley's family relationship to Joseph Nutt can only have been a distant one. Neither Wights nor Nutts directly mentioned each other, or any Bleays for that matter, in any of a series of detailed wills. The maiden name of poulterer Robert Wight's wife does appear in wills of the Nutt family, suggesting a possible link by marriage, but this tenuous connection is all that has been found. Therefore, while they may have been introduced by an uncle, it looks as though the two men cultivated each other's acquaintance out of friendship or mutual business interests, not through any sense of family obligation. Joseph Nutt was a very successful man, as prosperous as John Bley though seven years his junior, and he had many wealthy connections. His father Thomas Nutt had himself been a well-to-do brewer, based in Cripplegate, near the Brewers' Hall. His mother came from a leading Quaker family, that had built a Quaker meeting house in Uxbridge and had suffered fines and imprisonment for their faith. Joseph's sister had married Richard Morson, one of a very prosperous family of Lombard Street goldsmiths, while Joseph himself had married Ursula Manning from another prosperous City family. In short, Joseph Nutt was a very useful man to know.

Joseph's well-to-do background meant he was able to establish himself in business much more rapidly than John Bley had done. Within a few years of completing his apprenticeship he was running a large brewery at Execution Dock in Wapping, initially in partnership with rich merchant Gregory, later Sir Gregory, Page and subsequently with Joshua Russell. Page was one of the wealthiest dissenting merchants in the City and a director of the East India Company, as well as being a member of parliament, so had connections at the highest level. By 1711 the partners held a contract to supply beer to the Navy and in February that year Joseph was summoned to give evidence to a House of Commons committee investigating blatant abuses in the government victualling department. Joseph confirmed that he had been able to buy beer from the Queen's Hartshorne Brewhouse at 22 shillings a ton and sell it back to the Crown as superior 'store' beer for 48 shillings a ton. He was one of five 'contracting brewers' asked to sample a batch of suspect beer from the Queen's Brewhouse, confirming it to be 'fox'd, or stinking, and not fit for men to drink' and giving the opinion that this was due to its being brewed in the hot month of July. The accounts of the excise department for 1714 and 1716 mention refunds to Joseph of overpaid excise duty on exported goods, indicating that he was shipping beer overseas as well as supplying the home market.

The brewery at Wapping comprised an extensive group of buildings surrounding a courtyard, the brewhouse alone being 118 feet long. Other buildings included stables, storerooms, 'inn rooms' and dwellings and altogether they were insured for a total of £1550. The insurance was a wise move. When fire broke out at the brewery in October 1729 the insurance company's firemen proved far more effective than they had been for John Bley 15 years earlier; the Hand-in-Hand had to pay three men for a mere hour's work extinguishing the blaze. Execution Dock was a convenient spot for shipping out beer, but was also notorious, being where the infamous Captain Kidd and other condemned pirates were hanged. As a warning to others, pirates' corpses were left in place at low water mark until three tides had washed over them, so John Bley may have encountered some grisly sights when visiting his friend. Joseph Nutt's will shows he supported the dissenting meeting house in Shakespear's Walk, Shadwell, not far from where he lived. He left two guineas apiece to the ministers, David Jennings and Thomas Harrison, and five pounds to the associated charity school. Jennings was a famous preacher and the meeting house drew in large congregations, including the mother-to-be of the celebrated slave trader turned evangelist and abolitionist, John Newton. Joseph Nutt may even have witnessed the christening of the future author of 'Amazing Grace' at the Shakespear's Walk meeting house in July 1725.

Another 'cousin', Edward Walmesley, was also eminently well worth knowing, though again he was younger than John Bley. Like Joseph Nutt he was only a distant relation, John's great-uncle George Wight having married a Walmesley (or 'Wansly') back in 1653. There had clearly been no shortage of family money to train Edward and set him up in business as a druggist. He had served his apprenticeship under a member of the Grocers Company – somewhat unusually, his 'master' had actually been a woman, one Mary Conyngsby. Belonging to such an elite livery company, Edward himself was able to charge premiums ranging from £100 for his first apprentice to £200 for his later ones. Within months of completing his apprenticeship in 1715 Edward had taken over the druggist's house and business on the east side of Snow Hill where he had been trained, two doors north of the junction with Cock Lane. The building, as recorded in the Hand-in-Hand register, was nearly double the size of John's house.

This house on Snow Hill had some distinctly interesting occupants, not least Edward's father-in-law Alexander Cleeve. Back in the 1680s, Cleeve had been the Royal African Company's representative in the Gambia and effectively the territory's governor. He could tell tales of captured ships, African gold and games of cat and mouse with a French man-of-war. Gold, of course, was only part of the Royal African Company's business; it sold English manufactured goods in Africa and brought back ivory and other luxuries, while the most lucrative part of its trade was transporting slaves from West Africa to the sugar plantations of the West Indies, where they may have produced some of John Bley's raw materials.

St Sepulchre's Church where Edward Walmesley was a member of the vestry and his son-in-law was vicar (Maitland, 1756)

Edward Walmesley was a staunch churchman and in due course married his daughter Theodora off to Rev. Dr John Dry, the local vicar. He was also involved in local politics, being elected to the Common Council in 1731 and serving on the council until his death 15 years later. John left Edward Walmesley £100 but did not expect him to go into mourning, so of his two distant cousins it was the dissenter Joseph Nutt to whom he appears to have been closer – perhaps a clue to John's own religious preferences, insofar as he had any. One incident in Edward Walmesley's life graphically illustrates the workings of the judicial system in John Bley's lifetime, as well as prevalent attitudes and social values.

Edward was a cultured man and a bibliophile, his name appearing on book subscription lists ranging from a 1721 *History of the Arians* to a 1744 edition of *Hudibras*. On Saturday 26 March 1726, about four in the afternoon, he was walking in the fields near his home, with his nose in a book, when he was set upon and robbed at knife point. He suffered several cuts and was deprived of his silver watch, his hat and a small amount of money, but recovered himself sufficiently to spread a description of his assailant. The man's distinctive flattened nose made him easy to spot and he was seen that evening selling the watch in a nearby alehouse. Henry Vigus was arrested the next day and Edward was called out of church to identify him. A mere three weeks later Vigus was on trial at the Old Bailey, charged with assaulting Edward, 'putting him in fear' and robbery.

The scene in the court and the conduct of the trial were very different from those in a modern courtroom. For one thing, the court was open to the sky, a ploy to prevent judges and their officials catching jail fever which was rife. Trials were short and there were no professional advocates. Edward, as victim, was expected to act as prosecutor and the prisoner was expected to conduct his own defence, though both could call witnesses. Juries rarely retired but huddled together in court to decide their verdict and on this occasion it was treated as an open-and-shut case. On the testimony of Edward Walmesley, together with the arresting officer and the man who had seen the watch being sold, Vigus was found guilty and sentenced to be hanged.

Altogether 16 criminals were condemned to death at this assize, three for sodomy, three for murder and the rest for burglary or highway robbery.

Four had their sentences commuted and two died in prison, leaving ten to take the road to Tyburn in a procession of carts on 9 May. The sole woman prisoner, Catherine Hayes, was not to be hanged, but to be burnt at the stake. She had been party to the murder of her husband, deemed 'petty treason', and this was the punishment prescribed. Accordingly, Hayes did not join her male accomplices, seated on their coffins in the carts, but was dragged on a hurdle behind the rest of the procession. The prospect of a burning in addition to the hangings drew a massive crowd and there were chaotic scenes even before the executions started. An overloaded section of scaffolding, carrying 150 spectators, collapsed killing two people and injuring others. Vigus and another prisoner tried to escape amid the chaos but were quickly restrained and finally succumbed to their fate. The next day's newspaper completes the story:

> Catherine Hayes, as soon as the others were executed, was, pursuant to a Special Order, made fast to a Stake, with a chain round her waste, her feet on the Ground, and a Halter round her Neck, the End whereof went through a Hole made in the Stake for that Purpose: the Fuel being placed round her, and lighted with a Torch, she begg'd for the Sake of Jesus, to be strangled first; whereupon the Executioner drew tight the Halter, but the Flame coming to his Hand, in the Space of a Second, he let it go, when she gave three dreadful Shrieks; but the Flames taking her on all Sides, she was heard no more   *Daily Journal 10 May 1726*

It was only in 1790 that the Treason Act finally put an end to such burning of women.

Joseph Nutt and Edward Walmesley were very comfortably off, but some of John Bley's relatives were more in need of financial support. From his will we know that John lent money to the Essex based Thomas Wight who may have been instrumental in apprenticing him to Thomas Gilson. He also lent money to his cousin Samuel Wight, a Trinity House pilot who lived across the river in Jacob's Street, Southwark – a place that Charles Dickens made notorious over a century later when he used it as the setting for the death of Bill Sykes. So John was clearly in touch with his Wight relatives. He may have had frequent contact with Samuel's brother George also, since the latter described himself in his own will of 1744 as a 'cooper of St Dunstans in the East'. Indeed George may have approached John for financial advice; his name appears in a later list of investors in the 1717 issue of 5% Lottery Annuities, probably the very issue that John had advised Thomas Jury to buy.

It is clear from John's will that he was keen to help his younger relatives get a start in life, especially those who were fatherless as he had effectively been. Both John Hopkins, grandson of John's aunt Mary Hopkins, and Caleb Moore, grandson of uncle Robert Wight had lost their fathers before they were old enough to be apprenticed. In April 1725 John Bley was probably instrumental in getting John Hopkins apprenticed to his friend William Parker who traded as a cooper nearby in Harp Lane and he may also have helped to establish Caleb with the brushmaker William Thorp the previous September. Half of Caleb's £10 premium was paid by Christ's Hospital, which provided education for the children of deceased citizens, so Caleb must have been one of their former pupils.

Details of John Bley's business and financial dealings in the later part of his career are sparse. On 11 November 1716 he paid £307 10s into Hoare's Bank at the Sign of the Golden Bottle in Fleet Street and immediately drew it out again. The amount, £300 + 2$^{1}/_{2}$%, may be the payout from a short-term

investment or loan, for example six months at 5%. The Bank of England apart, this is the only one of John's banking records to have survived. We do not know where he did his day-to-day banking, though he was most likely to use one of the City banks in Lombard Street or in Fenchurch Street. These were much closer to Thames Street than the West End banks favoured by the gentry, such as Hoare's, Child's, or Coote's, but unfortunately far fewer

The Sign of the Golden Bottle, still displayed outside Hoare's Bank

147

of their records survive. One bank he may have used was Henry Hankey & Co. of Fenchurch Street, run by Henry Hankey, Robert Godfrey's friend and executor. John's holdings of Bank of England stock did increase, their face value rising from £2200 in 1715 to £2250 in 1720, £3250 in 1725 and finally £4000 at the end of 1730. The market price of the stock rose gradually over time also, the price quoted in the Daily Courant of 30 June 1730 making John Bley's holding at that date worth £5730.

John held onto at least part of his South Sea stock through the upheaval of the 1720 'bubble'. In the summer of that year the price of a £100 share rocketed to £1000 during a period of fevered speculation, then fell back within the space of a few weeks, catching out many people who had bought into the company unwisely when the frenzy was at its height. A list of £1000 stock holders from 1723 still included John's name and also showed some of the after-effects of the buying frenzy; the number of shareholders had doubled to around 5000 from the 1714 figure and the list now featured many of the aristocracy, the main sufferers of the 'bubble'. The social prominence of so many bubble victims ensured a great furore and the South Sea directors had their assets seized. However, the company itself, holding a large part of the national debt, could not be allowed to fail, was restructured and was permitted to continue operating. John's investment was therefore safe. In fact if he had sold off some of his shares at the height of the boom, like Thomas Guy the founder of Guy's Hospital, he could have made a killing and East Leake might have gained a hospital as well as a school! But all the evidence suggests John Bley invested for the long term rather than playing the market.

This then was the London in which John Bley lived and prospered. It was a place of huge contrasts, wealth and financial sophistication side by side with squalor, Georgian refinement alongside violence and barbarism. Disease was rife and life was cheap. London was a place in transition, but one from which a recognizably modern world was evolving.

Chapter 8

The final years

By the end of 1725 John was winding down his business activities. The land tax returns indicate that he handed over part of his Thames Street premises to Samuel Holmes at some time between October 1724 and October 1725 and moved out of his house altogether shortly after. Seemingly he was cutting down his London commitments so as to spend more time in East Leake. By this time his investment income must have approached £1000 per year, more than sufficient for a very comfortable retirement. John did not want to bury himself in the country completely, though; his will shows that he took a room, or rooms, at the Garter Coffee House and moved in some of his furniture. The bustle of the City obviously still exercised its pull and John felt the need to maintain a London base.

Possible further evidence of John's retirement is provided by an advertisement from the Daily Post of 28 January 1726:

To be LETT

The Person leaving off Trade, a convenient Shop, with Stills, Backs, and other Utensils, for the making Molosses Spirits, well situated for Trade, and Room capable of great Improvements, with the Lease of the House. Enquire at Mr William Green's, over-against Bear-Key, near the Custom-house, Thames-Street.

The word 'backs' commonly meant tubs or vats, in particular those used by brewers and distillers. The Mr William Green of this advertisement was John Bley's ex-apprentice who was certainly not vacating his own premises or giving up distilling, a trade he was still pursuing at the time of his early death eight years later. The only distiller in the vicinity nearing the end of his career was John himself. Samuel Holmes, John's tenant and successor, was a brandy merchant, but apparently had no interest in running a shop or making his own spirits. If planning to be in Nottinghamshire for much of the time John may well have commissioned his former apprentice, based close by, to act on his behalf and if William had a share of the proceeds it would explain why he was the only one of John's ex-apprentices who was left nothing in John's will.

Moving to East Leake at this time made a lot of sense. John could keep an eye on his new school and look after his elderly mother who had only a couple of years to live. The clinching evidence of a return to East Leake comes in the form of the 1727 parliamentary poll list. John cast his votes for the Whig parliamentary candidates for the City, but his address was given as 'Leak, Nottinghamshire', not Thames Street, indicating very firmly that his East Leake house was now his main address and main home.

Dividend Hall, South Sea House, where investors such as John Bley could collect their half-yearly dividends (Ackerman, 1808)

Around this time John rearranged and diversified his investments, with an emphasis on safe investment and a steady income. We know from his will that John invested several thousand pounds in South Sea Annuities and bought seven or eight London properties other than his own house. He may have had other investments of which no details have been preserved, but the good match between the total value of his known assets and the total of his legacies (see chapter 9) suggests that any unknown assets were fairly minor. The South Sea Annuities were much safer investments than company shares; being backed by the government, they were almost the equivalent of modern 'gilts'. Like these, they provided a steady income and at a time of falling interest rates they would appreciate in value. Local historian Sidney Potter, in one of his 1934 newspaper articles, described these South Sea Annuities as a bad investment, but this was based on a double misunderstanding. Firstly they were not the same thing as South Sea Company stock and secondly the company continued to trade and to issue fresh annuities for many years after the 'bubble'. Indeed by 1724 the company had retrenched so well that it had embarked on the construction of a handsome new building to house its activities. The annuities were actually worth slightly more than their face value when John died, trading at about 6% above par.

John Bley's London properties also brought in a steady income. One of his tenanted houses stood on St Dunstan's Hill and two others were close by in Cross Lane. He renewed the insurance on the Cross Lane properties with the Hand-in-Hand on 24 January 1726, so may have bought them seven years earlier when the policies were first issued or acquired them at a later date with the policies already in place. These houses were brick built and insured for £150 and £100 respectively. The tenants in 1730, when Bley made his will, were Joseph Gladman, Henry Bennett and James Long, one property presumably being split. No insurance record has been found for the St Dunstan's Hill property, but it may have been quite substantial. The 1730 tenant, Thomas Woodbridge, was a cooper and his family retained a base on St Dunstan's Hill as the headquarters for a large and expanding business through to the 1790s, importing rum and sugar from the West Indies. When house numbers were introduced in the 1760s, their address became known as No. 19 St Dunstan's Hill, though there is no guarantee this was the exact building that John Bley had once owned.

The other properties were a little further afield. Three quite substantial properties lay on the east side of Fetter Lane and were later known as

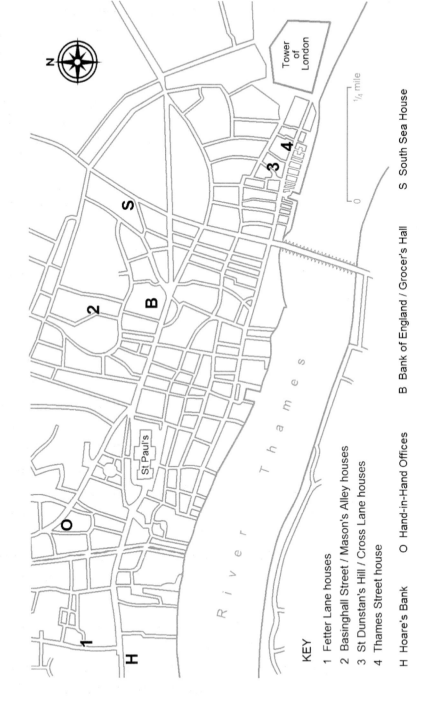

John Bley's London property in 1730 and financial institutions he used

KEY

1 Fetter Lane houses
2 Basinghall Street / Mason's Alley houses
3 St Dunstan's Hill / Cross Lane houses
4 Thames Street house

H Hoare's Bank   O Hand-in-Hand Offices   B Bank of England / Grocer's Hall   S South Sea House numbers 19, 20 and 24. They were insured for £250 each, John renewing this insurance on 7 January 1726. Another, smaller, property stood in Mason's Alley, just off Basinghall Street, and was insured for £125. This last policy was a new one, first issued on 29 November 1726, so this may well mark the date John bought the property. Again, the houses were all constructed of brick and all insured with the Hand-in-Hand. John's tenant in Mason's Alley in 1726 was a Widow Beardsley and in 1730 it was George Green. In 1730 John also owned a house in Basinghall Street itself, tenanted by the hosier Gabriel Small. This tenant had a chequered business career ahead of him, being declared bankrupt twice, once in 1735 and again in 1745. Between them, John's London properties may have brought in £200 per annum in rent.

Such investment in property was normal. For example, we know from insurance records that the Townleys owned and let out a substantial house in Queen's Square, Holborn, and that Thomas Bird owned a group of nine houses in King's Court, near Aldgate. All the investments mentioned to date, property, bank stock and annuities, were indeed exactly what one might expect of a successful London tradesman looking for a spread of sound investments likely to generate a substantial and dependable income. But one asset mentioned in John Bley's will stands out as unusual. In this will, drawn up in October 1730, Bley listed small shares in four ships.

The first ship was the *St George* of Hull, displacing 80 tons and captained by Robert Osborne. This vessel was presumably engaged in coastal trade. The other three were Great Yarmouth based, ocean-going vessels whose principal owners were apparently the Killett family of the adjoining town of Gorleston. These ships were described as the *Three Brothers*, 400 tons, master Jeffrey Killett, the *Godfrey,* 380 tons, master Samuel Killett and the *Samuel and Rebecca*, 300 tons, master John Cock. The tonnages had probably been rounded up; when put up for auction in 1745 the displacement of the *Three Brothers* was given as 327 tons, and this four years after a double keel had been added to extend its life. Nonetheless, these were three typical and substantial ocean-going merchant ships of the time. Bley left his share in the *St George* to owner Abraham Thompson, mariner of Hull, and his shares of the Yarmouth ships to Jeffrey Killett senior, Samuel Killett and Jeffrey Killett junior respectively, along with legacies to their families.

A search of all 106 wills of London distillers proved at the Prerogative Court of Canterbury in the ten year period 1726 to 1735 reveals many mentions of real estate, Bank of England stock and South Sea Annuities, but the only will to mention shipping shares was John Bley's. So it is natural to ask why a distiller, even one trading as a rum and brandy merchant, owned such shares. As long as the vessels remained afloat and trading the shares would generate a small annual dividend, but their capital value would depreciate steadily. Such ships had a typical useful lifespan of 25 years and these three had used up more than half this allowance. This hardly suggests a worthwhile investment – unless John had a special interest in what the ships were carrying.

John Bley's interest in the *St George* is relatively easy to explain. The east coast was the preferred route for the carriage of heavy goods from London to the north-east or, via the Trent, to the East Midlands and we already suspect John had dealings in Nottinghamshire, so this Hull based vessel may have carried his liquor to customers in those areas. Being a part owner might give John favourable carriage rates, priority when it came to loading and unloading cargoes and some influence over the timing of voyages – all very useful for his business.

The Yarmouth based vessels are more of a puzzle. We have suggested the Killetts may have helped to distribute John's goods within Norfolk, but while this may explain the business link, it does not explain John's interest in these three particular vessels. Nearly all customs records for the Port of London were destroyed by fire in 1814, but fortunately most of the three ships' movements can still be traced via the shipping reports in contemporary newspapers. The reports have a few gaps, but give a fairly clear picture of what the vessels were doing in the years either side of John Bley's death, with 126 definite or probable mentions. All three ships were principally engaged in trade with Norway in the five years before John died and two of them continued for some time afterwards, as the table of recorded destinations shows:

Date	Samuel & Rebecca	Three Brothers	Godfrey
1720	Baltic		
1723	Norway	Norway	
1724	Petersburg		
1725	Norway (3 times)	Norway (2 times) Archangel	New England
1726	Norway (3 times)	Norway	Greenland Norway (2 times)
1727	Norway (4 times)	Norway (4 times) Mediterranean	Norway (5 times)
1728	Norway (5 times)	Norway (3 times)	Norway (5 times)
1729	Norway (4 times)	Norway (4 times)	Norway (4 times)
1730	Norway (4 times)	Norway (4 times)	Norway (2 times)
1731	Norway (4 times)	Norway (4 times)	Norway (5 times)
1732	Norway (5 times)	Norway (5 times)	
1733	Norway (5 times)	Norway (3 times)	
1734	Norway (5 times)	Norway (2 times)	Newfoundland
1735	Norway (3 times)	Norway	
1736	Norway (3 times)	Norway (3 times)	
1737	Norway (4 times)	Norway	
1738	Norway	Norway	
1739	Norway (2 times)		
1740	Norway		
Total	59	41	26

Some of the ships may have fitted in some coastal trade as well, for example shipping East Anglian corn or Newcastle coal to London, but such domestic voyages were not included in the newspaper listings and go unrecorded. Four or five voyages to Norway would occupy a whole summer season, though, which left little time for other work. So in the last years of John Bley's life, from 1727 to 1731, we can see that all these three vessels were trading almost exclusively with Norway.

The one important import from Norway during the 18th century was timber, which clearly begs the question: just why would John Bley have been interested in the import of timber, of all things? All John's other business activities – distilling, importing rum or brandy, selling brandy – were so closely linked to each other. A possible answer may lie in a 1955 article on the 18th century Anglo-Norwegian timber trade published in the Economic History Review by H.S. Kent. This described how by the middle of the century 'a major industry' had developed in supplying French brandy to Norway so that it could be smuggled to Britain under cover of the timber trade. The 1711 Scottish incident mentioned in an earlier chapter shows that this illicit trade was already established in John's time. So it is just possible that he was using the Killetts' timber trade as cover to supplement his brandy imports with untaxed spirits.

There is one further piece of evidence to support this notion. As the table above shows, five years after John's death, the *Samuel and Rebecca* was still making several voyages a year from Norway to London. On 23 June 1736 the vessel arrived off Gravesend in company with Jeffrey Killett's *Three Brothers* and was boarded by two customs officers, Edward Stone and Thomas Davy. They remained on board for the two days it took the *Samuel and Rebecca* to work her way up the Thames, with the clear intention of staying put until the cargo had been unloaded. Several days after the ship had anchored the officers were still there and unloading had not started; the crew obviously had something to hide. Then, in an attempt to put the customs men out of action, some crew members plied them with a drugged alcoholic concoction. The London Evening Post takes up the story:

> [They] sate down to drink; and after a short Time Thomas Davie finding himself out of Order, judg'd it at first to be the Cholick; but was soon after seiz'd with a violent Vomiting, a great Pain in the Stomach, and very thirsty, which occasion'd him to drink very plentifully of Small Beer. Mr. Stone found himself much worse than the former, having taken a larger Quantity; and to relieve his Agony drank Brandy, tho' to no Purpose, for his Pain continuing he was carried ashore, where he dy'd the next Morning: On Tuesday his Body was open'd, and a Quantity of Arsenick found in the Stomach, the Parts about it being black and burnt

A coroner's inquest was convened immediately and on Friday 9 July a verdict of 'willful murder' was returned. The Customs authorities reacted immediately and drafted a 'wanted' notice:

Custom-house, London, 9 July 1736

The Commissioners of His Majesty's Customs having received certain Information, that Edward Stone, a Tideman belonging to his Majesty's Customs in the Port of London, was lately poison'd: And it appearing, by the Coroner's Inquest taken this Day, that Robert Stimpson, Boatswain of the Ship Samuel and Rebecca, John Cock Master, lately arrived from Norway, whereon the said Stone was boarded for the Security of his Majesty's Customs, and Thomas Banks, otherwise Vanbrank, Mariner, belonging to the said Ship, are guilty of Murder, by poisoning the said Stone and others; and it also appearing on Oath, that Gabriel Alexander is also guilty of the same Offence, in order therefore to bring the said Murderers to Justice, the Commissioners of his Majesty's Customs do hereby promise a Reward of Fifty Pounds each, for seizing any of the aforesaid Persons, so as they may be brought to Justice.

The said Stimpson is aged about 21 or 22 years, of a fair Complexion, and about 5 Feet 2 Inches high.

The said Banks is aged between 30 and 40 Years, of a swarthy Complexion, blind of one Eye, and about 5 Feet 10 Inches high.

The said Alexander is aged about 30 Years, of a swarthy Complexion, very wide Mouth'd, short, black, curl'd hair, a lusty Man, about 5 Feet 6 Inches high.

The wanted men were soon rounded up but they, in turn threw suspicion on the ship's mate, James Moulds, who was thrown into Newgate prison, then released for lack of conclusive evidence. Five years elapsed before Moulds was rearrested and brought to trial at the Old Bailey, with the bosun, Robert Stimpson, acting as the chief prosecution witness. The jury was unconvinced by the evidence and Mould was acquitted. The key fact relevant to our story emerged from the evidence given by Thomas Davy at the trial; after the poisoning, the customs men found casks of brandy hidden beneath the ship's cargo of deal. The brandy was in 'half ankers', the small casks favoured by smugglers and this alone meant it would be seized as contraband. By law, as a deterrent to smuggling, brandy had to be imported in casks with a capacity of at least 60 gallons.

So, were the crew of the *Samuel and Rebecca* indulging in a little private enterprise or did the owners know what was going on? If such smuggling was taking place in any volume in John Bley's time, he was surely shrewd enough to realise it. So was he actively involved? If so, he needed somewhere the brandy could be unloaded discreetly and stored, but John had many years to build up a network of contacts. For example no-one was better placed than his friend Robert Godfrey to provide suitable facilities, with the 'wharves, quays and cranes' mentioned in his will. Indeed there would be a direct incentive for Godfrey because of the thriving trade in smuggling corn into Norway where it was in short supply. Ships on the Norwegian run normally returned to Norway 'in ballast' and it would be easy for the 'ballast' to be supplied from Godfrey's grain stores. Smuggled goods were at risk of confiscation but Customs officers might be bribed and

John must have built up contacts in the customs service in all the years he had been operating so close to the Custom House. We have also seen that his uncle Edward Weight may have been in a position to provide inside information. The pattern of voyages shown in the table above indicates that if John had any influence on the ships' activities it was to increase their concentration on Norway. Finally, while he disposed of the shipping shares in his will he said nothing of any share in the cargo, though all three ships were to be on their way home from Norway on the day of his death, presumably fully laden. But if John's real interest lay in clandestine cargoes he could hardly mention them in his will.

All this is conjecture, of course, and may be no more than a series of coincidences. As we have seen, John apparently retired from business before the main concentration of Norwegian voyages started and the smuggling would have needed to be on an improbably large scale to make much difference to his income. And there were other reasons for the Killetts to prefer northern waters at this particular time. In 1726 rumours of impending war with Spain were strong enough to trigger a run on the Bank of England and must have alarmed the Killetts. They had fallen foul of the Spanish once before, in January 1719, when their ship the *Prince of Wales* had been seized by Spanish authorities, together with a valuable cargo, and they still awaited government compensation for losses totalling around £2500. On the other hand, it is a singular coincidence that the one case of brandy smuggling via Norway to come to light in the 18th century annals of the Old Bailey just happens to involve one of the four ships in which John owned shares, sailing under John Cock, the very captain he named in his will.

One loose end left by John's retirement was his apprentice, Gustavus Brooke. There is no record of a transfer to another master in order to complete his apprenticeship, although any of Messrs Saunders, Green and Holmes might have been persuaded to take on someone with five years' training under John Bley. Brooke may have preferred to return to the family inn at Coleshill; at any rate, the £20 legacy left him in John's will suggests they parted on good terms.

John was still a member of the Distillers Company and in retirement, or semi-retirement, he showed a belated interest in its affairs. By 1727 he was one of the most senior members of the company not to have been made an Assistant – his name was now fourth on the list of 97 ordinary members of the livery. There were two vacancies for Assistant that year and John's was one of three names put forward, but it was the other two candidates who were elected. Perhaps John's failure to act as Steward seven years earlier was held against him, perhaps his move to Nottinghamshire was the stumbling block.

John's mother, Elizabeth Wight, died in November 1727 and her loss may have led John to spend more of his time in London. Elizabeth drew up her will shortly before she died, leaving £5 to the three year old son of her brother Edward and £5 apiece to three other very young children, John Lambert, Dorothy Hunt and Dorothy Hardy, grandson and great granddaughters respectively of Elizabeth's late sister Mary. There was no mention of Elizabeth's son in the will, but her choice of East Leake grocer Hugh Hardy, husband of her great niece, as executor may well have been at John's suggestion; Hugh was to be one of John's own executors three years later. The most intriguing aspect of Elizabeth's will was the bequest of 'all my real estate' and 'the rest and residue of my personal estate' to Thomas Banks, cheesemonger of Thames Street. Banks lived not far from John, almost opposite Billingsgate dock, and clearly knew John well; we saw in chapter six that John had given him two of the ducks sent by Sir Thomas Parkyns. Whether he was acting on John's behalf or had some direct link with Elizabeth we can only speculate. The word 'widow' was inserted against Elizabeth's name in the East Leake burial register, perhaps because the clergyman responsible for the entry was aware she had a son. However, Elizabeth described herself as 'single woman' in her will.

The few clues to the final two years of John's life come from London where he eventually died, so that is where we have to look for any sign of his physical decline. Records suggest that John normally paid his debts very promptly – indeed a reputation for prompt payment may have been one secret of his business success. Thus, unlike many masters, he had always been very quick to pay the requisite duty when taking on a new apprentice, the day after the enrolment in the case of William Green. In 1722, as on previous occasions, John renewed the insurance on his Thames Street house nearly a week before the seven year term ran out, probably as soon as he received a reminder from the Hand-in-Hand. It was most unusual, therefore, that he apparently failed to renew the insurance on his house when it fell due in December 1729. Possibly he was ill at the time and possibly the fault lay with the company. When the policy was eventually renewed on 7 July 1730 the premium was paid 'in trust for John Bley' by William Mount, that year's company treasurer. This was the only time Mount acted for a third party in this way, and may indicate that the two men were closely acquainted. The board minutes reveal that the company had recently dismissed its secretary for incompetence and Mount was the person charged with sorting out the mess he left behind. So perhaps John's payment had simply gone unrecorded by the secretary; on the other hand this just might be the first sign of failing health.

Some of John's movements in the final year of his life can be tracked. On 8 June 1730 he was in East Leake witnessing the will of Thomas Hopkins, but he was apparently back in London by the end of the month. On 30 June, John transferred £600 of Bank of England stock to Edward Weight. Then he purchased three more lots of bank stock on 31 July, 16 October and 10 November amounting to £500, £500 and £350 respectively. So it appears he may have been tidying up his affairs by selling off assets, calling in debts, or both. While he was in his lodgings at the Garter that October, John drew up, or more probably revised, his will. As the next chapter shows, he was as precise and thorough as ever in setting out his bequests, so whatever the state of his physical health there is no sign of mental deterioration. John took care to choose people of good character and repute to witness his will. One was Henry Marshall of St Mary's Hill, merchant and member of the Grocers Company, a future Lord Mayor and knight of the realm. A second witness was the cooper Henry Neale of Mincing Lane, another merchant of substance who traded in wine and spirits.

Beside all his London friends, John may have had visitors from Nottinghamshire during his final winter. A recent act of parliament required all solicitors to be registered before they could appear in court and John's friend and executor Samuel Sterropp of Nottingham appeared for registration at the High Court of Chancery on 11 November. Sir Thomas Parkyns had an altogether more colourful reason for coming to town; on Boxing Day the Daily Post announced that Sir Thomas, 'author of a book on that curious subject called The Inn-Play or Cornish Hugg Wrestler', would appear on 28 December at Mr Figg's amphitheatre in Oxford Road to demonstrate all the 'rules and postures' mentioned in his book.

We do not know when John's health started its final decline, but his death in May 1731 seems to have been expected. Both his Nottinghamshire based executors were on hand to prove his will in much less time than it could take news of his death to reach East Leake and a return coach to arrive in London. On 28 May 1731, at his Thames Street lodgings, the 56 year old distiller passed away.

Aftermath

Following John Bley's death, his London property was sold. Thomas Bird acquired the houses in Mason's Alley and Basinghall Street and mentioned them in his 1738 will, still tenanted by George Green and Gabriel Small. Thomas Woodbridge probably bought his own home on St Dunstan's Hill and may also have bought the nearby houses to add to his growing business empire. Samuel Sterropp acquired and kept the Fetter Lane property, renewing the insurance when it fell due and mentioning the houses in his will. Samuel Holmes stayed in John Bley's former home on Thames Street until his death in 1739, when he was succeeded by his widow. Eventually the house was bought by the Excise Commissioners, always on the lookout for extra accommodation near the Custom House to help cope with rapidly expanding trade. At one point, the Excise used the property to auction off confiscated liquor – a trifle ironic if John had indeed been selling smuggled brandy.

Samuel Holmes became a member of the Common Council and his success as a businessman fully matched Bley's own. In March 1739 the

Daily Post listed the members of the new Common Council, describing Samuel Holmes as a 'brandyman' – implying someone who kept a brandy shop. A reader took exception to this, writing 'He is such an eminent Distiller and Importer that for several years past he has paid to the Crown for Duty above Twenty Thousand Pounds a Year'. Perhaps the anonymous reader was Holmes himself! This does sound as though Holmes had taken over John's import business along with his house. We are not told exactly what he was importing, very likely a mixture of goods, but one pointer is that in 1741 his widow was granted a warrant for imported rum.

Uncle Edward Weight died three years after John Bley at the ripe old age of 83 and was buried in his native village where his handsome headstone still stands alongside John's tomb. Although he spent his last years in East Leake, Edward's choice of the Londoner Henry Saunders as one of his executors shows that he retained London interests. He left his money in trust to provide an income for his young wife Eleanor, but on her death or remarriage it was to devolve to young Edward Weight junior, their son. Uncle Edward said that £50 should be spent putting his son out as an apprentice and also stipulated the payment of 'two hundred and fifty pounds and no more unto my said Son Edward Weight when he shall be out of his time or apprenticeship to sett him up in his trade'. We know nothing more of Eleanor, but the London Gazette of 6 April 1754 declared the bankruptcy of 'Edward Weight of

Edward Weight's headstone

Loughborough, Mercer'; if this was young Edward it was a sad end to his inheritance.

Joseph Nutt retired to Ponders End, near Enfield, and died leaving a reputed fortune of £40,000 and a very eligible widow, Ursula. She was rapidly snapped up by an ambitious merchant, Alderman William Bridgen, whose first marriage had been to a much wedded, wealthy and elderly widow. This new marriage was not a happy one and Ursula obtained a legal separation. She died shortly before her estranged husband was installed as Lord Mayor of London. Ursula shared her first husband's dissenting views and, like him, remembered Rev. David Jennings in her will. She also asked to be buried at Bunhill Fields, the main cemetery for London dissenters and the last resting place of such luminaries as John Bunyan, George Fox and Daniel Defoe.

The Killetts prospered and even obtained belated compensation for the ship seized by Spain in 1719. In April 1745 the House of Lords awarded them £1400 compensation for the ship and the very precise sum of £1147 17s 10d for the cargo. A year later a lavish banquet took place in Great Yarmouth to mark William Killett's appointment as Mayor. Their ship the *Three Brothers* was sold off in 1741 and ended its days as a collier; the final fates of the *Godfrey* and the *Samuel and Rebecca* are not known.

While we do not know what became of John Bley's fourth vessel, the *St George*, we do know the likely fate of Abraham Thompson and Robert Osborne, her owner and master respectively. North of Great Yarmouth lay a notorious stretch of coast known as Winterton Ness where sandbanks lay in wait for the unwary and even experienced mariners could come to grief in bad weather. Such was its reputation that in 1720 Daniel Defoe chose the spot for the fictional shipwreck of Robinson Crusoe on his very first voyage from Hull to London. One of many real life tragedies was reported in the Daily Journal of 30 March 1737:

> Yesterday by Express came the melancholy News of seven sail of Ships having been lost near Winterton Ness, the north-east point of Norfolk, viz. the John and Frances, Abraham Thompson, with a valuable Cargo of Woollen Goods from Hull for London; the ---, Capt. Norton, and

another (feared to be the Henry and Frances, Robert Osborn) bound from London to Hull; a Vessel from Scotland with Corn, of whose crew only one man was saved; and three Colliers.

William Green's name appeared annually in the list of Distillers' members, his address given as Thames Street each time, and he was elected Steward in 1732. He prospered sufficiently to acquire a house in the country near Enfield but died in 1734, leaving a widow and a young family. The inventory of his effects listed various pieces of distilling equipment, such as a copper still valued with its fittings at £16 10s, a worm valued at £14 8s and a tub valued at £1 10s.

Charles Townley, son of John Bley's old master, became extremely prosperous. He bought a house in fashionable Clapham and educated his three sons, Charles, James and Kirkes, at Merchant Taylors School. All three had distinguished careers. Charles rose steadily through the College of Heralds, was knighted by George III after overseeing the coronation of 1760 and eventually became Garter King of Arms. He inherited the Wilde family estate of Long Whatton in 1753 – his mother had been Sarah Wilde – and spent the last years of his life there. Kirkes became a merchant and philanthropist and his portrait now hangs in the National Portrait Gallery. James Townley was ordained, was appointed headmaster of his old school, became a friend of William Hogarth and David Garrick and enjoyed great success as a playwright. When Hogarth published his most famous set of engravings in 1751 he asked James to provide a set of matching verses. James had no compunction about attacking the trade through which his grandfather had repaired the family fortunes; he accompanied the famous *Gin Lane* with the following much quoted lines:

Gin, cursed fiend, with fury fraught,
Makes human race a prey; it enters by a deadly draught,
And steals our life away. Virtue and Truth, driven to despair,
Its rage compels to fly; but cherishes, with hellish care,
Theft, murder, perjury. Damned cup, that on the vitals preys,
That liquid fire contains; which madness to the heart conveys,
And rolls it through the veins.

This fully captured the public mood of the 1750s, for by now distillers of gin were being castigated for poisoning and debasing London's entire labouring class. Even Samuel Johnson's famous dictionary joined in, defining a distiller as 'one who practises the art or trade of distilling; one who makes and sells pernicious and inflammatory spirits'.

Distiller Henry Saunders, meanwhile, quietly prospered in his house on the corner of Water Lane. He rose to high office in the Distillers Company, being elected an Assistant in 1737, serving as Warden from 1743 to 1745 and becoming Master of the company in 1746. He then reverted to the status of Assistant for the rest of his life, appearing on the Court list for the last time in 1770. Life for Henry and his wife Mary appears to have been long and largely untroubled, although their peace was rudely disturbed late in the evening of 4 June 1732 by the dramatic arrival of Henry's brother Robert:

> On Sunday Night last, about 10 o'Clock, Capt. Robert Saunders, Commander of the Ruby (which is ready to go down the River on her Voyage for Leghorn, Messina, and Venice) returning from Eltham, was attack'd about 200 Yards on this side of New Cross, by two Foot-pads, who came out of a Ditch, one of whom swore, and at the same Instant fir'd at him; the Ball enter'd the Side of his Right Breast, and grazed on the Bone, went out near the Pit of the Stomach, when a third came up on the other Side the Horse, and seized the Bridle, and then they knocked him off, and dragged him up a Lane which leads to Peckham, where they rifl'd him: They staid by him till they had recharged, and then commanded him to sit there until he heard them whistle, threatening him if he stirred: But in Half a Quarter of an Hour they came back to him, and one of them taking Pity on him, prevail'd on the rest to let him go, which they did, giving him a Shilling for a Coach: The Captain getting to the Half-Way House found his Horse again, and having had some Refreshment, he mounted, and coming to his Brother's (a Distiller in Thamestreet) Mr Girle, an eminent Surgeon, was sent for (who, dressing the Wound, found a Piece of his Coat and Waistcoat in it) and Yesterday he was in a fair way of doing well.
>
> *Daily Journal 6 June 1732*

John Girle was a surgeon of St Thomas's Hospital with an excellent reputation and Robert received highly effective treatment. Within a week, the Daily Journal reported, he had made such a good recovery that he was able to set off for the Mediterranean.

Seafaring was in the Saunders blood and even the name of Robert's ship was part of the family tradition; in 1653 a Captain Robert Saunders had commanded an earlier *Ruby* when it received orders to transport men for Cromwell's army. Both Henry's brothers Robert and Jacob plied the Italian trade for many years and when war broke out with France and Spain they swapped trade for privateering. In March 1742 the Daily Post reported 'a fine new Galley, call'd the Ruby, of 400 Tons, was launched ... for Capt. Robert Saunders, in the Mediterranean Trade' and by September 1744 the London papers were reporting the capture of a string of prizes in the Mediterranean by this new *Ruby*. Brother Jacob, however, was less fortunate:

> The Boscawen Privateer (late the French Medea Man of War, of 26 Guns) being on a Cruize, fell in with a Spanish Ship of 300 Tons, 26 Guns, and 180 Men, from Corunna for Cadiz, as Convoy to a Lubecker, loaded with Naval Stores; who maintained a Fight for two hours, most of which was Yard-Arm and Yard-Arm; in which Capt. Saunders, his Second Lieutenant, and 20 Men were killed before the Prize struck. ... The Prize is brought into Portland road. Capt. Saunders was many Years Commander of a Ship in the Italian Trade, and establishe'd so fair a Character that his Death is greatly regretted.
>
> *London Evening Post 23 August 1744*

A few months later, Henry Saunders had the melancholy task of identifying the handwriting on Jacob's unwitnessed will.

Until he reached old age, Henry managed his business largely without apprentices. He did employ one while acting as Warden and Master, but as soon as he had completed these duties he passed the apprentice on to another distiller. Eventually Henry felt the need for another pair of hands and recruited Matthew Bell, who in due course became his assistant. When Henry died in 1771, Bell succeeded to the business assisted by his brother Robert. On 22 June 1772, Matthew Bell was reluctantly persuaded to attend a public firework display on Tower Hill, was struck by a rocket stick and died. Robert advertised his intention of continuing the business but died soon after, reportedly from the shock of losing his brother. A third brother, Thomas, took over but sadly went out of business in 1778 and the property was sold along with all the furniture, stock and distilling equipment. The equipment included four large copper stills and eight 300 gallon vats, significantly more than the two stills left to Matthew Bell in Henry's will. So the Bells may have fallen victim to their own ambitious plans for expansion. The inclusion of a large parcel of juniper berries in the 1778 sale confirms that they were manufacturing gin, while the stock also included brandies, rum and 'a great quantity of peppermint water'.

Henry's house on the corner of Thames Street and Water Lane later earned a unique place in both the history of transport and the history of working class leisure. Early in the 19th century the house was taken over by a father and son team of notaries called Lewis Gilson – no relations of John Bley's old master. From 1815, the younger Gilson used the building as the headquarters of one of the world's first steamship businesses, plying between London and Margate a decade before Stephenson's Rocket init-iated the first passenger railway. This revolutionised travel on the Thames, cutting a tortuous journey which could take several days, even with a favourable wind, to a voyage of a few hours. Gilson was soon running weekly Sunday excursions to Gravesend so that ordinary Londoners might savour the clean air. A decade before Thomas Cook ran his first railway outing from Leicester to Loughborough, these excursions were proving so successful that Lewis Gilson was summoned before an 1832 parliamentary inquiry into Sunday observance. In the face of hostile questioning, he gave an idyllic description of artisans and mechanics from London climbing the hill to Gravesend windmill with their families, 'spreading their little cloths, and taking their refreshment on the grass'.

Over the years Thames Street became increasingly dominated by offices and warehousing and most of the residents were squeezed out. The street retained much of its insalubrious reputation, however, as the following pungent article in a Punch Magazine of 1880 made all too plain:

Lower Thames Street is a narrow passage at the side of the Thames, about broad enough for a wheelbarrow. It is called Lower Thames Street, it being almost impossible for the Corporation to sink lower, or for the street to be in a lower condition. It is guarded at one end by an old fortress called the Tower, where big guns, some Beefeaters, and a small army are kept to repel any foreign invasion. The guns and the army might be sent where they are more wanted, as no foreigner in his senses would invade Lower Thames Street, or come willingly within a mile of it. If the delicate odour did not kill him, it would drive him away as a warning to other invaders.

Nothing now remains of the buildings that lined Thames Street in John Bley's time. Some were swept away by the construction of a huge new Custom House to the west of its predecessor in the early 19th century and others were displaced by Victorian rebuilding. The remainder succumbed to the blitz in the Second World War or to post-war redevelopment. Even the course of the street has changed. So for a lasting memorial to John Bley we must look not to London but to East Leake.

Chapter 9

'A great many legacies'

Following John's death on 28 May 1731 his two executors, Hugh Hardy and Samuel Sterropp, lost no time in applying for probate. Because John had possessions in both East Leake and London his will had to be proved in the capital at the Prerogative Court of Canterbury, the only ecclesiastical court with jurisdiction over both areas. The executors swore their oaths at this court on 29 May, leaving at least one of them free to accompany the body back to East Leake. The other may have stayed in London to collect the grant of probate when it was issued the following week, or returned to deal with it after the funeral. The ceremony took place on Thursday 3 June 1731, six days after John's death. Lord of the Manor Sir Thomas Parkyns may have had a hand in the choice of burial site, as John was buried just outside the church close to the east window. Such a prominent position was normally reserved for lords of the manor or other important landowners.

John Bley's Tomb

No account of the funeral survives, but one can imagine a large turnout of villagers and it may not be too fanciful to picture schoolmaster Richard James lining up his pupils to pay their last respects to their benefactor. Some time later a stone tomb was erected over the grave with a slate plaque that read:

> Here lyeth interr'd the Body of Mr. John Bley,
> Citizen and Distiller of LONDON; Born in this Town; Whose
> Charity in his Lifetime, and at his Death, was very extensive; he Built the
> Charity-School-house in this Town, and by his Will gave Four hundred
> and fifty Pounds for the Purchase of Lands, to be settled on ye said School;
> and also Ten Pounds to each Farmer, and five Pounds to each Cottager,
> living here in Leake; And likewise Ten Pounds to the Poor of each
> Parish that border upon this Lordship, with a great many other
> large legacies to his Relations and Friends: he died in London May
> the 28th, An Dom 1731, and was here Buried June the 3^d following
> in the 57th Year of his Age.

As this inscription implies, John may already have spent or given away considerable sums of money in his lifetime, but he still had much more to leave.

The value of the estate

One estimate of John's wealth can be obtained from his known assets, namely those mentioned in his will together with the amount of stock he held in the Bank of England at the time of his death. The bulk of his known assets were in the form of South Sea Annuities (nominal value £3400) and Bank stock (nominal value £4000). We can assign precise values to these using market valuations published in the daily press in June 1731. From what we know of the insurance valuations his London property was probably worth somewhere between £1500 and £2000. The shipping shares were unlikely to be worth more than £400; bearing in mind the age of the three main vessels, a figure of £200 seems more likely. To this we can add estimated values for his East Leake properties, furniture, horses, etc.:

	nominal value	market value
Bank Stock	£4,000	£5,880
South Sea Annuities	£3,400	£3,604
London property		£1,750
EL house, horses, etc.		£400
school site & building		£400
named debts		£300
ships		£200
Total (estimate)		**£12,534**

There were almost certainly other assets; the will mentioned ready money, arrears of rent and 'securities for money' all of which would add to the total. We know also that John had at least £1000 worth of South Sea Company stock (as distinct from annuities) some years earlier, although this may have been sold to buy property. An overall estimate between £13,000 and £15,000 would therefore seem reasonable.

We can compare this estimate with the total value of the legacies listed in John's will:

villagers + poor	£600
named individuals (cash)	£5,230
individuals (South Sea Annuities)	£3,604
individual (Bank of England stock)	£1,470
school site and building (estimate)	£400
school privies + endowment	£470
individuals (ship shares) (estimate)	£200
clothes, horses, furniture (estimate)	£100
Total	**£12,074**

John named no fewer than 16 people he wanted to share the residue of his estate once all the specific legacies had been paid, so he presumably expected a fair amount to be left over. Again, an estimate of £13,000 to £15,000 seems reasonable.

By City standards this was a substantial amount but by no means exceptional. Joseph Nutt would die worth two or three times as much and Joseph's former partner Sir Gregory Page reputedly left well over £600,000. By village standards, however, John Bley had accumulated an immense fortune. Probate inventories of East Leake tradesmen for the period 1700 to 1750 amounted to between £6 and £80 while those of farmers ranged from £17 to £320; John was in an utterly different league.

Conversions of the value of John's estate into modern terms can only give a very rough idea of its worth. Using the retail price index, £15,000 in 1731 equates to just under £2 million in 2010 (the latest available date) while a conversion based on average earnings gives £25 million. Such differing amounts remind us how unreliable these comparisons are.

The will

John's will was dated 28 October 1730 and probate was granted on 2 June 1731. The document was eleven pages long and contained no fewer than 55 separate legacies together with instructions for the disposal of his property. Two versions survive in the National Archives at Kew. The original was written in a typical clerk's hand and signed by John on every page, with his seals at the beginning and end. The registered copy which is available online differs only in minor respects; various spellings have been corrected and superfluous apostrophes removed. Clearly and precisely worded and unusually detailed, the will may well have been revised several times over the years, one obvious likely occasion being the death of John's mother three years earlier. A full transcript of the registered copy is included in appendix B.

Unlike most wills at that time it was prefaced by only the briefest religious statement: 'In the name of God Amen'. There was no testament to John's faith or beliefs, nothing was said about his soul and there were no directions about the disposal of the body – separate instructions had probably been issued verbally. Once more we are left with the impression that John was not very interested in religion.

The first page of John Bley's will

As soon as the content of the will became known, the extensive local bequests must have made it the talk of the countryside. Thus shortly after the funeral Rev. Robert Marsden, Rector of Rempstone, made notes in his Commonplace Book (page 93):

Mr Bley's will

He was a distiller

Put out … £100, he got 20[000] or £30,000

He never mix'd his brandy but sold it as it came to him.

He gave £10 apiece to 15 Farmers and £5 to 70 Cottagers of Gt. Leake & left out one as being a lazy man.

He gave £10 a town to ye poor of the 7 towns bordering on Gt. Leake – and cautioned agst his house being sold to Major Gery, a rude hunter

As a summary of the will this is not entirely accurate; the caution about Major Gery did not actually appear anywhere in the document. However Marsden's figures for the number of villagers who benefited are very useful and fit quite well with the 94 East Leake families reported in Rev. Granville Wheler's 1743 Visitation return.

Distributing wealth

By the custom of the City of London a citizen was expected to leave one third of his estate to his widow and one third to his children, with only the last third being left to his own discretion. Having no immediate family, John was free to distribute his wealth more widely, as chart 1 shows. Here we can see that a significant amount (5%) was left as charity to the villagers of East Leake, both rich and poor, and to the poor of the other villages bordering on

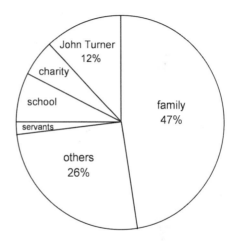

Chart 1 Who got the money

the parish. When the value of the school and its endowment is added, John's charitable donations amount to around 12% of the total.

The village community

The very first item in the will set out the gifts to John's fellow villagers, £10 to each farmer and £5 to every other householder. At a time when almost all villagers tended holdings in the open fields, even if their main income came from trade, the term 'farmer' needed careful definition. John specified that they should be farming on a sufficient scale to own their own plough team: 'every husbandman or husbandmans widow that follows husbandry and keeps at least one teame with plowe carriages'; there were 15 farmers who met this qualification if Marsden is to be believed.

The amounts sound small until one realises that £10 would buy 50 or 60 sheep or half a dozen cattle and might represent a year's rent for a tenant farm, while the maximum wage for a head farm labourer was set by the Nottinghamshire Quarter Sessions at £5 per annum. The one exception to John's generosity was for 'that idle family of George Doughty' – clearly wanton idleness was one thing that John could not stand!

A more conventional bequest was money for the poor of John's native village, with £10 to be paid 'for the use and benefit of the poor of East Leake in the severities of winter' in each of the next three years. But John went much further than convention dictated by leaving another £10 apiece to each of the seven parishes that bordered on East Leake for the benefit of their poor.

John's most important bequests to his village related to the school. First, there was the school itself, placed in the hands of trustees, along with £450 to buy land which would provide a perpetual income to maintain the building and pay the schoolmaster's salary. Next he secured the continued services of the schoolmaster Richard James with an immediate bequest of £20 to be followed by 'ten pounds per Annum for three years if he the said Mr James so long Continues to teach my said Schoole (as and for his yearly Sallary)'. Ever attentive to detail, John even left a further £20 for the construction of privies, or 'necessary houses', for the school.

The family

John made extensive provision for members of his mother's family, distributing nearly £6000 amongst them (chart 2). He was especially generous to three fatherless members of the younger generation who were about to complete apprenticeships and would need money to set them-selves up in trade. John and Robert Hopkins, grandchildren of John's aunt Mary Hopkins, and Caleb Moore, grandson of uncle Robert Wight, each received £600 in South Sea Annuities – an amount that could either provide a modest long-term income or be used to establish a substantial London business. Caleb was also left all the clothes in John's London lodgings, a personal touch that suggests John had taken a particularly close interest in this youngster.

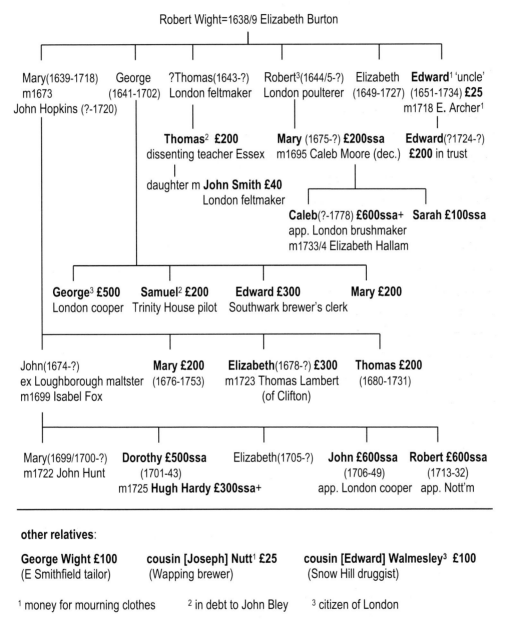

Chart 2 Wight family tree, showing legacies

---

other relatives:

George Wight £100
(E Smithfield tailor)

cousin [Joseph] Nutt[1] £25
(Wapping brewer)

cousin [Edward] Walmesley[3] £100
(Snow Hill druggist)

[1] money for mourning clothes   [2] in debt to John Bley   [3] citizen of London

Female relatives also fared well. Dorothy Hardy, another of Mary Hopkins' grandchildren, received £500 in South Sea Annuities while her husband Hugh, one of the two executors of the will, was given a further £300 worth, a horse and first choice of John's clothing. Aunt Mary's daughter Elizabeth received £300 'for her own separate use' – in other words it was to go to her, not her husband. Elizabeth had married Thomas Lambert of Clifton and probably lived in the house where Thomas had grown up. This is now listed grade 2* as an unusually fine example of a timbered 14th century hall farmhouse and still carries the initials of Thomas' parents over the door.

Altogether some 21 relatives received legacies.

Other beneficiaries

The table below lists the other beneficiaries. John's London friends feature strongly in the list and there were bequests to four current servants as well as a former one. The proprietor of the Garter Coffee House, Mary Gigg, was generously rewarded for her hospitality, receiving £300 in South Sea Annuities along with John's London furniture, while her sister Sarah was left a further £100 worth of annuities. Again John showed sympathy with fatherless youngsters, leaving £100 apiece to the four orphaned children of his friend Robert Godfrey.

Some legacies are intriguing. Besides a generous bequest of £400, friend and executor Samuel Sterropp was left 'the chest in my closet'. We can speculate that it may have held money and important documents, but have no real clue to the contents. The inclusion of the Ticknall schoolmaster, Richard Bryan, is something of a mystery; perhaps he had helped to set up the East Leake school. If Elizabeth Garland of Prestwold was related to former master of Prestwold school, John Garland this would make another school link. Clearly elderly and frail, Elizabeth was granted her £20 'if living at the time of my death'; in the event she died just weeks before John himself. Another unexplained beneficiary on an altogether different scale was a young boy called John Turner. He received a nominal £1000 in Bank of England stock, worth well over £1400 at the prevailing market price, which is considerably more than was left to any of John's known family. John Turner's story is told in the next chapter.

Name	Occupation / address	Legacy
Mary Gigg	coffee house keeper; Thames St	£300 SSA + furniture
Sarah Gigg	Thames St, London	£100 SSA
William Parker	cooper; late of Harp Lane, London	£300
Henry Saunders	distiller (ex-apprentice); Thames St	£100
Gustavus Brooke	ex-apprentice	£20
George Quinton	gilder; East Leake, ex-London	£100
Thomas Garrett	salter; Thames St, London	£150
Richard Fendall	grazier; Southwark, London	£50
Daniel Berry	ex-distiller; Felmersham, Beds.	£100
John Bird	ex-cooper; Barrow upon Soar, Leics.	£50 + debts forgiven + suit
Elizabeth Hickling	former servant	£75
William Angrave	servant	£50 + horse
Jane Lambert	servant	£40
Sara Crosse	servant	£35
Richard Callis	servant (a minor)	£10
Robt Godfrey's 4 chn	orphans (minors); London	£400
Thomas Bird	cooper; London	£500
John Turner	a minor; address unknown	£1000 Bank stock + tankard
Elizabeth Pratt	painter stainer; London	£50 debt forgiven
Joseph Matthews	salter; Buckler's Bury, London	£90 debt forgiven
Elizabeth Garland	Prestwold, Leics.	£20
Samuel Sterropp	attorney; Nottingham	£400 + chest
Mary Sterropp	Nottingham	10 guineas for mourning
Killett families	ship owners/captains; Gorleston	£120 + ship shares
Abraham Thompson	mariner; Hull	ship share
Richard Bryan	schoolmaster; Ticknall, Derbys.	£20

non-family beneficiaries

Overall John's will was clearly the result of much thought and deliberation; it seems he was determined to leave out no-one he knew whom he might benefit. The sums left to the villagers appear very carefully calculated: large enough to be of serious use but not sufficient to induce a change of lifestyle and totally disrupt the fabric of village life. The amounts given to family and friends were probably geared in part to need; a cash handout to Joseph Nutt, significantly richer than John himself, would have been meaningless, so he received only £25 for mourning. It seems that John took previous pay-outs into account. Thus Samuel Wight received less than his brothers but had debts forgiven. The £200 left to uncle Edward's son was a relatively modest amount for one of the closer relatives, but John had made over £600 of Bank of England stock to uncle Edward himself a few months earlier.

John's treatment of men and women was remarkably even-handed. He worded his will carefully to make sure farming families headed by women did not lose out – at any given time there were likely to be several such families in the village. The four orphan children of Robert Godfrey received equal amounts, even though the eldest was a boy and the others were girls. And, of course John's school catered for boys and girls alike. Perhaps we should not be surprised; given his mother's story, John must have been more aware than most of women's financial needs.

Perhaps the strongest theme running through John's will is his determination to give young people an easier start in life than he had enjoyed. All East Leake youngsters now had ready access to schooling and individuals who might otherwise have toiled for years to establish themselves could set up businesses of their own as soon as they completed their apprenticeships.

John Bley's signature and seal on the original will

Implementing the will

It was several months before the executors were in a position to pay all the legacies because John had specified that all his East Leake and London property should be sold to help finance them. The executors simplified the task by acquiring some of the property themselves, Hugh Hardy taking on John's East Leake house and Samuel Sterropp purchasing the properties in Fetter Lane. As mentioned in the last chapter, one of the principal beneficiaries, Thomas Bird, acquired two of the houses and others may have been sold to the tenants. A nominal £3000 of John Bley's Bank of England stock was sold off between 25 November and 1 December and should have realised about £4400 in cash, according to the prices given for Bank stock in the Daily Courant that week. Together with the money from the houses this should have provided just enough to cover all the cash legacies.

Distributing the money must have been a tedious task, involving several journeys to places as far apart as Gorleston near Great Yarmouth and Ticknall in Derbyshire and the transport of considerable amounts of cash. Hugh Hardy had the additional chore of identifying deserving poor villagers in East Leake over the next three winters. At least as a grocer he was well placed to know everyone in the village and would have a fairly shrewd idea of their family circumstances. He could also involve the village overseers of the poor if he needed assistance. As we shall see in the next chapter, Samuel Sterropp also had continuing responsibilities. All-in-all, before they had finished, the two executors must have felt they had earned their generous legacies.

The impact of the will

John's bequests had an immediate short term impact on the lives of East Leake's villagers. Debts could be paid off, new livestock purchased, a daughter's dowry paid or money just put aside for a rainy day. John's memory must have been toasted a good few times in local ale houses over succeeding months. One legatee, ex-servant Jane Lambert, took quick advantage of her forthcoming £40 windfall by marrying John Cox, husbandman of Normanton on Soar, just seven weeks after the funeral.

There must also have been long term effects on the local economy. As chart 3 shows, much of John's money went to friends and relations in London but there was still a massive injection of wealth, around £4000, into his native village.

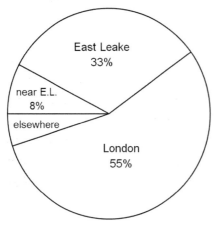

Chart 3 Where the money went

The destiny of some of this wealth can be traced. Within five years of receiving his legacy of £600 in annuities, Caleb Moore paid £660 for a farm in East Leake, married a local girl and settled down in the village. Rural life seems to have palled, however, and he later moved back to London and resumed a career in trade. Robert Hopkins, another recipient of £600 in annuities, returned to East Leake from his Nottingham apprenticeship to begin trade as a carpenter, but died within two years. His money, £450 of which was still in South Sea Annuities, stayed within the family – some of it going to his sister Dorothy. Together with her husband Hugh Hardy, Dorothy certainly made good use of their new wealth and by the end of the century their son John was second in importance only to the Parkyns family as an East Leake landowner.

The school endowment had the greatest impact of all, for it meant that a sound basic education was available to every child in the village, no matter how poor. With the school came the schoolmaster and he too would play an influential role in the village. The story of the school and its masters is told in full in the final chapter.

The will is far-sighted, generous and humane, sensitive to individual needs and circumstances, but also comprehensive and essentially businesslike. For its time it can be read as unusually and carefully egalitarian. It is the final and defining expression of a rich and fruitful life with all the loose ends neatly tied up – with just one exception.

Chapter 10

The mystery of John Turner

Halfway through John Bley's long and detailed will lies a bequest that is both the largest and also the most mysterious of his legacies:

> Item I do give and bequeath to John Turner one thousand pounds Bank of England Stock to be Transferred to him on his Attaining the age of one and twenty years and in the mean time the Severall Dividends to be applied for his benefitt as well for his Maintenance as also for the placing him out an Apprentice to some Trade or business and I do also give to the said John Turner one Silver Tankard markt at the bottom with the Letters J T being in weight twenty five ounces and twelve penny weights

There is no clue in the will as to who John Turner was, only the indication that he was not yet old enough to become an apprentice. No address is given and, even though the beneficiary is clearly a minor, no parent is named. The youngster's name was an extremely common one, yet John Bley clearly expected his executors to know exactly who was meant without needing any further identification. This suggests that John Turner was someone very close to him, as does the exceptional amount of the legacy. The silver tankard, too, was the kind of gift that might be given to a favourite relative. The records of the Bank of England confirm the transfer of the stock to John Turner's name shortly after John Bley's death, giving just one further piece of information – when the will was proved in June 1731 the boy was just four years old:

So who was this young child? An immediate answer might be that he was John Bley's own illegitimate son; John would have been about 52 years old at the time of the boy's birth. But there is no direct evidence of such a relationship. Given Bley's own background in East Leake, it might seem unlikely that he would have refused to marry the boy's mother. The young-ster never took the name Bley, none of John Bley's relatives mentioned John Turner in their wills, though they frequently named each other, and John Turner's will mentioned no known relative of John Bley. So it certainly appears no relationship of this kind was ever acknowledged. A more likely explanation, perhaps, is that this was a destitute orphan whom John Bley had taken under his wing. There were no official adoption records at the time, so there are no direct means of checking such a theory. There were many homeless orphans in 18th century London and in time this would lead to the founding of several charitable orphanages, but in John Bley's lifetime their only recourse was the parish workhouse. Even this refuge was denied to some, for not all London's floating population could claim the settlement in a specific parish that would entitle them to relief. John Bley may have been motivated in part by memories of his own difficult start in life; he may also have wanted an heir. After his mother's death in 1727 he had no immediate family to inherit his wealth.

It is also possible that John Turner spent most of his childhood in Nottingham with one of John Bley's executors, for Samuel Sterropp's own will indicates he did much more than John Bley had asked. Written in 1766 but proved in 1773, this will made John Turner Sterropp's principal heir. This suggests Sterropp may have brought up John Turner himself, with the help of his sister Mary, and, in the absence of a family of his own, may have come to look on the young man as a son. Mary Sterropp died when young John was 14 years old, leaving Samuel, like John Bley before him, with no close family to provide for.

John Bley doubtless intended that John Turner should have enough money to set up in business when he came of age and this may have happened. Bank of England records show that John Turner disposed of his bank stock to Samuel Sterropp soon after attaining his majority. The face value of the stock transferred was £1025, presumably including interest for the current year, and the market value more like £1300. This should have been enough to set up or buy into a business as a mercer – the occupation given for John Turner at the time of the Bank of England transaction. If the young man did start his own business it cannot have been a success, for Sterropp's will reveals that by his late thirties John was working as an employee of Charles Lowth, a 'men's mercer' with a shop in Paternoster Row, just north of St Paul's cathedral.

John may have been working for Lowth for some time. An advertisement in the London General Advertiser of 26 July 1744 indicates that Charles Lowth had a trade connection with Nottingham in the period that John Turner was growing up and possibly some connection, direct or indirect, with Samuel Sterropp's friend Abel Smith:

> Lost or mislaid: a bill for £27-4s on Mr Sam Smith ... drawn by Mr A Smith of Nottingham. ... Whoever brings the said bill to Mr Charles Lowth in Paternoster Row shall have 10 shillings reward.

This may just be coincidence and John may equally well have received his training elsewhere. On 6 December 1743, when our youngster was 16 years old, a member of the Drapers Company called Charles Salkeld took on an apprentice called John Turner. Three months later, on 23 March, the Daily Advertiser announced that 'Charles Salkeld, Mens-Mercer, is remov'd from the Seven Stars in Ludgate-Street to the Seven Stars and Woolpack, the Corner of the Old Baily, on Ludgate-Hill'. So this John Turner was the same age as John Bley's former protégée and was trained in exactly the same trade. Moreover, Salkeld's new premises were less than five minutes' walk from Paternoster Row and it would be a short move for John Turner to transfer to Charles Lowth's employment when his first master Salkeld was declared bankrupt in 1762. However, caution is needed. The name John Turner was such a common one that we cannot be certain that Salkeld's apprentice and the youngster mentioned in the wills of John Bley and Samuel Sterropp really were one and the same person. The details in the Register of Apprentices do not help much. No father was named, which is not surprising given what we know about John Turner, but his place of residence in December 1743 is given as Southwark and this would raise further questions about where and by whom he was brought up. Did he move from Nottingham to Southwark in London when Mary Sterropp died in 1741 perhaps? It seems that John Turner's early years will always remain something of a mystery.

Charles Lowth's will confirms John Turner's subordinate position in the Paternoster Row business; whereas £100 was left to Lowth's junior partner James Pitts, there was just £20 apiece for 'my Servants John Turner William Morgan and James Moffatt'. Indeed, Lowth's footman came out rather better, receiving £10 together with all of Lowth's clothing. Samuel Sterropp knew that John was not free to travel as and when he pleased for he wrote in his will that his friend the banker Abel Smith was to see to the funeral arrangements 'in the Absence of my said Executor John Turner'.

Chapter Coffee House

Charles Lowth was a man of wide interests and no mere shopkeeper. He was a member of both the Society of Antiquaries and the Society for the Encouragement of Arts, Manufactures and Commerce. He was also a director of the Union Fire Office, governor of various charities and one of His Majesty's Commissioners of Lieutenancy for the City of London. Paternoster Row was the centre of the publishing trade, Longmans being perhaps the most famous business that started there in the 18th century, and the local coffee houses attracted many figures from the worlds of literature and the theatre. One such figure was James Quinn, renowned for his performances as Falstaff and England's leading actor before the rise of David Garrick. Lowth became Quinn's intimate friend and when Quinn died in 1766 the mercer was named as one of his executors and main beneficiaries. Lowth & Co.'s shop at the sign of the King's Head, 48 Paternoster Row, stood roughly halfway along the south side of the street very close to the Chapter coffee house. The Chapter was particularly known as the haunt of publishers and was probably favoured by Charles Lowth; two of the witnesses to his will gave the establishment as their address. Given all Lowth's social and cultural activities, much of the day-to-day running of the business must have been left to his employees.

When Lowth died in 1769 the business passed to his young partner James Pitts, but Pitts himself died the following March and the shop closed down. The stock in trade, consisting of 'a large assortment of goods for gentlemen's wear … in exceeding good condition and of the best manu-factories', was advertised for sale and the employees mentioned in Lowth's will had to seek alternative employment. To judge by a later sequence of advertisements, William Morgan switched to selling ladies' wear before opening a business of his own. James Moffatt appears to have made a far more radical change of career, for in his will John Turner left £50 to 'James Moffatt of Castle Street Shoreditch Salt Peter Refiner'. John too had to find a new employer, since it was not until 1773 that his inheritance from Samuel Sterropp would make him financially independent. In his will 16 years later John described himself as a linen-draper so, unlike Moffatt, he remained in broadly the same line of business.

John's legacy from Samuel Sterropp must have made a huge difference to his life. Sterropp left John his three houses in Fetter Lane 'of the present yearly rent of fifty six pounds', which alone should have enabled him to live quietly in lodgings without having to earn a living. Tax records confirm that these houses were the very ones John Bley had once owned, so they were a singularly appropriate legacy. Sterropp went on to make John his sole heir, the only other legacies being three mourning rings for his friends Sir Thomas Parkyns (son of the wrestler), Henry Athorpe and Abel Smith and the bequest of Samuel's clothes to his servant John Clayton. We have no valuation for Sterropp's estate, but after a long career as attorney for the Parkyns family and others he might be expected to leave a large fortune in addition to the Fetter Lane houses. However, there is no sign of any such fortune in John Turner's 1789 will; if it existed, it may have been frittered away in further attempts to establish an independent business.

The details of John's will suggest strongly that he spent the last years of his life in the household of John Danvers, a wholesale hosier living at 1 New Court, Broad Street, in the parish of St Benet Fink and in the heart of the City. John gave only the parish as his address, but the will is dominated by members of the Danvers household and family. John Danvers himself was the residual beneficiary and sole executor. All four of Danvers' surviving children were mentioned, along with the son-in-law Dr William Hamilton. Danvers' four servants shared a 20 guinea legacy and his apprentice received £10. Furthermore, the apprentice and one of the servants were each left articles of John Turner's clothing. All this suggests that John may have lived there for some time.

John Danvers was a philanthropic gentleman and was by religion nonconformist. He had all his children baptised at the nearby dissenting meeting of 'Bartholomew Close and Pinners Hall' and was an active supporter of the dissenting Orphans Working School. His name appeared in the lists of governors, or guardians, for both the Orphan Working School and the London Hospital. Such governorships were not in themselves a mark of great involvement, since any payment of 30 guineas or more made the donor a guardian or governor for life, as well as conferring the right to present potential residents. More significantly, though, Danvers acted as a steward for each of the charities and his name appeared in newspaper advertisements as an organiser of fund-raising events. He also took a turn chairing the House Committee that oversaw the day-to-day running of the London Hospital. The bequests in John Turner's will clearly reflect the influence of Danvers' charitable activities.

John Turner wrote his will shortly before he died in the autumn of 1789 and made it clear he had not forgotten his Nottingham connections:

> I also give to John Clayton of Saint James's Lane in the Town of Nottingham one hundred pounds as a Gratuity for his long and Faithful Service to my late Friend Saml Sterropp Esqr of Nottingham And it is my Will if the said John Clayton die before me that the said sum of £100 go to his children share and share alike

John's principal asset consisted of 'the sum of Forty four pounds sterling per annum consolidated of 1780 for 28 years standing in my name and transferable at the Bank of England'. This stock was left in trust to John Danvers with the instruction to sell it to cover some £600 of legacies. There is no indication that any of the 26 people named in John's will were related to him – reinforcing the notion that he had been orphaned at an early age. The Danvers household and children account for half the names and several others were connected to the men's clothing trade. James Moffatt was presumably the man who had worked with John at Paternoster Row, John Brockway and Maynard Dixon were both hosiers, Mary Stalker and Mary Scott were the widow and daughter of a tailor and Alice Roberts may have been married to a tailor. John may have encountered at least some of the others through his trade. So a wide circle of friends did not necessarily mean a wide range of interests. However, those interests did include at least three charities and it is John's bequest of £50 apiece to the London Hospital, the Asylum for Orphan Girls and the Orphan Working School that perhaps constitute the most interesting part of his will.

The London Hospital on Whitechapel Road as depicted
in the Corporation's 1796 report

These charities were typical of the institutions that sprang up in the decades following John Bley's death. The London Hospital was the oldest of the three, founded in 1740 and housed since 1750 in a large, handsome purpose-built mansion on Whitechapel Road. It treated the poor free of charge and admitted accident victims without question. Sufferers from disease, however, were strictly vetted:

> no person of known ability to pay for advice are allowed to partake of this charity: nor are any admitted into the house with infectious distempers; or, who are asthmatic or consumptive, or deemed incurable or improper by the physicians or surgeons; but such may be relieved as out-patients.

At any one time, there were typically 130 in-patients at the hospital and 400 or more receiving treatment as out-patients. The hospital was served by three physicians and three surgeons who gave their services free and worked in rotation. One of the physicians listed in 1796 was John Danvers' son-in-law Dr William Hamilton.

The 'Asylum for Orphan Girls situated at the Surrey side of Westminster Bridge' was founded in 1758 at the instigation of magistrate John Fielding, anxious as he was to divert homeless children from a life of crime and prostitution. This institution took in orphan girls between the ages of 9 and 12 whose parish of settlement could not be determined. London's floating population of soldiers, seamen and labourers meant there were many such children and by 1789 there were some 200 girls in residence. The orphanage may have been a model of benevolence in its time, but the admission rules reflected contemporary attitudes to race and disability:

> No negro or mulatto girl can be admitted.

> No diseased, deformed or infirm child can be admitted.

The girls were trained as domestic servants and as soon as ready they were placed in carefully vetted homes on seven year apprenticeships. To show they were ready to be put into service, the girls had to

> produce to the Committee a shirt cut out, made, washed, and ironed by their own hands.

> be able to cut out and make their own linen, to clean rooms, and make beds, to understand plain cookery, and to clean kitchen, and other household, furniture.

read a chapter in the Bible, write a legible hand, and cast up a sum in addition.

Every detail of the girls' lives was minutely controlled. They were to wash their hands and faces every morning and their feet every Friday evening. They were to have clean linen twice a week and clean sheets once every four weeks. In the summer they were roused at six a.m., spent four hours in the classroom each morning and afternoon and were allowed two or three hours of play time. Meals were taken at 8 a.m., 1 p.m. and 8 p.m. and the girls went to bed at 9 p.m. In winter they rose an hour later and went to bed an hour earlier, with one hour less being spent in the classroom each morning and afternoon. A writing master attended twice a week to instruct the older girls, but most lessons were devoted to needlework, with the girls being expected to perform paid mending to help defray the cost of their upkeep. The prescribed diet was frugal, as befitting prospective servant girls, but was fairly nutritious with meat provided at midday five days a week. Weak beer was the staple drink – much safer than water – but strong drink was strictly prohibited.

	Breakfast	Dinner	Supper
Sunday	bread & butter	roasted beef & vegetables	bread & butter
Monday	milk-porridge	boiled mutton & vegetables	rice milk & treacle
Tuesday	water-gruel	boiled beef & vegetables	milk & water with bread
Wednesday	milk-porridge	suet pudding with plumbs	bread & butter
Thursday	water-gruel	roasted mutton & vegetables	rice milk & treacle
Friday	milk-porridge	suet pudding with plumbs	bread & butter
Saturday	water-gruel	boiled mutton & vegetables	milk & water with bread

Orphan Girls Asylum report (1789) p54: 'Table of diet for the children'

The newest of the three charities, the Orphan Working School had been founded in 1760 and had moved in 1773 to purpose-built premises on the City Road. It was half the size of the Orphan Girls' Asylum and a dissenting foundation, its governing body dominated by businessmen rather than the aristocrats and Church of England bishops who featured prominently among the guardians of the Orphan Girls Asylum. Children were admitted between the ages of six and nine and stayed until they were at least 14. Some were orphans, others were children whose parents were incapable of looking after them. As at the Girls Asylum, admission was subject to medical examination, but only children carrying an infectious disease were rejected. Both boys and girls were taken in, but they were kept strictly apart, except at times of worship. The boys were trained to become apprentices and the girls to be domestic servants.

In their prospectus, the Governors of the Orphan Working School were anxious to stress that children were not given notions above 'the lower sphere of life in which Providence hath intended them to move', with 'their diet, their dress, and their instruction, such as every honest manufacturer would wish an apprentice should have been trained up in; and every worthy master and mistress would desire the lowest of their servants should have been accustomed to'. The children kept similar hours to the girls at the Asylum. They too were allowed time for play, but most of their day was divided between lessons in reading and writing and physical work. The boys made carpets that could be put up for sale and the girls were employed in 'sewing and knitting and in assisting the mistress and servant in the domestic affairs'.

The rules of the Orphan Working School were less prescriptive about diet than those at the Girls Asylum, but went into great detail about religious observance and the forms of prayer that children should be taught. Though the school described itself as 'non-sectarian' the children were to 'attend the public worship of God, in some congregation of Protestant Dissenters under the inspection of the master', besides attending house prayers twice daily. Disciplinary procedures were also set out in great detail, giving an insight into what was considered appropriate in an

18th century school. Wilful lying was not to be tolerated. A lie 'known only to the master or mistress' was to be dealt with in private, but public lies were to be punished in public. The options were to turn the offender out of the room during prayers, to place him or her face to the wall at meal-time with 'a paper pinned to his or her back wrote upon *Lyar*', to keep the offender in at play time, or to make him or her miss a turn to read before prayers or say grace. Cursing or blaspheming, 'though such a thing can scarce be imagined', was to be punished in a similar way.

Corporal punishment was also used. Although 'great care must be taken not to terrify the children by confining them in the dark or with any idle tales' and the master was to be 'tender in correcting the children', disobedience and obstinacy were punished by public whipping. As a final recourse, a troublesome child might be expelled. There were also positive inducements to industry and good behaviour. At the weekly governors' inspections good work was rewarded financially, with money being set aside until the child was ready to leave.

All three charities grew and flourished in the years that followed. While John Turner's choice of charities clearly showed the influence of John Danvers, his interest in the fate of orphans may also reflect his own origins. At any rate, the founder of East Leake School would surely have approved.

If John Bley had hoped his protégé would follow in his footsteps and become a successful businessman, he would have been disappointed by John Turner's career. If, however, he shared the aim of the orphanage founders, rescuing a needy youngster from a possible life of crime on the streets and turning him into a productive member of society, he would have been well content with the result of his bequest.

Chapter 11

Legacy and conclusion

The local legacy

The most immediate and outstanding legacy left by John was the successful survival of his school. Following John's will, from 1731 the Bley School was well endowed by contemporary standards. The house, adjoining orchard and land to the value of £450 represented a substantial investment and ensured the survival of a new, lively and evidently very popular institution in the village.

The main task facing the executors of the will was to purchase land from which rent could be raised. The first of several purchases was of 20 acres of land (Nether Walton Brook Close) in Burton on the Wolds. It seems that this process triggered the formulation of the first trust deeds which were recorded at the Charity Commission, in the Court of Chancery, on 18 November 1733. Here the trustees John Clifton, Samuel Earby and Daniel Woodroffe were required to use the income from the land 'perpetually to repair the schoolhouse, and, when necessary, to rebuild it' which shows long-term thinking indeed. Then they were to 'dispose of the residue of the rents and profits of the premises, as a salary for the maintenance of a schoolmaster, to be employed to teach the children of the inhabitants of East Leake only, to read and instruct them in the principles of the Christian religion, according to the usage of the Church of England, and in other useful learning, for ever...' On 9/10 October 1733 the trustees paid a further £64, from the Bley estate, to Daniel Hickling for nine acres of land in Wymeswold. The school was now well endowed.

How was the school to be run from now on? The new foundation reasserted Bley's original intention, expressed in his will, that the money was to be used to teach the children of East Leake *only* – 'for their sole use and benefit'. But this did not prevent Richard James or any of his successors from taking in children from elsewhere, at their own expense. We have clear evidence from Robert Marsden at Rempstone that children from his village were being taught before 1733, even though someone had to pay for them. We have no knowledge of what Bley himself intended for the curriculum apart from handwriting and arithmetic, either before his death or in the will itself. The absence of any specific religious requirement is unusual both locally and nationally at this time. Whatever conditions applied before 1733, we now find that the trustees required instruction 'in the principles of the Christian religion, according to the usage of the Church of England'. The rest of the curriculum is reduced to 'other useful learning'. The rector in 1733 was a notorious absentee, Michael Stanhope, so it is likely that any religious influence came from the churchwardens Thomas Carver and Daniel Woodroffe. It is also significant that Francis Greene, about whom we know nothing more, had seen it necessary to donate a large Bible to the school in 1733. Perhaps the Bley School simply did not possess one until then. How closely would the master follow these new requirements?

The Trust was registered as a charity in London. In 1743 Bishop Herring requested information from the churchwardens as part of his visitation. The resulting report on the Bley School was succinct and positive. Serving 94 families (and two dissenters) in the village,

> The present Master, a very Careful Man, teaches constantly threescore or fourscore Boys and Girls to read and write, instructs them diligently in their Church catechism, and brings 'em duly to Church on Wednesdays and Fridays, taking care as far as he is able that their parents do so on Sundays.

This was not an independent inspection by Victorian standards for one of the churchwardens involved was the schoolmaster himself, Richard James. But it is likely to be an accurate summary of the school's position since the next rector Granville Wheler was a conscientious man who would not sign it off otherwise. On the other hand the number of dissenters was probably an understatement in order to avoid embarrassing the rector. Despite the interest shown in the school by higher clerical authorities, however, it is interesting that control of its governance remained in secular hands throughout the 18th century. The 1829 Commissioners' Report lists seven trustees throughout this period who served the village on the vestry and the other local charity, the Townlands Trust. All of them came from the local farming community: Daniel Woodroffe, John, William and Thomas Cooper Angrave, John Marcer, William Marcer and Edward Burrows. The rector and curate were never included as trustees.

Interest in nonconformity began slowly in East Leake with a Presbyterian meeting house in 1698 while an active Presbyterian group is recorded in 1717. Baptists built their East Leake chapel in 1757 and were a significant presence in the village in the second half of the 18th century. The first Methodist chapel was built in 1798. By 1800 nonconformist belief was widespread in the district and some of the Angrave family, well represented on the Bley School trustees, were influential Methodists. These facts may well explain the next shift in the religious requirements for the school: the 1829 Commission reported that the school took in an average of 40 poor village children a year aged from 4 to 14, of both sexes. But now the C. of E. catechism was only taught to 'those whose parents do not object.' Dissent continued to spread: from the 1851 religious census we know that about two-thirds of the villagers were nonconformists and in 1862 the school's position again came under scrutiny. The Diocesan inspector reported that 'Dissent is all powerful here', with only four out of 90 children able to say the [C. of E.] catechism and 'the Endowed School for Boys [was]… still closed to the inspectors ... a church endowment in the hands of Dissenters.' We can see here that only the boys are now mentioned – yet another modification of Bley's original vision. So the school suffered the strains and challenges of changing religious preferences through its history. As far as we know, from 1829 no teacher ever allowed a diocesan inspection and no log-books or attendance registers were kept. The school remained resolutely, even defiantly, outside the influence of church and state. A photograph shows the building to be in a fair condition in the mid-19th century, but inflation and material degradation steadily ate away at its position. By 1829 the premises were thought to be worth only £10 per annum. We think that the masters were now teaching older boys such as the Normans for a fee in order to make up their salaries. Faced with similar problems many schools elsewhere in the country either abandoned their original status, as grammar schools or as dissenting academies, and adopted the boarding public school model in order to pay their way. In the 19th century the school took boarding pupils according to Potter, though the venture may have been short lived – no boarders appear in any of the available census returns (from 1841 onwards).

As well as his role as schoolmaster Richard James soon began to make an impact on village life. He was churchwarden from 1742 to 1745. We find him acting, too, as witness to the wills or inventories of eight people from 1733 to 1755. From 1751 onwards his son Patrick assumed this role, witnessing the wills or appraising the inventories of at least 24 villagers to 1805. From the handwriting styles on these documents it would appear that it was Patrick who was responsible for drafting them. In 1807 Patrick's successor as teacher William Lester then witnessed the will of John Hardy, one of the school's trustees at that point and owner of Bley's former house. Thus through their position as literate and knowledgeable schoolmasters these three, Richard and Patrick James and William Lester, had developed the role of reliable legal scrutineers, an increased status for their occupation which 200 years later was to be considered a profession. Thus they became members of an expanding group of middling local authorities, the new and growing band of officials in Georgian society. Through their educational and literary qualities these professionals were to join if not replace the clerics and the landed gentry as the natural authorities in village life. Together with the Parish Clerks, the Constables and the Overseers of the Poor, successive teachers at John Bley's school provided an example of the *ex-officio* secular leadership required in local government for the next, more democratic age.

The future of the school was assured, then, by the generous terms of the original endowment, by the size of the village supplying the core of its pupils, by the skill and status of the masters and by the survival of the building itself. Over the years inflation, of course, gradually ate into the value of the endowment. The succession of Norman schoolbooks shows how masters increasingly offered basic schooling to all children free of charge, as required, but also gave additional and higher level tuition to fee-paying older students, some of whom appear to have been dissenters. At two points (1824 and 1826) the Norman books make reference to the school being an Academy which suggests a dissenting character, while the English exercises in the books show practically no religious tenor. What we may now term the 'upper school' seems to have retained a commercial curriculum with a secular ethos. But eventually and inevitably the school fell into disrepair. The 1870 Education Act offered a way out of this local dilemma; the Bley School was pulled down in 1877 and a new Board School was erected on the same site. It is this building which survives as a section of the current Brookside School. The original plot is still there of course – almost the final legacy. John Bley's original endowment is worth but a few pounds, and is held – still in perpetuity – by the Local Education Authority.

John's impact on the village

John's investment in two large buildings added interest to the lives of the villagers. Other building work was in progress throughout the period but it was the creation of the Bley School that really broke new ground locally. Across the country literacy rates had been rising from a moderate level in Tudor times and in our village must have been boosted after 1723. Children were now educated to more than a level of functional literacy. They were taught to read and write and above all to calculate as part of a properly organised and regulated scheme of work, and all for free for very local children. Others travelled in from neighbouring villages, at minimal cost to their parents. For all children this must have been a vast improvement on the somewhat casual and sporadic learning offered by parents and by individual clerics over the previous centuries. And the new school employed some notable teachers over the following 200 years, among them Richard and Patrick James whom we have already met, and later on Richard Hawley. He was described by Potter as 'a geologist of some repute' who possessed a good collection of geological specimens. One of his daughters married the eminent geologist, Professor Etheridge. Under Hawley's tutelage we can be sure that the children of the village were at least taught a more up-to-date version of Creation, and possibly full evolutionary theory.

John's life also had an impact on the growth of capitalism in the village. The local legacies put thousands of pounds of cash into what was for many poorer people a mixed cash/barter economy. For the wealthier families, and for the Hardy family especially, this injection of capital came just as agriculture everywhere was being modernised. In a way the financial revolution came to the whole of the village and local area with John Bley's will. In 1798, the landholding system of the whole village was reorganised following the Enclosure Award. Within a few generations East Leake had entered the world of modern commercialised farming.

Local memorials

Within the church are two religious books purported to derive from John Bley. A Bible dating from the early 17th century and measuring approximately 22 by 17 centimetres was owned for many years by the family of Thomas John Burrows of Rempstone. In 1934 Potter claimed that this belonged to John Bley whose name appears in several places, along with those of H. Hallam, Eliz. Wisher, Thomas Richardson and Robert Wilde who was resident in West Leake in the previous century. But are these genuine signatures? Only one looks anything like that of the real John Bley, but it is rather immature and lacks a number of significant features. The book predates our John Bley as it has a hand written date at the top of one early page: either 1660 or 1670. Whether this really did belong to John, or was ever owned by him, must remain doubtful. Then there is 'The works of Bishop John Jewel' which was printed in 1611 and measures approximately 22 by 32 centimetres. Inside the front cover is the signature of 'Mr. Bley' in another style again. It has been claimed that this could well be the signature of John's father William but for this the spelling is surely wrong. Further signatures are also appended: John Chamberlain whose Bible it is more likely to have been originally and John North (both of this parish) and John Willett. It must be said however that none of these books can be ascribed with any certainty to John Bley himself. A third 'Bley Bible' dated 1717 and printed by John Baskett is attached to a chain with two brass clasps, but has no mention of John Bley himself.

In the village today we can see five major memorials to John Bley's life and achievements. First there is his tomb in a prominent position below and just to one side of the east window of the church. This table tomb has an impressive plaque on the side summarising his life. The writing is still legible but the whole tomb has been restored twice. Railings have been erected, taken away and renewed. Primary-school children still visit the tomb as part of their work on the locality. Brookside School has, of course, a particularly close relationship with Bley. The Bible given to the school by Francis Greene in 1733, and called 'The John Bley Bible', is kept in the Headteacher's office. The County Council Education Committee's recent request to wind up the remaining endowment was politely refused by the Brookside School governors.

Standing at the tomb one can see both John Bley's house on Main Street and the site of his school. At the time of writing the frontage of John's house is a photographer's shop and the house was much restored recently with renewed windows and roofs, repointing and internal restoration. The well is still visible in the back yard, with many original cobblestones beneath the tarmac. The house was used as the village Post Office in the twentieth century. The surrounding land has been sold and built up but the plot is still quite large and impressive. John's house stayed within the family until 1872 when the High Court of Chancery ordered it to be sold. No longer fashionable in the 19th century, but in a prime position for commercial use, the building was rented out either to the tenant of the associated Hill Farm or to one of a succession of tradesmen. In 1899 the property was bought by Harry Hill, a provision merchant, and became owner occupied once more. Hill was probably responsible for developing the site by constructing the two pairs of semi-detached houses that still stand on either side of Bley's building. According to the 1911 census he had seven habitable rooms in domestic use; other rooms may have been used for storage. Subsequently the house was bought by basket manufacturer George Mather and then sold to the Clarke family who ran it for many years as a Post Office. It was during these latter years of owner occupation that John Bley's frontage was altered. Besides those already mentioned, families thought to have occupied Bley's house at some time include Felstead, Oldershaw and Wilson.

Not too far away, in a newer post-war section of the village, we can find Bley Avenue.

On the south wall of the chancel in the church can be seen an impressive stained-glass window commemorating John's life. According to Potter 'Charity' is based on a painting by Sir Joshua Reynolds in New College Chapel, Oxford. Closer examination shows that this is incorrect. The image is much closer to an 1867 painting by Sir Edward Burne-Jones, currently part of a private art collection. Below the East Leake church window is written: 'In memory of John Bley who built and endowed the Free Schools [sic]: he died AD 1731'. Apparently the window was donated by Annie Harwood who was a direct descendant of Hugh and Dorothy Hardy via the Burrows family from Ruddington. Detailed documentation for the window's origins is scarce; the Diocesan Faculty for the new church window only mentions its installation in about 1900 'in consequence of a generous offer'.

Finally in the Nottingham Weekly Guardian on 28 April 1934 Potter claimed that 'a rat-tailed silver spoon marked JB, and a memorial ring, heirlooms in her family, were given by Miss Harwood' to the church. Potter also added that 'Thirty years ago, in 1900, during the removal of the floor of a stable at John Bley's house, a much-worn silver spoon … bearing his initials J.B., was unearthed'. No trace of these interesting objects can be found today.

Conclusion

The trajectory of John Bley's life is clearly recoverable from the records he and others left behind. Most of this material is to be found in various archives in London and Nottinghamshire. There are some significant gaps in this record. Apart from village folklore we know nothing of John's early life in East Leake, his education and the means by which he was able to arrive in London. The origins of his relationship with Sir Thomas Parkyns, Lord of the Manor of Bunny, are probably also out of reach. More importantly the parentage and background of John Turner must remain a mystery. There are many John Turners in the records but none can be directly linked to John Bley.

One weakness of the evidence on John Bley is the absence of any trace of his appearance; we have no idea therefore what he looked like. Personal portraits were then a vanity property of the very rich and very famous. As for his personal characteristics, these we have to infer from his behaviour and his letters to Parkyns. He seems to have been a well organised, hard-working and enterprising businessman, cautious but successful in his investments and careful with his friendships and business relationships. With so many friends and his lasting attachment to the bustling scene of Thames Street we can infer that he was outgoing and gregarious. Probably quite charismatic, too, since he seems to have had some success in getting people to do what he wanted and certainly he must have been very shrewd. It would also seem reasonable to suppose that he was a very energetic person and deplored indolence (hence the Doughty family comment in his will). One could even speculate that he and Sir Thomas Parkyns recognised each other's drive and energy and that this helped to draw them together.

Clearly John was trustworthy and reliable. He supported the City entrepreneurs in politics and contributed modestly to the governance of London. Perhaps his most endearing feature was his continued interest in his home village and in the maintenance of his friendships and family contacts. His interest in the education of his village led to the creation of a very successful school, a model of its time. He was loyal to his extended family and generous to business colleagues both in his life, as the tomb eulogy states, and in death.

What else may be inferred about his personal life, his attitudes, beliefs and desires? In London John had established contacts with several nonconformists. There is no evidence of any contact with his local churches either there or back in his home village. His will does nothing to acknowledge the place of organised religion in his life or work. These are, we would argue, indications that John may have had nonconformist sympathies or even have been of quietly nonconformist persuasion himself. He may even have been atheistic though there is absolutely no evidence of this. As to more personal matters, the evidence suggests that he did not, so far as we know, either marry or have any close sexual relationships with other people, men or women. The age of marriage was high at this time and a significant proportion of men remained bachelors throughout their lives. Homosexuality had been a quietly ignored feature of London life for some time, and although homosexual acts were still a capital offence there were surprisingly few convictions and many 'molly houses' within easy reach in the city. Such temptations were available to those interested. On these matters however the documentation of John's life is silent. We must conclude therefore that many aspects of John Bley's personal life will remain hidden.

…………………………..

'Complex changes in history are thus revealed in the fortunes of ordinary families'. In this one sentence Michael Wood summarised one of the major themes of English local history. The life of John Bley exemplifies this idea in many ways.

Our hero's story confirms the generally accepted picture of English rural life at that time. By the middle of the 17th century the inhabitants of an average, medium-sized village in the East Midlands were by no means members of backward communities. Most of them were not seriously impoverished, some were in contact with the wider world of commerce, and others were not slow to take up new ideas. Some of the better-off villagers here as elsewhere were socially and geographically mobile. East Leake was a complex open society because amongst other things its agricultural base had developed a commercial edge since feudal times. Extensive family networks had been laid down over many years and could be called upon when needed. The Wights and their neighbours were no longer tied to the soil in subservience to their semi-feudal lords. Although only a small handful, some villagers had travelled to London where there was work, opportunity and the possibility of personal growth.

Within the village there remained many limitations on the extent of personal freedoms. If anything, social mobility was more restricted than physical travel. Certainly feudal constraints on marriage had gone, but overwhelmingly people were expected to remain in the 'sphere of life in which Providence had placed them' as the orphanage guardians put it – and they nearly always did so. Poverty continued to be a significant feature of village life. According to Arkell 'about one quarter of the population lived in some form of poverty and one seventh perhaps in or near destitution' and 'up to 25% of the households may have received some form of charity in the course of a year'. There are plentiful indications of debts that could not be paid in contemporary East Leake inventories – £23 13s of 'desprat debtes' owed to Richard Sheffield in 1692/3, debts 'hopeful and desperate' owed to Robert Hardy 1693, £23 of 'desperate debts' owed to Thomas Black in 1699 (after a succession of bad harvests), the £30 'debts good and bad' owed to Enoch Watson in 1707. Then we have the substantial arrears of rent owed to the Parkyns manor – £48 7s owed to Sampson Parkyns in 1713 and £120 owed to his widow in 1719. Average per capita incomes had increased since Tudor times but by contemporary and modern standards many of the villagers were still in need. This puts John Bley's bequests in rather a different light. For the poor his will must have been an exceptional windfall and a lifesaver – for the time being.

The public shaming of Elizabeth Wight by the churchwardens was for 'having a bastard' and 'she refusing to tell who is the father of it'. Whatever her motivation at the time, Elizabeth lived as an unmarried mother when all official morality and convention worked against her. Meanwhile the alleged father William Bleay was supported by the local clergy in his move to Worcestershire, for whatever reason, and was able to pursue his profession.

These events must raise many questions for the modern reader. Was William really John Bley's father? Why did Elizabeth not marry the father of her child, whoever he was? What was the nature of their relationship? How much did the churchwardens know, and what did the Rector himself think of it all? Whatever the truth of the matter, as we said in chapter 1, tongues must have wagged. At the height of her crisis Elizabeth was compelled to turn inwards to her own close family, but we have no real idea of how her position was perceived within the community. Given the circumstances of his inauspicious birth, John Bley's achievements are a testament to his mother and to her family.

In a smallish Nottinghamshire village in the 17th century there must have been few opportunities for social and economic advancement. Only London, perhaps, could provide the space and the economic outlets – the growing thirsty (and weary) population – to ensure real commercial success. In this respect John was fortunate in the timing of his arrival in the capital. The banking system and developing financial markets offered the chance to build on business profits and to reinvest in trade. The creation of annuities enabled enterprising investors to ensure a continuing income for family and friends, in life and in death. We hear much about the growth of the City at this time. Its economic weight, measured in financial infrastructure, in population and in commercial variety and trading expansion, created the springboard for modern enterprise and industrialisation.

Betterment migration, as opposed to enforced migration, was now making an enormous impact on English local and national history. In increasing numbers people were moving from the countryside to the growing towns and cities, especially London. But where did that migrating population come from? Most of those on the move are unknown to us; they are largely anonymous and their lives remain unrecorded. Who was it who made their own fortunes, who made the investments, who travelled the road and left their villages behind them? Who, apart from the few well-known cases of individual aristocrats with an eye for luxury and perhaps for debauchery, who apart from the already wealthy, saw the capital as a shining adventure with glittering prizes on offer? There were many thousands of would-be Dick Whittingtons in the late 17th century but few indeed who emerged with gold in their pockets at the end of their journey. John Bley gives us a fine and detailed example of how Britain emerged from an agricultural countryside to become a commercial and urban powerhouse.

So what did it take for John Bley to set out and to succeed from such an unpromising beginning? Where did his enterprising spirit come from? In many respects John demonstrates the classic characteristics of what has become known as 'the spirit of capitalism.' His family were from yeomen and tradesmen stock, modestly wealthy but with significant local status in village and city. John was educated locally though quite how far, and in what, we cannot say. Most likely the family were themselves literate at some level though we remember that his mother only signed with a mark when witnessing Luke Hallam's will in 1709 and her own will 18 years later. That he was hard-working and shunned extravagant living is evident from his first business venture to his last. The basic commercial knowledge and skills required for a successful business career in London were acquired there as part of the livery companies' apprenticeship system which, via the guilds, was medieval in origin. The immediate and necessary financial support almost certainly came from the family. Personal qualities of courage, ambition and business acumen, a quick mind and a grasp of social and economic realities must have been developed at some point in order to take advantage of the opportunities on offer. But it was the Wight family networks that created those opportunities. They had in abundance what we now recognise as the most important ingredient of all – social capital. They had the confidence, the optimism and the initiative to invest in John's future in an expanding market. They seem to have played little part in his later career however. And John himself saw how beneficial it was to develop and extend his own contacts whilst keeping in touch with his social and geographic origins. Finally he had, perhaps, the wisdom to turn away from the temptation to commit himself too deeply to London politics during an age of political turbulence. He kept his eye firmly fixed on his stills, his barrels, his ships and his accounts. He returned the investment his family and his village had made, and he returned it with wisdom and generosity.

Date	National events	John Bley's life
1642	English Civil War	
1645	Siege of Leicester	William Bleay born in Leicester
1660	Restoration of Charles II	
1666	Great Fire and rebuilding of London	
1674/75		John Bley born in East Leake
1685	King James II	
1688/89	'Glorious Revolution'	
1689	William III and Mary	
1690		Bley goes to London and is apprenticed to Distillers Company
1694	Bank of England founded	
1697		Apprenticeship ends
1702	Queen Anne	
1714	King George I	
1715	First Jacobite Rebellion	Builds house in East Leake
1723/24		Builds John Bley Free School
1725		Probable retirement from business
1727	King George II	Elizabeth Wight dies
1731		John Bley dies
1874		Bley School demolished
1877		New Board School on same site
1902		Council school
2008		Restoration of John Bley's tomb

John Bley's Will

The following transcript is taken from the probate copy of John Bley's will held on microfilm at the National Archives in Kew. The original spelling and capitalisation have been preserved, but the text has been divided into short paragraphs for ease of reading; as is normal for such legal documents there are no paragraph divisions in the original.

In the Name of God Amen I John Bley Citizen and Distiller of London do make my last Will and Testament as follows that is to say

I do give and bequeath to every Husbandman or Husbandmans Widow that follows Husbandry and keeps at least one Teame with Plowe Carriages and other Implements of Husbandry and lives and employs such Teames within the Lordship of East Leake in the County of Nottingham the sume of ten pounds to each and every of them and also to every Cottager or Inhabitant in East Leake aforesaid the sume of five pounds to each of them (Except that Idle family of George Doughtys)

Item I do give and bequeath to the poor of Bunny Costock Remston Stanford Normanton upon Soare Little Leake and Gotham all in the County of Nottingham aforesaid ten pounds to each of the said Towns and I give and bequeath to Hugh Hardy of East Leake aforesaid ten pounds per Annum for three years to be Computed from the time of my death to be by him the said Hugh Hardy Employed and paid to and for the use and benefitt of the poor people of East Leake aforesaid in the severities of Winter

Item I do give and bequeath to the said Hugh Hardy fifty pounds in Trust for him to pay the same to Mr Richard James Schoolmaster of my Schoole at Leake aforesaid in manner following (that is to say) twenty pounds part thereof Imediately after my decease as a gift from me to him and the remaining thirty pounds by ten pounds per Annum for three years if he the said Mr James so long Continues to teach my said Schoole (as and for his yearly Sallary but if the said Mr James does not Continue to teach Schoole as aforesaid Then what Remains of the said Thirty pounds unpaid I give the same to the said Hugh Hardy for his own use and benefit

Item I give to Thomas Wight (now a dissenting Teacher in Essex and son of Thomas Wight late of London feltmaker two hundred pounds and forgive all Bonds Notes and Booke debts due from him to me

Item I do give and bequeath to John Smith of London feltmaker (Son in Law of the abovesaid Thomas Wight) forty pounds

Item I do give and bequeath to George Wight Citizen and Cooper of London five hundred pounds

Item I do give and Bequeath to Samuel Wight late a Waterman and since Master of a Coasting Vessell and now a Pilot of Trinity House London and Brother to the abovesaid George Wight two hundred pounds and I forgive all debts due from him to me

Item I do give and bequeath to Edward Wight (Brother to the aforesaid George and Samuel Wight) sometime since Clerk to a Brewer in Southwarke three hundred pounds

Item I do give and bequeath to Mary (only Sister to the aforesaid George Samuel and Edward Wight) two hundred pounds in case she shall be living at the time of my death But if she shall then be dead I order and direct that the said two hundred pounds be paid to the said George Wight her Brother to be by him distributed to and amongst any Child or Children of her the said Mary as he shall think fitt and do direct in that case the receipt of the said George Wight shall be a good discharge in Law to my Executors hereinafter Named for the said Legacy

Item I do give and bequeath to Mary Hopkins (Daughter of John and Mary Hopkins of East Leake aforesaid) two Hundred pounds

Item I do give and bequeath to Thomas Hopkins (Brother of the aforesaid Mary) two hundred pounds

Item I do give and bequeath to Elizabeth Lambert (Wife of Thomas Lambert of Clifton in the County of Nottingham aforesaid) three hundred pounds for her own separate use and do direct that her receipt shall be good to my Executors for the said Sume Notwithstanding her Coverture

Item I do give and bequeath to Caleb Moore (Son of Caleb and Mary Moore) now Apprentice to Mr Thorp a Brushmaker in London six hundred pounds South Sea Annuitys to be Transferred to him at the Expiration of his Apprenticeship and till that time to be found and provided with apparell and Necessaries out of the Dividends ariseing therefrom and I do alsoe give to the said Caleb Moore all my Wearing Apparell at my Lodgings at the Garter Coffee House in Thames Street London

Item I do give and bequeath to John Hopkins (Son of John Hopkins late a Malster at Loughborough in the County of Leicester now an Apprentice to Mr William Parker of London Cooper Six hundred pounds South Sea Annuitys To be Transfer'd to him at the Expiration of his Apprenticeship and till that time to be found and provided with Apparell and Necessarys out of the Dividends Ariseing therefrom

Item I do give and bequeath to Robert Hopkins Brother to the aforesaid John Hopkins) now Apprentice to Mr Storer of Nottingham Six hundred pounds South Sea Annuitys to be Transferred to him at the Expiration of his Apprenticeship and till that time to be found and provided with apparell and Necessaries out of the Dividends ariseing therefrom

Item I do give and bequeath to Mary Moore Daughter of Robert Wight Citizen and Poulterer of London (widow of Caleb Moore deceased) two hundred pounds South Sea Annuitys

Item I do give and bequeath to Sarah (Daughter of the aforesaid Mary Moore) one hundred pounds South Sea Annuitys

Item I do give and bequeath to Dorothy the Wife of Hugh Hardy of East Leake aforesaid five hundred pounds South Sea Annuitys to be Transfered by my Executors to John Garrat of London Salter as soon as maybe after my decease in order for the said John Garratts Acceptance of the same in his own name but for the sole and seperate use of the said Dorothy Hardy

Item I do give and bequeath to the said Hugh Hardy three hundred South Sea Annuitys and the Choice of any Horse I shall dye possest of and also the Choice of one Suite of my Apparell with all Boots Shoes and Stockings six Shirts and all my Hatts

Item I do give to George Wight Taylor in or near East Smithfield London one hundred pounds South Sea Annuitys

Item I do give and bequeath to Mary Gigg Daughter of John Gigg of Saint Dunstans in the East London three hundred pounds South Sea Annuitys and alsoe my bed and bedding that I use to lye on together with the Chest of Drawers Chairs and all other goods or furniture that shall be in my Lodgings at the time of my death but nothing Contained in any drawers

Item I do give and bequeath to Sarah Gigg (Sister to the aforesaid Mary Gigg) one hundred pounds South Sea Annuitys

Item I do give and bequeath to my Couzen Nutt Brewer in Wapping twenty five pounds to buy Mourning for himselfe and Wife

Item I do give and bequeath to Hugh Hardy of East Leake aforesaid in Trust for Edward Son of Edward Wight of East Leake aforesaid two hundred pounds To be paid to the said Edward Wight the son When he Attaines the age of one and twenty years but if he dyes before that time then I order that the said Hugh Hardy may Retaine the said two hundred pounds to and for his own use and benefit

Item I do give and bequeath to Mr William Parker late of London Cooper three Hundred pounds

Item I do give and bequeath to Henry Saunders of London Distiller one hundred pounds

Item I do give and bequeath to Gustavos Brook (son of John Brook of Coleshill in the County of Warwick) twenty pounds

Item I do give and bequeath to Elizabeth Hickling that was lately my servant (if living at my decease seventy five pounds

Item I do give and bequeath to Mr George Quinton of East Leake aforesaid one hundred Pounds

Item I do give and bequeath to Mr Thomas Garrat Salter of London one hundred and fifty pounds if he happens to survive me but if he dyes before me then the same to be divided equally between his widow Lydia Garratt his son John Garratt and his Daughter Mrs Lydia Lance

Item I do give and bequeath to Mr Richard Fendall Grazier in Southwark fifty pounds

Item I do give and bequeath to Daniel Berry of Felmersham in the County of Bedford one hundred pounds

Item I do give and bequeath to John Bird Citizen and Cooper of London now living at Barrow in the County of Leicester fifty pounds and one Suite of my Cloaths (if any left after Hugh Hardy hath taken his) and I forgive all debts due from the said John Bird to me

Item I give to my Servant William Angrave if in my Service at the time of my Death fifty pounds and my Horse or Mare that I dye possest of (after Hugh Hardy hath made his Choice

Item I do give and bequeath to my Servant Jane Lambert if in my Service at the time of my Death forty pounds

Item I do give and bequeath to my Servant Sarah Crosse (if living with me at the time of my Death) thirty five pounds

Item I do give and bequeath to Richard Callis of East Leake aforesaid ten pounds to place out his son Thomas (my Servant) to some Trade (if the said Thomas Callis shall be in my Service at the time of my decease)

Item I do give and bequeath to Robert Elizabeth Henrietta and Amy Godfrey Children of Mr Robert Godfrey late of London Cornfactor Deceased) one hundred pounds to each of them and I do direct that the Discharge of the Executors of the said Robert Godfrey shall be a good Discharge to my Executors for payment of the said Severall Sumes of one hundred pounds to each of the said four Children

Item I do give and bequeath to Mr Thomas Bird Citizen and Cooper of London five hundred pounds

Item I do give and bequeath to John Turner one thousand pounds Bank of England Stock to be Transferred to him on his Attaining the age of one and twenty years and in the mean time the Severall Dividends to be applied for his benefitt as well for his Maintenance as also for the placing him out an Apprentice to some Trade or business and I do also give to the said John Turner one Silver Tankard markt at the bottom with the Letters J T being in weight twenty five ounces and twelve penny weights

Item I forgive a debt of fifty pounds (more or lesse) due to me from Elizabeth Pratt Widow of London Painter Stainer

I also forgive a debt of about Ninety Pounds due to me from Joseph Matthews Salter in Bucklers Berry

Item I do give and bequeath to my Couzen Walmsley Druggist on Snow Hill London one hundred pounds

Item I do give and bequeath to Elizabeth Garland of Prestwould in the County of Leicester aforesaid (if living at the time of my decease) twenty pounds

Item I do give and bequeath to Samuel Sterropp of the Town and County of the Town of Nottingham Gentleman the Sume of four hundred pounds

Item I do give and bequeath to Mrs Mary Sterrop of Nottingham aforesaid ten Guineas to buy her Mourning

Item I do give and bequeath to my Uncle Mr Edward Wight twenty five pounds to buy Mourning for himselfe and Wife

Item I do give and bequeath to the three familys of Mr William Killett Mr Jeffery Killett and Mr Samuel Killett of Golstone neare Yarmouth forty pounds to Each of the said familys

Item I do give and bequeath to Richard Bryan of Ticknall in the County of Derby Schoolmaster twenty pounds

and I direct that the Said Severall Legacies herein before by me given and bequeathed shall be paid to the Respective Legatees within one year next after my Decease and if any of the Said Legatees herein before mentioned shall happen to dye before his her or their Legacy or Legacys become payable Then the Legacy or Legacies of him her or them so dying Shall be Deemed and taken as part and parcell of my personall Estate and added to the rest and Residue thereof that shall remaine after payment of the other Legacies my Just debts and funerall Expences

Item I do give and bequeath to the said Samuel Killett Senr of Golstone near Yarmouth aforesaid Mariner my one two and thirtith part of all that Katt or Vessell called the Godfrey of Yarmouth of the Burden of three hundred and Eighty Tuns or thereabouts (the said Samuel Killett being now Master

Item I do give and bequeath to the said Jeffery Killett Senr of Golstone neare Yarmouth aforesaid one Sixteenth part of the good Ship or Vessell called the three Brothers Burthen about four hundred Tuns (the said Jeffery Killett now Master)

Item I do give and bequeath to Jeffery Killett Junr my one two and thirtieth part of that good Ship or Vessell called the Samuel and Rebecca of Yarmouth (John Cock now Master Burden three hundred Tuns or thereabouts

Item I do give and bequeath to Abraham Thompson of Hull Mariner my one Sixteenth part of the St George (Robert Osborne now Master) Burden Eighty Tuns or thereabouts

Item I do give and bequeath to Samuel Sterropp of the Town and County of the Town of Nottingham aforesaid Gentleman the Iron Chest in my Closett

Item I do give and devise to John Clifton Samuel Earby and Daniel Woodruffe and others the Trustees for the time being of the Common Meadow In East Leake aforesaid their Heirs and Successors all that my Schoolhouse Erected at East Leake aforesaid with the Orchard thereto Adjoining To hold to them the said John Clifton Samuel Earby and Daniel Woodruffe their Heirs and Successors In Trust only and for the sole use and benefitt of the Children in the Township of East Leake aforesaid

Item I do order and direct that the Sume of four hundred and fifty pounds be paid by my Executors to the said John Clifton Samuel Earby and Daniel Woodruffe and such others of the Trustees for the time being of the Common Meadow belonging to East Leake aforesaid as shall be living at the time of my Death so soone as a Convenient purchase of Lands can be made after my Death and which when made my will that the same be Setled John Clifton Samuel Earby and Daniel Woodruffe their Heirs and Successors In Trust only that the Rente and profitts of Such Purchased Estate may be applyed in the first place for the keeping my said Schoole house in good repaire and the Residue of the Rents and profitts to be paid halfe yearly for the Maintenance of the said Schoolmaster of the said Schoole

Item I do order and direct that the Sume of twenty pounds be paid to Hugh Hardy of East Leake aforesaid to build two Necessary Houses of Brick to the said School house in such place or places as may be Judged proper (In case I shall not have built them myselfe in my life time) and what sume remains of the said twenty pounds after the building thereof the said Hugh Hardy to apply to his own use and benefit

and I Do hereby give devise and bequeath all my Messuages Lands Tenements and Hereditaments Situate and being in Thames Street St Dunstans Hill Crosse Lane Fetter Lane and Basinghall Street in the City of London now or late in the Severall Possessions of Samuel Holmes James Long Henry Bennett Woodbridge Joseph Gladman George Green Gabriel Small and Richard Heath together alsoe with my House att East Leake aforesaid now in my own possession with the Land and Common right thereto belonging and all others my Lands Tenements and Hereditaments whatsoever or wheresoever within the Kingdom of Great Brittaine with their and every of their rights members and Appurtenances unto Samuel Sterropp of the Town and County of the Town of Nottingham aforesaid Gentleman and Hugh Hardy of East Leake in the County of Nottingham aforesaid Grocer their Heirs and Assignes to the use of them The said Samuel Sterropp and Hugh Hardy their Heirs and Assignes for ever upon Trust Nevertheless that they the said Samuel Sterropp and Hugh Hardy and the

Survivor of them and the Heirs of Such Survivor shall and do with all Convenient Speed After my Decease Sell and dispose of the said Messuages Lands Tenements Hereditaments Either Entirely or in parcels unto any person or persons that shall be willing to purchase the Same for the most money and best price and prices that can be had or gotten for the Same and shall and do apply and dispose of the money ariseing by such sale or sales and of the Rents and profitts of the same premisses untill Such Sale or Sales shall be made for the ends Intents and purposses hereinafter mentioned

and I do hereby give and bequeath all my ready money Arrears Rent Securityes for money Stocks in the Public funds goods Chattells and personall Estate whatsoever and wheresoever to the said Samuel Sterropp and Hugh Hardy their Executors Administrators and Assignes upon the Trusts and to and for the ends Intents and purposes hereinafter mentioned and declared and my Will is that the Said Samuel Sterropp and Hugh Hardy their Heirs Executors Administrators and Assignes respectively shall and do apply and dispose of the produce of my personall Estate and alsoe the money ariseing by sale and out of the Rents of my reall Estate hereby Devised unto and vested in them In Trust to be sold as aforesaid in the first place for the payment of my funerall Expences and all the just debts that I shall owe at the time of my Decease and afterwards and subject thereto in and for the payment of the Severall Legacies herein before given and bequeathed and which I shall by any Codicill or writing under my hand hereafter give and Dispose of

and also shall and do pay apply and dispose of the residue of the money ariseing and to be produced out of my personall Estate and by Sale and the Rents of my reall Estate afore mentioned which shall remaine after payment of my funeral Expences debts and Legacies hereby Directed to be paid and Satisfyed thereout unto and amongst the before mentioned Thomas Wight George Wight (Citizen and Cooper) Samuel Wight Waterman Edward Wight (Brother to George and Samuel Mary (only Sister to George Samuel and Edward Wight) Mary Hopkins of East Leake aforesaid Thomas Hopkins of East Leake aforesaid Elizabeth Lambert (Wife of Thomas Lambert of Clifton) Caleb Moore John Hopkins (son of John Hopkins) Robert Hopkins Joyner Dorothy Wife of Hugh Hardy Mr William Parker Cooper Mr Thomas Bird Cooper and them the said Samuel Sterropp and Hugh Hardy to and for their own use and benefitt proportionably and in Equall proportions According to their respective legacies herein before by me Respectively given and bequeathed

and my Will is and I do here[b]y Declare that the receipt or Receipts of the said Samuell Sterropp and Hugh Hardy or the Survivor of them or the Heirs of such Survivor shall be good and Effectuall Discharges to the Purchaser or Purchasers of my said Reall Estate hereby Devised to be sold for the purchase money of the premises so to be sold or any part or Parcell thereof and after such receipt or Receipts such Purchaser or Purchasers shall not be Answerable or Accountable for any Losse or Misapplication of the said Purchase money or any part thereof and my Will is and I do hereby further Declare that the said

Samuel Sterropp and Hugh Hardy shall not nor shall either of them be Answerable or accountable for any money to be received by Virtue of or under the Trusts of this my Will any otherwise than each person for such Sume or Sumes of money as he shall respectively Actually receive and that neither of them shall be Answerable or Accountable for the Acts Receipts Neglects or defaults of the other of them and also that they the said Samuel Sterropp and Hugh Hardy their Respective Executors Administrators and Assignes shall and may out of my reall and personall Estate hereby vested in them for the purposses aforesaid retain to and Reimburse themselves for all Costs Charges Damages and Expences that they respectively shall or may Sustain be put unto in and about the Execution of the Trusts hereby in them reposed

and I do hereby make Constitute and appoint the said Samuel Sterropp and Hugh Hardy Executors of this my Will upon the Trusts aforesaid and I do hereby revoke all former Wills by me made In Witness whereof I the said John Bley the Testator to this my Will Containing Eleven Sheets of paper have to each of the first ten of the said sheets Subscribed my name and to this last Eleventh Sheet have Subscribed My Name and Sett my Seale and alsoe have Sett my Seale to the Ribbon affixt at the top of the said sheets this twenty Eighth day of October in the fourth year of the Reigne of our Soveraigne Lord George the Second by the Grace of God of Great Brittaine France and Ireland King Defender of the Faith et[c] and in the year of our Lord one thousand seven hundred and thirty

Jn° Bley

Signed Sealed published and declared by the said John Bley the Testator as his last Will and Testament in the presence of us and we in the presence of the said Testator have Subscribed our Names as Witnesses

Hen: Neale in Mincing Lane Henry Marshall Grocer on St Mary Hill London John Edwards on Saint Dunstans Hill.

[left hand column]

1717, Sʳ: Tho: Parkyns Baronᵗ: is Debtor

			£ s d
Oct 12	To 12 lb Chocalate box & porter		02:02:06
Nov 25	To one gall: French Brandy & Runlet		00:10:06
Dec 23	To Richd: Stevens for 112 lb: graind tin & firkin to put it in		04:06:06
	To Coach hire from ye Inn to my own house thence to Lady Parkyns & one of ye boxes of plate back to my house againe & portrage to ye Mansfield Carrier & expences in ye Inn Examining of plate before I took it away from ye Carriers		00:06:06
Jan 10	To Lady Ann Parkyns Carew Rawleige Ann & Tho Weeks parties in A parcel of plate Bgt: of them for Sr: Tho: Parkyns		55:12:08
	To Daniel Shilling for bill of Saile		00:04:00
Jan 18	To expenses at Inn with Mr Carter		00:03:01
	To Coach hire from ye Inn to Mrs Tollets & back to Mr Carters & 1: to ye Nottingham Coachman		00:04:00
Jan 20	To Porter with ye Books to Westminster		00:01:00
	To Dr Friend	3:3:00	
	To Mr Nickols	2:2:00	
	To ye Usher	1:1:00	06:06:00
	To Mrs Tollett		05:05:00
Feb 1	To A Bewrow		01:14:00
Feb 6	To A Gown for ye Young Gentlman		00:17:00
Feb 14	To A Box of Petters pills		00:01:00
Feb 15	To portrige of ye Verjuice from ye Carriers to Mrs Tollets		00:01:06
Feb 24	To A hat & Lace		00:07:00
	To 2 Neckcloths		00:08:00
	To 4 handkercheifts		00:05:04
	To Porter for 2 pr stockings & two shirts from one Mr Norton		00:00:06
Mar 10	To Peck Chesnuts bag & porter		00:03:09
Apr 11	To A pr Shoos for Mas[ter]		00:02:00
	To A pr Gloves		00:00:08
	To Tho Plampin for 2 Wiggs		01:17:00
Apr 28	To Drugett & Shalloon as p[er] bill p[ar]cels		01:00:00
May 8	To Mrs Tollets Bill for Quarters board & other Necisaries ending the 18 Aprill 1718		05:12:11
June 5	To A pr Rouling hose		00:02:06
	To Ribbon for's shirt sleves		00:00:02¼

June 10	To Taylors bill	01:11:00
June 24	To Cash pd Mr Carew Weeks	91:13:06
	To expences & porter going of an errand at Signing	00:01:09
July 19	To porter to assist me to bring ye money from Mansfield Carrier	00:00:06
	To Cash pd: Mr: Carew Weekes in acc:	1000:00:00
	To portrage of ye 3 shirts from Smithfield	00:00:06
Aug 4	To Cash pd: Mr: Maddon as p[er] his bill & Receipt	166:11:00
Aug 11	To Cash paid ditto as p[er] his bill	132:04:06
Aug 12	To Mrs Tollet for ¼ years board & contingency due 18th July	06:01:10
Aug 22	To Mrs Tollet to Drink Ld Chesterfields health	00:10:00
Aug 27	To A packet of writings from Smithfield	00:00:06
Aug 28	To Mr: Maddon as p[er] his bill p[ar]cels & Receipt	75:00:00
		1561:10:02:¼
	To ballance	205:00:01: ¾
		1766:10:04

[right hand column]

1717 Contre Creditor

		£ s d
Jan 11	By Cash to Mother at Leak	05:00:00
Jan 17	By A bill on Saml: Smith	55:09:08
March 10	By ½ years Dividend on ye New River due Xmas Last	21:09:04
June 14	By A bill on Mr: Saml: Smith for	100:00:00
July 11	By bill on ditto for	1200:00:00
July 19	By Cash p[er] ye Mansfield Carrier	160:00:00
July 25	By bill on Mr: Saml: Smith for	200:00:00
	By ½ years dividend due at Michs: Last on 1/5 part of an adventurers Share in ye Newriver Waters	24:11:04
		1766:10:04

[beneath both columns]

This acc.t: examin'd & approv'd & ye Balance being two hundred & five pounds 1:¾ Carried to ye Credit of Sr: Tho: Parkyns Baron.t: in A Suckeeding acc.t: which when Sattisfied will be in full of all acc.ts: Sep.tr: ye 22: 1718.   Jn.o: Bley

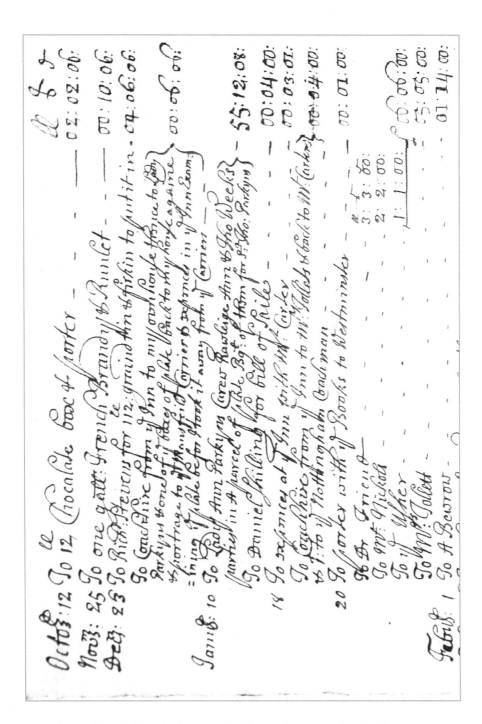

Extract from John Bley's accounts for work undertaken in London on behalf of Sir Thomas Parkyns 1717/8 Pa A 64

Bibliography and Sources

General Sources

Books

Ashton, J. (1919) *Social life in the reign of Queen Anne* Chatto and Windus.

Berlin, M. (1996) *The Worshipful Company of Distillers: a short history* Phillimore.

Clark, P. (1988) The 'Mother Gin' controversy in the early eighteenth century *Transactions of the Royal Historical Society*, Fifth Series, 38, pp. 63–84 London.

Dickson, P.G.M. (1967) *The financial revolution in England: a study of the development of public credit 1688–1756* MacMillan.

Earle, P. (1989) *The making of the English middle class: business, society and family life in London 1660–1730* Berkeley: University of California Press.

Godfrey, J.T. (1907) *Notes on the churches of Nottinghamshire* Phillimore.

Holmes, G. (1993) *The making of a great power: late Stuart and early Georgian Britain 1660–1722* Longman.

Nichols, J. (1795-1812) *History and antiquities of the town and county of Leicester* four Vols. London.

Potter, S. P. (1903) *A history of East Leake* East Leake, Notts.

Rule, J. (1992) *Albion's people: English society 1714–1815* Longman.

Venn, J. (1922) *Alumni Cantabrigienses: a biographical list of all known students, graduates and holders of office at the University of Cambridge, from the earliest times to 1751* Cambridge UP.

Webb, C. (1997–2007) *London apprentices* 44 Vols London: Society of Genealogists.

Online sources

Ancestry at www.ancestry.co.uk (London trade directories 1736–1800, apprenticeship indentures, etc.)

CCEd Clergy database at www.theclergydatabase.org.uk

International Genealogical Index at www.familysearch.org

Newspapers

London Gazette Online at www.london-gazette.co.uk

Newspaper sources from Burney Collection of Early Newspapers and Nineteenth Century Newspapers at British Library and online at subscribing public libraries.

Potter, S. P. East and West Leake *Nottingham Weekly Guardian*, 1934.

Maps

Fer, N. de (1700) *London and Westminster* Paris.

Feuille, J. de la (1690) *London* Amsterdam.

Morgan (1682) *Map of the whole of London.*

Old London Maps at www.oldlondonmaps.com
        Horwood, R. 1792–9 32″ to 1 mile
        Strype, J. Tower Street Ward; Billingsgate Ward 1720.

Strype, J. London map in Strype's 1720 edition of *Stow's survey of London.*

Wills

Several hundred wills have been consulted during the writing of this book. The more important ones are listed under individual chapters.

Sources used in individual chapters

Chapter 1

Blackmore, R. D. (1869) *Lorna Doone, p320* Reprinted by Daily Express Pubs. 1933.

Blagg, T. M. (ed) (1942) *A history of Colston Bassett* Thoroton Society Record Series, 9, 1942 [extracts available from Colston Bassett website].

Chapter of Collegiate Church of Southwell v Bishop of Lincoln (1675) In Colquitt, A. (1682) *Modern reports, or, Select cases adjudged in the Courts of Kings Bench, Chancery, Common-pleas, and Exchequer since the restauration of His Majesty King Charles II collected by a careful hand.* London: Basset.

Hyde, E., Earl of Clarendon (1702–4) *The history of the rebellion and civil wars in England, begun in the year 1641* Reprinted Dublin (1719) Vol. 2, p 470.

Meadowcroft, H. *Notes on John Davys and Joice's Manor East Leake* (unpublished).

Postles, S. *The agricultural year* Talk to Notts. LHA, Ollerton 12 Oct 1991 (unpub'd).

Tren, J. (1728) *A funeral sermon occasion'd by the death of the late Reverend Mr Daniel Gilson who departed this life February 8. 1727–8, in the LXXIst year of his age preached at Colchester: February 13.* London.

Young, Rev. E. (1942) *A history of the county of Essex* Hornchurch: religious history, Vol. 7 (1978), pp. 46–51; Brentwood, Vol. 8 (1983) pp. 90–109.

Manuscript sources

AC 27/422 folio 3064, AC27/430 folio 72 Bank of England Archives.

Apprenticeship bond, George Wight of Charlton in Kent, yeoman, to Charles Pearce of Hereford, to instruct Edward Wight, his son, in the managing and converting of timber 20 Mar 1701 6683/4/4; *Papers related to his debts 1703–23* 6683/4/7 Shropshire Archives.

Archdeaconry of Nottingham Presentment Bills East Leake 1610 AN/PB/295/1/49; 1666 AN/PB/316/325; 1675 AN/PB/317/457; 1681 AN/PB/318/167; Colston Bassett 1670–9 AN/PB/317 University of Nottingham Dept of Manuscripts & Special Collections.

Distillers Company *Apprenticeship records* CLC/L/DA/C/014/MS06212/001 London Metropolitan Archives.

East Leake Parish Registers East Leake Library.

East Leake Parish Register Bishop's Transcripts March 1771 DR1/5/56/133 Nottinghamshire Archives

East Leake probate inventories 1692–1733 Nottinghamshire Archives.

Four Shillings in the Pound Aid May 1694 COL/CHD/LA/03/004/005 London Metropolitan Archives.

Hearth Tax Return for East Leake 1674 E179/254/30 University of Nottingham Dept of Manuscripts & Special Collections.

John Bley's Account 1718 *Parkyns Papers* Pa A64 University of Nottingham Dept of Manuscripts & Special Collections.

Land tax returns for the Ward of Farringdon Without, City of London 1705/6 CLC/525, London Metropolitan Archives.

Letter Books of the Royal Society of London 1661–1740 at http://royalsociety.org

Letter of resignation from living of Hatcliffe by Thomas Bleay 1675 RES1675/4 Lincoln Record Office.

London Inhabitants within the Walls 1695 British History Online at www.british-history.ac.uk

Marsden, Rev. R. *Commonplace and memoranda book, 1724–35*, p93 DD/TS/14/2 Nottinghamshire Archives.

Notes concerning the case of Sir Thomas Parkyns against John Davyes concerning the manor of East Leake, Nottinghamshire [1714] *Parkyns Papers* Pa L20 University of Nottingham Dept of Manuscripts & Special Collections.

Parish Registers for Charlton (near Woolwich) Kent Available online.

Parish Registers for Colston Bassett Nottinghamshire Archives.

Parish Register Leicester St Mary Record Office for Leicestershire, Leicester & Rutland.

Poll Lists for City of London 1701, 1710, 1713.

Poll Lists for Nottinghamshire 1698, 1710, 1722 Nottinghamshire Archives.

Registration of Schoolmasters QS43 Record Office for Leicestershire, Leicester & Rutland.

Rental for East Leake and Thorpe for the whole of the year 1701 *Parkyns Papers* Pa M32 University of Nottingham Dept of Manuscripts & Special Collections.

Testimonial for William Bleay August 1675 732.21–BA.2051 Worcestershire Archive & Archaeology Service

Trial of Robert Foulks 16 January 1679 *Proceedings of the Old Bailey Online.*

Will of Thomas Bleay 1706 Record Office for Leicestershire, Leicester & Rutland.

Will of William Bleay (nuncupative) 1721 Borthwick Institute, York.

Wills of George Wight 1651, George Wight 1744, George Wight 1777, Samuel Wight 1734 PROB 11 PCC National Archives.

Wills of Luke Hallam 1712, John Hopkins 1720, Elizabeth Wight/Weight 1728 Nottinghamshire Archives.

Chapter 2

Anon. (1707) *The freemen of London's necessary and useful companion: or, the citizens birth-right, ... treating of the city's antiquity, ... The duty and office of constables, ... and other useful things* London.

Anon. (1715) *The merchants and traders necessary companion for the year 1715* London.

Anon. (2004) *Tracing the Townleys,* available online as a freely downloadable pdf file from www.burnley.gov.uk/towneley/downloads/TTv4_web.pdf [accessed 24/12/2008]

Campbell, R. (1747) *The London tradesman. Being a compendious view of all the trades, professions, arts, both liberal and mechanic, now practised in the cities of London and Westminster. Calculated for the information of parents, and instruction of youth in their choice of business.* London: Gardner.

Defoe, D. (1726) *The complete English tradesman, in familiar letters; directing him in all the several parts and progressions of trade. ...* London: Charles Rivington.

Distillers Company (1698) *The Case of the Distillers; (1698) The London Distiller; (1708) Abstract of the Bye-Laws of the Company of Distillers* London.

Pelling, M. (1994) Apprenticeship, health and social cohesion in early modern London *History Workshop*, No. 37 (Spring), pp. 33–56 Oxford.

Porter, R. ((1994*) London: a social history* Hamish Hamilton.

Salmon, T. (1731) *Modern history: or, the present state of all nations. Vol. XIV. Treats of the Islands of Britain, and more at large of the South Part of Great Britain call'd England, .., and herein more particularly of the County of Middlesex and City of London* London.

Smith, G. (1725) *The Compleat Art of Distilling* London.

Stow, John (1720) *A survey of the cities of London and Westminster: containing the original, antiquity, increase, modern estate and government of those cities. Written at first in the year MDXCVIII. By John Stow, citizen and native of London. ... Now lastly, corrected, improved, and very much enlarged ... by John Strype, ... In six books....* Vol. 1.

Y-Worth, W. (1705) *The compleat distiller: or the whole art of distillation practically stated, ... To which is added, Pharmacopœia spagyrica nova: ....* 2nd edition. London.

Manuscript sources

Four Shillings in the Pound Aid May 1694 COL/CHD/LA/03/004/005   London Metropolitan Archives.

Land Tax returns for Tower Ward, City of London 1692/3, 1703/4–1706/7   CLC/525 London Metropolitan Archives.

London Inhabitants within the Walls 1695 British History Online as above.

Order of Justices at General Sessions of the Peace that Vintners, Coffee-sellers, Alehouse-keepers, Victuallers etc. shall not suffer any person to continue in their house tipling and drinking after 10 p.m. (1695) CLA/047/LR/004/007 London Metropolitan Archives.

Petition of Edward Weight and others 18 February 1696/7 HL/PO/JO/10/1/491/1116 annexe (b) House of Lords Archives

Wills of Wm Mackley 1702, Samuel Robinson 1708. PROB 11 PCC National Archives.

Chapter 3

Defoe, D. (attrib.) (1734) *A general history of the lives and adventures of the most famous highwaymen, murderers, street-robbers, &c. To which is added, a genuine account of the voyages and plunders of the most notorious pyrates.* London.

Encyclopædia Britannica; or, a dictionary of arts, sciences, &c. On a plan entirely new: 1778 Edinburgh.

Lackington, J. (1791) *Memoirs of the forty-five first years of the life of James Lackington* 2nd edition. London: 1793.

Mathias, P. (1952) Agriculture and the brewing and distilling industries in the eighteenth century *Economic History Review*, Vol. 5(2), pp. 249–57.

Phillips, F. A. (1909) *The romance of smuggling* London: C. Arthur Pearson.

Roseveare, H. (1991) *The financial revolution 1660–1760* Longman Seminar Studies in History Longman.

Shaw, W.A. and Slingsby, F.H. (eds) (1952–7) *Calendar of Treasury Books*. Vols. 25, 27, 28, 29: warrant books. Warrants by Treasurer Oxford to the Excise Commissioners to permit importers to make post entries of brandy and rum imported over strength, 20 July 1711, 21 October 1713, 21 July 1714, 30 April 1715 Institute of Historical Research London, via British History Online as above.

South Sea Company (1712 & 1714) *A list of the Names of the Corporation of the Governor and Company of Merchants of Great Britain, Trading to the South-Seas, and other Parts of America, and for Encouraging the Fishery* London.

Whiston, W. & Diston, H. (1714) *A new method for discovering the Longitude both at sea and land, humbly proposed for the consideration of the public* London.

Manuscript sources

Apprenticeship Registers, Vol. 1 (1711/12). IR/1/1 National Archives.

Distillers Company *Apprenticeship records* CLC/L/DA/C/014/MS06212/001 London Metropolitan Archives.

Entries relating to John Bley AC 27/422, folio 3064 Bank of England Archives.

Hand-in-Hand Insurance Company *Registers* Vols. 4,5,6,8,11 CCC/B/055 MS08674 London Metropolitan Archives.

Land Tax returns for Tower Ward, City of London 1706–14 CLC/525 1706–14; *Victuallers licences for Tower Ward 1708* CLA/047/LR/03/1708/029 London Metropolitan Archives.

The Names and Surnames of the Inhabitants of the said Ward [Tower Ward] Who are Willing to take out Licences according to the Act of Parliament for Retayling of Brandy and other Distilled Liquors wth their securities and also the Severall Parishes of their Abodes 22 October 1701 CLA/047/LR/03/B/1701/028 London Metropolitan Archives.

Plan (scale 1: 192): The charities of St. Dunstans in the East: property in Lower Thames Street ... / William E. Clifton, architect & surveyor; Waterlow Bros. & Layton Limd. [printers] [c. 1900] Bib Id 369761 London Metropolitan Archives.

Will of Thomas Nutt 1704 PROB 11 PCC National Archives.

Chapter 4

Andrews, W. (1887) *Famous frosts and frost fairs in Great Britain: chronicled from the earliest to the present time*, pp. 40–4 London: G. Redway.

Anon. (1715) *A Full and Particular Account of that Sad and Deplorable Fire which happen'd on Thursday the 13th of January 1715* Printed for J. Cuxon, London.

Anon. (2004) *Tracing the Townleys* available online as above.

Maitland, W. (1739) *The history of London, from its foundation by the Romans, to the present time. Containing A Faithful Relation of the Publick Transactions of the Citizens; Accounts of the several Parishes; Parallels between London and other Great Cities; its Governments, Civil, Ecclesiastical and Military; Commerce, State of Learning, Charitable Foundations, &c. With the several Accounts of Westminster, Middlesex, Southwark, and Other Parts within The Bill of Mortality.* London: printed by Samuel Richardson, in Salisbury-Court near Fleetstreet.

Rogers, N. (1978) Popular protest in early Hanoverian London *Past and Present,* No 79 (May) pp70–100 Oxford.

Shaw, W.A. (ed.) (1933) *Calendar of Treasury books* Vol. 15: warrant books. Warrant relating to Edward Weight 19 January 1699/1700. Institute of Historical Research, London, via British History Online as above.

Shaw, W.A. and Slingsby, F.H. (eds) (1957) *Calendar of Treasury books* Vol. 29: warrant books. Warrants relating to Edward Weight 7 February 1715, 25 February 1715. Institute of Historical Research, London, via British History Online as above.

Manuscript sources

Account and plan of the fire in Thames Street 1714/15 (erroneously dated 1716) CLC/297/MS00046 London Metropolitan Archives.

Book of plans by George Gwilt of the company's 'east walk' estates 1772 *Book of Plans of property of Worshipful Company of Fishmonger* CLC/L/FE/G/043/MS21536 London Metropolitan Archives.

Hand-in-Hand Insurance Company *Minutes* Vol. 5 CLC/B/055/MS08666/005; *Registers* Vol. 15 CCC/B/055/MS08674 London Metropolitan Archives.

Land Tax returns for Tower Ward, City of London 1714–6 CLC/525 London Metropolitan Archives.

Leases relating to property of Fishmongers Company at corner of Thames St and Water Lane London CLC/522/ MS01812, MS 1911, MS 1912, MS01929 MS01931 London Metropolitan Archives.

Minutes of a Whig club 1714–7 British History Online as above.

Petition to Lord Chancellor on behalf of sufferers from Thames Street fire 11 July 1715 CLA/047/LJ/13/1715/005 London Metropolitan Archives.

Chapter 5

Dickson, P.G.M. (1967) *The financial revolution: a study in public credit 1688–1756* Macmillan.

Ellis Flack, G. (1945) Sir Thomas Parkyns of Bunny *Transactions of the Thoroton Society*, XLIX.

Marshall, V. A. (2000) *Parkyns* Bunny, Notts: Bunny & Bradmore Charities.

Parkyns, Sir T. Bart (1716) *A practical and grammatical introduction to the Latin tongue. By Sr. Thomas Parkyns of Bunny, bart. for the use of his grand-son and of Bunny-School*; (1724) *A method proposed for the hiring and recording of servants in husbandry, arts, mysteries etc.* Nottingham.

Sergeaunt, J. (1898) *Annals of Westminster School* Methuen.

Thoroton Society (1902) Thoroton Society excursion, Spring 1902: Bradmore and Bunny *Transactions of the Thoroton Society*, No. 6.

Trevor-Roper, H. (1953) The gentry 1540–1640 *Economic History Review* Supp. 1.

Twelvetrees, B. (1973) *Sir Thomas Parkyns of Bunny* Nottingham: B. Twelvetrees.

Manuscript sources

East Leake Enclosure map 1798 EA 21 Nottinghamshire Archives

Land title deed 1874 for John Bley's house QDE 1/4 Nottinghamshire Archives

Parkyns papers Pa. University of Nottingham Dept of Manuscripts & Special Collections.

Record of Old Westminsters Westminster School Archives.

Wills of Anne Parkyns 1711, Sir Thomas Parkyns 1741 PROB 11 PCC National Archives.

Chapter 6

Barley, M. (1963) Double pile houses in Nottinghamshire In *The house and home* London: Vista Books.

Brunskill, R.W. (2000) *Vernacular architecture: an illustrated handbook* Faber & Faber.

Buchanan, W. (2001) Robert Marsden B.D. – Rector of Rempstone 1702–48 *Leake Historian* No. 5, pp. 4–8.

Ellis Flack, G. (1945) Sir Thomas Parkyns of Bunny *Transactions of the Thoroton Society* XLIX.

Foden, P. (2008) The west gallery in East Leake *Leake Historian*, No. 10, pp. 35–37.

Grundy T. (2004) The Norman boys, pupils at the John Bley Endowed School *Leake Historian* No. 8, pp. 6–10.

Hodgkinson, K. and Van Laun, B. and G. (2010) John Bley's house *Leake Historian* No. 12, pp. 15–21.

Meadows, W., Gilliver, L., and Clarke, J. (1738) *The intelligencer: or merchants assistant* London Guildhall Library.

Twelvetrees, B. (1973) *Sir Thomas Parkyns of Bunny* Nottingham: B. Twelvetrees.

Wood, R.O. *Notes on the deeds of John Bley's house* (unpublished).

Manuscript Sources

Confirmation of East Leake property transfer to John Woodroffe and John Bley National Archives CP 25/2/1048/9GEO1 TRIN

For East Leake: census returns 1841–1911; electoral lists 1836, 1850–5, 1885; land tax returns 1780 –1832 QDE 1/4; land values 1910; taxation map 1910 (part of the Rushcliffe section of the taxation maps); trade directories 1891–9 Nottinghamshire Archives.

Marsden, Rev. R. *Commonplace and memoranda book, 1724–35* DD/TS/14/2 Nottinghamshire Archives.

Newspapers: *Loughborough Advertiser* July 1872; *Loughborough Monitor & News* 7/9/1899; *Nottingham Weekly Guardian* April 28 1934.

The Norman schoolbooks DD/2533/1 (1723) Nottinghamshire Archives.

Poor rate books PR 2677, 2679–2683 Nottinghamshire Archives.

Chapter 7

Abel, E. L. (2001*)* The gin epidemic: much ado about what? *Alcohol and Alcoholism,* Vol. 36(5) pp. 401–5, 200.

Brown, J. (1733) *The Interest of the Compound Distiller Considered* London.

Defoe, D. (1711) *An Account of the African Trade*; (1722) *Tour through the Eastern Counties of England*; (1726) *A brief case of the distillers, and of the distilling trade in England, shewing how far it is the interest of England to encourage the said trade, as it is so considerable an advantage to the landed interest, to the trade and navigation, to the publick revenue, and to the employment of the poor. Humbly recommended to the Lords and Commons of Great Britain, in the present Parliament assembled.* London.

Distillers Company (1729) *The Case of the Company of Distillers of the City of London: With Proposals for reforming the Abuses practised in the Distilling Trade* London.

Hayes, R. (1722) *Rules for the Port of London or the waterside practice* London.

Hoppit, J. (2000) The myths of the South Sea Bubble *Transactions of the Royal Historical Society*, 6th series, Vol. 12, pp.141–65.

Lillywhite, B. (1963) *London coffee houses* George Allen & Unwin.

London Pollbooks, 1713 *London Politics 1713–1717* British History Online as above.

Poll of the liverymen of the City of London at the election for Members of Parliament, begun Munday October 9th 1710 London.

Poll of the liverymen of the City of London at the election for Members of Parliament, begun Tuesday April 10th 1722 London.

Shaw, W.A. and Slingsby, F.H. (eds) (1955*) Calendar of Treasury Books. Vol. 29* to 'Declared Accounts: Excise'; *Calendar of Treasury Books Vol. 29: 1714-1715* (1957), pp. CCCXXXI-CCCLII Repayments for exports and overcharges on export of malt spirits, strong ale, etc. to Joseph Nutt and others Institute of Historical Research, London, via British History Online as above.

South Sea Company (1711) *Abstract of the Charter of the Governor and Company of Merchants of Great Britain, Trading to the South-Seas, and other Parts of America, and for Encouraging the Fishery*; (1723) *A list of the Names of the Corporation of the Governor and Company of Merchants of Great Britain, Trading to the South-Seas, and other Parts of America, and for Encouraging the Fishery* London.

Trials of John Jones 25 May 1721, Barthia Fisher 5 December 1722, Henry Vigus 23 April 1726 *Proceedings of the Old Bailey Online* at www.oldbaileyonline.org.

Manuscript Sources

Apprenticeship Registers Vol.10 (1724/25*)* IR/1/11 National Archives.

Attested Copy Book of a Poll for Common-Council Men for Tower Ward (1717) COL/CC/13/01/029 London Metropolitan Archives.

Distillers Company *Annual lists of members of the livery* (1724 to 1771) CLC/L/DA/C/001/MS06210/001; *Apprenticeship records* CLC/L/DA/C/014/MS06212/001; *Minutes of the Court of Assistants,* Vol. 1 (Jan 1714/ /15 to Jan 1730/31) CLC/L/DA/B/002/MS06207 London Metropolitan Archives.

Hoare's Bank Archive Entries relating to John Bley Ledger 19, folio 348 RBS Group Archives.

Journals of the House of Commons Second Parliament of Great Britain, 2nd session 15, 16, 27 February 1710 (evidence of Joseph Nutt).

Land Tax returns for Tower Ward, City of London CLC/525 1716–31; *Land Tax returns for the ward of Farringdon without, City of London* CLC/525 1730/1 London Metropolitan Archives.

St Dunstan's Charity, Lease Trustees: Lease to John Bley (1717) *Leases of houses in Thames Street 1669 to 1832* A/81/66/7/2/3 Lewisham Archives.

St Dunstan in the East parish registers Available online.

Wills of Alexander Cleeve 1741, Dr John Dry 1748, Robert Godfrey 1729, Richard Heale 1700, John Lucas 1736, Thomas Plampin 1738, Joshua Russell 1762, James Wyke 1728, Charles Townley 1719, Edward Walmesley 1746. PROB 11 PCC National Archives.

Chapter 8

Billingsgate Billingsgated *Punch Magazine*, October 1880 Punch Publications Ltd.

Defoe, D. (1719) *Robinson Crusoe*, pp.13–16 Reprint Odhams Press (early C20th)

Kent, H.S. (1955) The Anglo-Norwegian timber trade in the eighteenth century *Economic History Review*, Vol. 8(1), pp. 62–74.

Phillips, H. (1719) *The purchaser's pattern* London.

Trial of James Mould 28 August 1741 *Proceedings of the Old Bailey Online* as above.

Trusler, J. (1768) *Hogarth moralized. Being a complete edition of Hogarth's works*, p151 London.

Manuscript sources

Entries relating to John Bley AC27/426, folio 5181, AC17/425, AC27/430 folio 72 Bank of England Archives.

Hand-in-Hand Insurance Company *Minutes* Vol. 10 Ms08666; *Registers* Vol. 3, 26, 28, 29, 31, 32, 34, 35, 38, 41. CCC/B/055 MS08674 London Metropolitan Archives.

House of Commons Papers 1831–2: Reports of Committees. Report from Select Committee on the Observance of the Sabbath (evidence of Lewis Gilson).

Inventory: Green, William of St Dunstans in the East, London, 1735 PROB 3/34/48 PCC National Archives.

Land tax returns for Tower Ward, City of London 1730/1, 1739/40, 1745/6, 1752/3, 1760/1, 1768/9, 1776/7, 1831/2 CLC/525; *Victuallers licences for Tower Ward 1730* CLA/047/LR/03/1731/029 London Metropolitan Archives.

Wills of Matthew Bell 1772, Ursula Bridgen 1763, Elizabeth Holmes 1761, Samuel Holmes 1739, Joseph Nutt 1739, Jacob Saunders 1744, Henry Saunders 1771, Hester Saunders 1776, Edward Weight 1734. PROB 11 PCC National Archives.

Chapter 9

Manuscript sources

Archbishop Herring's Visitation returns 1743 Yorkshire Archaeological Society Record Series LXXI.

Marsden, Rev. R. *Commonplace and memoranda book, 1724–35*, p93 DD/TS/14/2 Nottinghamshire Archives.

Wills of John Bley 1731, Daniel Berry 1734, John Bird 1720, Thomas Bird 1738, Richard Fendall 1753, Dorothy Hardy 1743, Mary Hopkin 1753, Thomas Lambert 1804, Caleb Moore 1778, George Quinton 1733 PROB 11 PCC National Archives.

Will of Robert Hopkins of East Leake 1733 Nottinghamshire Archives.

Chapter 10

London Hospital (1796) *General State of the Corporation of the London Hospital for the Reception and relief of Sick and Wounded Seamen, Manufacturers and Labouring Poor their Wives and Children* London.

Orphan Girls Asylum (1789) *An account of the institutions and proceedings of the Guardians of the Asylum, or house of refuge, situate in the parish of Lambeth in the County of Surrey, for the reception of Orphan Girls, the settlements of whose parents cannot be found.* London.

Working Orphans School (1779) *The Plan of the Charity for the Maintenance Instruction and Employment of Orphans and other Poor Children erected at Hoxton in the year 1760 now in the City Road* London.

Manuscript sources

Apprenticeship Registers Vol.17 (1743/46) IR/1/17 National Archives.

Entries relating to John Turner AC27/467; Will extracts M1/95 Bank of England Archives.

Land tax returns for the Ward of Farringdon Without, City of London 1720–73 CLC/525, London Metropolitan Archives.

Wills proved at Prerogative Court of Canterbury: John Bley 1731, James Quinn 1766, Charles Lowth 1769, Samuel Sterropp 1773, John Turner 1789, John Danvers 1803. PROB 11 PCC National Archives.

Chapter 11

Arkell, T. (1987) The incidence of poverty in the later seventeenth century *Social History*, Vol. 12(1), pp. 23–47.

Bray, A. (1995) *Homosexuality in Renaissance England* New York: Columbia UP.

Coward, B. (1988) *Social change and continuity in early modern England* Longman.

Lewis, B (2004) Schools in East Leake before 1875 *Leake Historian* No. 8, June 2004.

Rosenheim, J. M. (1997) *The emergence of a ruling order: English landed society 1650–1750* Longman.

Wood, M. (2010) *The story of England: a village and its people through the whole of English history* Viking/Penguin.

Manuscript sources

East Leake Inventories Nottinghamshire Archives.

Faculty document for East Leake St Mary's Church PR21, 417/2, December 29 1899 and PR21, 417/3 23rd January 1900 Nottinghamshire Archives.

Index